May God
richly bless you
for your faithfulness.
Prayerfully,
Thompson   Eph 6:18

To pray the Word of God is to pray the will of God. That's why I'm so excited about Mary Ann Bridgwater's *Prayers for the Faithful*. Nothing I have ever seen regarding how to pray for faithful Christians in global ministry activity is so well-designed and so powerfully practical as *Prayers for the Faithful*. Because our ministry has over 12,000 workers worldwide, I intend to give every intercessor I know a copy of this timely guide.

Dr. Dick Eastman
International President
Every Home for Christ

For most Christians, "good intentions" is usually the best way to describe our prayer life. *Prayers for the Faithful* is a wonderful tool to move us from good intentions to prayerful action. I recommend this book to sit on your nightstand, not just your bookshelf.

As Mary Ann's pastor, I can assure you her life matches her words. Without a doubt, every prayer she will lead you to pray, she will have already prayed several times herself. After you purchase this book, make sure you have patches for the knees of your pants because you will wear holes in them.

Gregg Matte
Senior Pastor
Houston's First Baptist Church

The first time we prayed together, I was undone—I was drawn—and I wanted to be her student. When Mary Ann Bridgwater prays, she connects to a spiritual reality in the unseen dimension that I long to touch. *Prayers for the Faithful* takes me to the front lines of the spiritual battle on behalf of the nations, their leaders, and the message-bearers who serve among them. No more casual or uninformed praying. This is prayer meant to shake the heavens and change eternity.

Carol Davis
Director
LeafLine Initiatives

If you want to have a more comprehensive, kingdom focused, and strategic intercessory prayer life, this book is for you. *Prayers for the Faithful* is a tool that can revolutionize the way you pray for missionaries and mission work around the world.

Jerry Wiles
President
Living Water International

A book on prayer is best evaluated by knowing the practice of its author. No one I know more fervently represents the power of praying the Word than Mary Ann.

Steve Riggle
Senior Pastor
Grace Community Church, Houston

Spiritual warfare is a fierce and daily reality for missionaries working to share the gospel of Jesus Christ with unreached peoples. *Prayers for the Faithful* effectively combines real-life stories from these modern-day Christian workers with the powerful Word of God to lead the church to intercessory prayer on behalf of missionaries in the thick of the battle.

Doug Floyd
Team Leader, Office of Mission Personnel
International Mission Board, SBC

Prayers for the Faithful strikes at the heart of the greatest and most constant needs for missionaries on the field: families who have left their homes, elderly parents, children who are stateside studying, and the work itself. God answers the prayers of the faithful at home who lift up our faithful on the field. This book and these personal testimonies will be a great motivator to "pray without ceasing."

Harvey Kneisel
Minister of Missions Emeritus
Houston's First Baptist Church

MARY ANN BRIDGWATER

INTRODUCTION BY JERRY RANKIN

Prayers
—for the—
Faithful

FERVENT DAILY PRAYER
and MEDITATIONS
for CHRISTIANS SERVING
AROUND *the* WORLD

FOREWORD BY
BETH MOORE

B&H
PUBLISHING GROUP

NASHVILLE, TENNESSEE

ISBN: 978-0-8054-4752-1
B & H Publishing Group
Nashville, Tennessee
www.BHPublishingGroup.com

Dewey Decimal Classification: 242.2
Subject Heading: Prayers / Meditations / Ministers

In Honor

I have such a heart of gratitude and appreciation for my former pastor, Dr. John R. Bisagno, and his wife, Uldine. Their "preparing God's people for works of service, so that the body of Christ may be built up" empowered both my family and me to believe that the promises of God are truly attainable in one's life (Eph. 4:11–13). I love you both and thank you for living lives that are true examples of the living Word of God.

Dedication

Reverend Harvey and Charlene Kneisel are two of the most dedicated and faithful Christians I have ever known who seek to fulfill the Great Commission. They live a life completely surrendered to the gospel of Jesus Christ, our Lord and Savior.

Brother Harvey, as Minister of Missions for Houston's First Baptist Church, as well as Charlene—you led Roger and me on our first missionary journey to India in 1989. Our lives are forever changed! Our whole family, in fact, has been greatly impacted, for they all are now involved in missions ministry. Charlene, you influenced my life to pray for missionaries and, in doing so, I learned how to pray the Word of God. The passionate love I now have with the Lord eternally burns in my heart like a fire! Indeed, I cannot hold it in! (Jer. 20:9).

I dedicate this book to you and to all those who have surrendered their lives to the work of God to fulfill the Great Commission in the local church, our nation, and throughout the world.

Table of Contents

Part One
The Messenger/The Missionary

SECTION A: STANDING READY

SECTION B: WALKING IN CHRIST

SECTION C: THE MISSIONARY'S MARRIAGE

SECTION D: THE MISSIONARY'S CHILDREN

SECTION E: THE MISSIONARY'S PARENTS

Part Two
The Harvest/The Nations

Foreword by Beth Moore

I am thrilled to recommend *Prayers for the Faithful* by my dear friend Mary Ann Bridgwater. One of the things I like about Mary Ann's ministry is that she does not sense a new call or come up with a new burden every other week. Her calling to urge and equip people to pray has remained consistent and passionate for many years. I am as excited about the equipping she offers for prayer in this particular realm as I've ever been.

I was raised in a church that indoctrinated us in a love and support for foreign and North American missionaries. About ten years ago, God began leading me to take a far more active role in missions in a number of ways, primarily through daily intercession. I recall wondering, "How does a person approach praying for the entire world?" God graciously placed tools in my hands along the way, but I can assure you I've never seen one quite like this one. Mary Ann has done her homework. This guide is packed full of Scripture. All we need to do is add some faith, open our mouths, and pray them! The testimonies she has included will cause our fellow servants on the field to become more than names to you. Their stories and requests will steal your heart and hopefully some of your prayer time.

God recently reminded me of a Scripture as I was preparing a Sunday school lesson on prayer. In 2 Corinthians 1:10–11, the apostle Paul says, "[God] has delivered us from such a deadly peril, and he will deliver us. On him we have set our hope that he will continue to deliver us, *as you help us by your prayers*" (emphasis mine). Scripture clearly teaches that some things only happen through prayer, but more astonishingly, God's Word goes further in Scriptures like these to infer that some things may only happen as a result of *others' prayers*. This may be one way God enforces His children to work as a team.

Can you imagine the ramifications of this concept regarding missionaries? Could it be possible that some breakthroughs in their ministries, their lives, and their work may only happen as a result of our prayers—indeed their deliverance from "deadly peril"? I don't believe that God is doing anything more exciting in our generation than rapidly fulfilling the prophecy of Matthew 24:14—"And this gospel of the kingdom will be preached in the whole world as a testimony to all nations, and then the end will come." I want to be part of what God is doing around the world. I want to join with my brothers and sisters on the field in any effective way I can. I think you do, too. We will never waste a prayer on missionaries. They need them, they want them, they *feel* them!

Thank you, Mary Ann, for providing us with the very words of God to pray over His servants. Heaven alone will bear witness of its profound harvest.

Keep believing and praying!
Beth Moore

Introduction

Ask any missionary what their greatest need is, and the answer will always be prayer. Yes, they could readily enumerate many other needs and practical things that may be more apparent. They are all over-extended and would like additional personnel to be called to join their team. They could use more financial resources to provide materials and support programs that would accelerate their outreach and make their ministry more effective. They yearn for more frequent communication from home and just to know that someone cares and is thinking of them.

But they would forego all of the above for a massive outpouring of prayer on behalf of them and their work. It doesn't matter how much education and experience they carry to the field, missionaries recognize it is only the power of God that will enable them to survive and communicate the gospel effectively. It is not the methodology and mission strategies they learn in orientation but only the power of God that can soften hardened hearts and enable the Holy Spirit to convict people of the truth of the gospel.

But it takes more than one humble missionary family pouring out their own hearts to the Father. If they are to be witnesses to the ends of the earth and claim the kingdoms of the world as the kingdoms of our Lord, the united hearts of God's people must be joined in massive intercession to invoke and claim the promises of the Father on behalf of the nations and those sent from our churches in obedience to His call.

For some reason, God has chosen to limit His activity in the world to the prayers of His people. This is not because of any limitation in His power and sovereignty but because of His desire for us to be involved and join Him in His activity. C. H. Spurgeon linked the action of God with the prayers of His people. He said, "God will bless Elijah and send rain on Israel, but Elijah must pray for it. If the chosen nation is to prosper, Samuel must plead for it. If the Jews are to be delivered. Daniel must intercede. God will bless Paul, and the nations will be converted, but Paul must pray. . . . Let me have your prayers, and I can do anything! Let me be without my people's prayers, and I can do nothing."

While there is power in prayer—and even more power in collective prayer—there is nothing more powerful than the Word of God. In this book, Mary Ann Bridgwater has linked these two powerful tools that God has made accessible to us. This is not simply a book of inspirational reading on prayer; it is a manual for engaging in spiritual warfare on behalf of missionaries around the world. It will be a guide for those to whom God has given a burden for a lost world. It will be a powerful tool to invoke the assurances and truths of God's promises on behalf of those who need them so desperately. It will enable families and church members to move beyond the shallow, general prayers of "God bless the missionaries" to claim the specific answers that are needed.

One does not have to wait for the periodic prayer letter to discern the needs of their missionary friends around the world. Every missionary needs us to pray for their health and safety and for the needs of their children. They need us to join them in expressing their desire for a closer walk with the Lord and to experience His power. They need wisdom and boldness as they plan their work and engage people with the claims of Christ. We would desire for them joy and fulfillment in their task, asking that they might have new opportunities of witness, that they would break through strongholds and obstacles and be able to claim victories for the glory of God on their field of service. All we have to do is claim His Word.

Prayers for the Faithful compiles the verses that apply to every imaginable situation and need. It is wonderful to think that we are not petitioning the Lord for selfish desires or things that come from our own mind, but requests that reflect the heart of God and the will of the Father for those for whom we pray. It will be an exciting prayer journey as you follow these Scriptures, lifting them to the Father on behalf of those missionaries you may or may not know personally. God has assured us that He hears and answers those prayers that glorify Him and are according to His will. Missionaries will be blessed and empowered, and we will be blessed by faithfully partnering with them in what God is doing around the world through prayer.

Dr. Jerry Rankin, President
International Mission Board, SBC

From the Author

I remember when the Holy Spirit revealed to my husband, Roger, and me in 1989 that we were to join others from our church family and go on a mission trip for eighteen days, halfway around the world to Hyderabad, India. It reminded me of the Lord saying to Abram, "Leave your country, your people and your father's household and go to the land I will show you" (Gen. 12:1).

Indeed, God was calling us to leave the USA, our two daughters, Kay and Jane Ann (who were six and nine at the time), other members of our family, friends, and all of our material possessions. I was willing to answer God's call and go, but there was no way that I was going to leave my family or attempt to serve God in another country without knowing that all was covered in fervent prayer. I needed my home church, family members, and our own team members to pray focused, fervent prayer—for my family; for the full measure of God to be accomplished through my life as His witness; and for others to know Jesus Christ as their personal Lord and Savior.

It was for this purpose that the Holy Spirit prompted me to write my very first prayer guide, built around the crusade our church was sponsoring and in which we were participating. Knowing that there were people on bended knee before the Lord, praying for God's purposes to be fulfilled, gave me peace and an expectant heart for wondrous miracles that only God could accomplish.

Upon reaching our destination and stepping off the airplane in India, the Holy Spirit immediately made known to me that I was on holy ground! We had crossed over into the land in which God wanted to use us. He was going to give us every place where we were setting our feet, and no one would be able to stand up against us. God was with us and would never leave us nor forsake us (see Josh. 1:1–5).

We made our way to our hotel to clean up and rest for the night. After only one hour of sleep, I awoke, drawn by the Holy Spirit to read and pray God's Word from my Bible. God had led me all the way to India to share the gospel fearlessly and prayerfully to others who would inherit the land of eternal life. I gained strength and courage as

He spoke to me from His Word. I was not going to turn to the right or to the left without knowing and being obedient to the plans He had for me. I was not about to let God's truth depart from my mouth. I was to meditate on it day and night so that I would be careful to do everything written in it. Then I would be useful, prosperous, and successful. I was to be strong and courageous, not terrified, not discouraged, for the Lord God was with me wherever I was—even in India, a long way from home and family (see Josh. 1:6–8).

While there, I had the incredible opportunity to share the gospel with over 30,000 men and women from the surrounding areas. I told about the importance and power of praying for our families and ourselves. One night while praying for a blind man, God immediately answered our prayers and restored his sight before our very eyes. What amazing miracles we saw during that time—physically and spiritually, visibly and invisibly. This is when God really began to show me how essential it is for God's people to be praying daily—deliberately—for missionaries. Just now, in fact, as I have been writing this testimony, I received an e-mail from Natalie, a very dear friend who has served as a missionary in Africa. One thing she said really struck home:

"Serving overseas seems to have a certain mystique for most folks in the American church. The concept that only spiritual giants end up serving on the field seems to pervade and is something that I experienced even on my brief trip home last summer. In reality, most of the folks that I meet here are simply the ones who dared to follow. So I challenge you to simply surrender to prayer and fellowship with Him, because walking in His steps is such a good place to be! Don't worry—He doesn't want us all in Africa!"

Beloved, we are all just regular, everyday people who have been called as followers of Jesus Christ—like Peter and John before us, who were ordinary and unschooled men. Yet the noted difference in their lives was that people "took note that these men had been with Jesus" (Acts 4:13). Whether we physically go and serve God in another country or we serve Him right where we are, we have all been called to surrender to God in prayer and to obediently follow Him. May this prayer book be one way He uses to draw you closer to His side.

Prayerfully, Mary Ann

How to Use This Book

The pattern used to guide you throughout this prayer book and into the worship of God is this acronym: P-R-A-Y .

P—PRAISE AND THANKSGIVING

We begin with praise and thanksgiving to God for who He is and what He has done. Beloved, we have the privilege and honor of receiving the blessing of instruction from God's Word to "enter his gates with thanksgiving and his courts with praise; give thanks to him and praise his name." (Ps. 100:4). "Everything that has breath praise the Lord. Praise the Lord" (Ps. 150:6).

Inside are fifty-two names of God (one for each week) that you can exalt and lift up in worship and praise to God. The scripture that supports each name of God is given so you can intentionally give Him thanks for what He has done personally in your life and for the work that is being completed on this earth through His salvation. There are also scriptures available for you to praise God and give Him thanks for the assurance of your salvation and for who you are in Christ.

R—REPENTANCE AND CONFESSION

It then becomes necessary to confess and wash with the Word of God. We are instructed from God's Word to take thought of the sin God reveals to us, to confess it, asking God to forgive us, and to take hold of the truth that will wash us and empower us to be holy.

Beloved, "without holiness no one will see the Lord" (Heb. 12:14). Our sin blinds our eyes and hearts from seeing the Lord's pathway we are to take for our daily life. The scriptures available in this portion of the book will assist you in searching your heart for any sinfulness you may have committed against God, helping you be certain that you are serving God's purpose with your life. "Blessed are the pure in heart, for they will see God" (Matt. 5:8).

A—ASKING

Asking is when we make intercession, praying in the Spirit on all occasions with all kinds of prayers and requests, praying that God's plans and purposes will be accomplished on this earth as they are in heaven, demolishing the strongholds of Satan. To do so, you'll be asked to rewrite selected Scriptures, personalizing them for missionaries. For when God's promises are prayed in faith, believing them wholeheartedly, they break the chains that bind, piercing the darkness that has come to invade the land of the living. "With this in mind, be alert and always keep on praying for all the saints." (Eph. 6:18).

Y—Yielding

Yielding is submitting your heart, soul, and mind before God, listening to His voice, and being obedient to His commands until, like Jeremiah, His words become like "a fire shut up in my bones. I am weary of holding it in; indeed, I cannot" (Jer. 20:9).

Again, you'll be asked to personalize Scriptures, directing them toward yourself and your current situation, believing God for all things as you submit to Him in gratitude and willingness of spirit. In this way, prayer will come full circle—from you to heaven, around the world, and right back to your door—trailing joy and blessing and the consuming presence of God.

Possible Uses of This Book by Your Local Church

· When planning commissioning ceremonies for missionaries or a time of prayer for missionaries home on furlough.

· When posting Scripture in the Sunday worship bulletin, in the weekly church newsletter, or on the screen in the worship services for corporate intercession before or after the sermon.

· When praying for specific needs and requests, for missionary families that are members of your church, for retired missionaries.

· When organizing prayer for short-term mission trips.

Possible Uses by Missionaries Themselves

· Individually during their own quiet time with the Lord.

· With their own family during times of prayer for one another.

· When having prayer with other missionary families on the field.

· When praying for family members left behind in the states.

· When praying for children who have gone off to college.

This book could also be used as a prayer guide for missionaries' family members, as well as by missionary kids when praying for themselves, their families, and others. Worshiping God wholeheartedly in prayer will minister His perfect will, and the church will do and see things like never before. May God be glorified and His kingdom expanded through our praying!

Part One

The Messenger
The Missionary

Be strong in the Lord and in his mighty power.

Put on the full armor of God so that you can

take your stand against the devil's schemes.

For our struggle is not against flesh and blood,

but against the rulers, against the authorities,

against the powers of this dark world and against

the spiritual forces of evil in the heavenly realms.

Therefore put on the full armor of God, so that when

the day of evil comes, you may be able to stand your ground,

and after you have done everything, to stand.

Stand firm then, with the belt of truth buckled around

your waist, with the breastplate of righteousness in place,

and with your feet fitted with the readiness

that comes from the gospel of peace.

In addition to all this, take up the shield of faith, with which

you can extinguish all the flaming arrows of the evil one.

Take the helmet of salvation and the sword

of the Spirit, which is the word of God.

And pray in the Spirit on all occasions with

all kinds of prayers and requests.

With this in mind, be alert and always

keep on praying for all the saints.

EPHESIANS 6:10–18

STANDING
READY

Week 1

BELT OF TRUTH

I am convinced that Satan is not happy about the Father's work led by missionaries serving overseas, so he relentlessly attacks in areas where we are most vulnerable. For some, it is health; for others, it is marriage and family relationships; for still others, it is relationships with colleagues. The Great Deceiver is doing all he can to discourage us, distract us from the calling God has placed on our lives, and render our testimonies powerless.

When I do deputation/mobilization in the U.S., I often ask this question: "How many of you have placed missionaries up on a pedestal?" When they respond in the affirmative (which they invariably do), I encourage them to take us down! I emphasize that we have the same problems and temptations they face daily.

What can we do to counter Satan's attacks? The Bible exhorts us to pray for one another—"always laboring fervently for you in prayers, that you may stand perfect and complete in all the will of God" (Col. 4:12, NKJV). I think we do pray for one another . . . to a certain extent. We pray for one another's ministries. We pray when we know of specific, special needs. But how faithful are we to really *intercede* for one another in the known and unknown struggles of life?

I challenge you to be intentional in your prayers for missionary families. Pray for your missionaries in the following areas: daily spiritual growth, time in the Word and prayer, relationship with spouse, children, freedom from temptation (movies, books, magazines, TV, Internet), purity of thought, attitudes, action, speech, "separateness" from the world while living and ministering in it, and wisdom in daily decisions which have eternal consequences.

Let us not allow Satan to have the victory! The battle is too important. Many souls still living in darkness are counting on our fighting the good fight. The best way to begin is on our knees.

Debbie—WESTERN EUROPE

> A most beneficial exercise in secret prayer before the Father is to write
> things down exactly so I see exactly what I think and want to say.
> *Oswald Chambers*

PRAISE & THANKSGIVING

Worship by using the name of God mentioned in this
Scripture—"the true God."

> *But the Lord is the true God; He is the living God and the everlasting King.*
> *At His wrath the earth quakes, and the nations cannot endure His indignation.*
>
> Jeremiah 10:10 (NASB)

REPENTANCE

Search your heart as you meditate on this Scripture.
What is the Holy Spirit revealing to you?

> *Let us examine our ways and test them, and let us return to the LORD.*
>
> Lamentations 3:40

ASKING

Read the following Scripture. Rewrite it, personalizing it
for missionaries, asking that they would have the "belt of
truth" buckled around their waists.

> *Righteousness will be his belt and faithfulness the sash around his waist.*
>
> Isaiah 11:5

_____

_____

_____

YIELDING

Now meditate on the Scripture again. Rewrite it below,
personalizing and praying it for yourself. How can you
respond to what God is saying to you in this Scripture?

_____

_____

_____

_____

Pray for missionary work in AFGHANISTAN
(Southern Asia, between Iran and Pakistan)

> The Holy Spirit is the greatest teacher of prayer.
> Lord, teach us to pray.
> *Anonymous*

PRAISE & THANKSGIVING
Worship the "true God."

> *But the Lord is the true God; He is the living God and the everlasting King.*
> *At His wrath the earth quakes, and the nations cannot endure His indignation.*
>
> Jeremiah 10:10 (NASB)

REPENTANCE
Search your heart as you meditate on this Scripture.

> *Let us examine our ways and test them, and let us return to the LORD.*
>
> Lamentations 3:40

ASKING
Rewrite this Scripture, personalizing it for missionaries, asking that they would have the "belt of truth" buckled around their waists.

> *The goal of this command is love, which comes from a pure heart and a good conscience and a sincere faith.*
>
> 1 Timothy 1:5

_____

_____

_____

_____

YIELDING
Rewrite it again, personalizing and praying it for yourself. Respond to what God is saying to you in this Scripture.

_____

_____

_____

_____

_____

Pray for missionary work in ALBANIA
(Southeastern Europe, between Greece and the Adriatic Sea)

> Pray, asking God for kingdom perspective
> and worldwide vision.
> *Jerry Rankin*

PRAISE & THANKSGIVING

> *But the Lord is the true God; He is the living God and the everlasting King.*
> *At His wrath the earth quakes, and the nations cannot endure His indignation.*
> Jeremiah 10:10 (NASB)

REPENTANCE

> *Let us examine our ways and test them, and let us return to the LORD.*
> Lamentations 3:40

ASKING

Personalize this Scripture for missionaries, asking that they would have the "belt of truth" buckled around their waists.

> *But the wisdom that comes from heaven is first of all pure; then peace-loving,*
> *considerate, submissive, full of mercy and good fruit, impartial and sincere.*
> *Peacemakers who sow in peace raise a harvest of righteousness.*
> James 3:17–18

_____

_____

_____

_____

YIELDING

Now personalize and pray it for yourself. How can you respond to what God is saying to you?

_____

_____

_____

_____

_____

_____

Pray for missionary work in ALGERIA
(Northern Africa, between Morocco and Tunisia)

> More things are wrought by prayer
> than this world dreams of.
> *Lord Alfred Tennyson*

PRAISE & THANKSGIVING

> *But the Lord is the true God; He is the living God and the everlasting King.*
> *At His wrath the earth quakes, and the nations cannot endure His indignation.*
> Jeremiah 10:10 (NASB)

REPENTANCE

> *Let us examine our ways and test them, and let us return to the LORD.*
> Lamentations 3:40

ASKING

Rewrite this Scripture, personalizing it for missionaries.

> *Do not withhold your mercy from me, O LORD; may your love and your truth*
> *always protect me.*
> Psalm 40:11

_____

_____

_____

_____

_____

YIELDING

What is God saying to you in this Scripture?

_____

_____

_____

_____

_____

_____

_____

_____

Pray for missionary work in AMERICAN SAMOA
(South Pacific islands about halfway between
Hawaii and New Zealand)

> The greatest answer to prayer is that I am
> brought into a perfect understanding with God,
> and that alters my view of actual things.
> *Oswald Chambers*

PRAISE & THANKSGIVING

But the Lord is the true God; He is the living God and the everlasting King.
At His wrath the earth quakes, and the nations cannot endure His indignation.

Jeremiah 10:10 (NASB)

REPENTANCE

Let us examine our ways and test them, and let us return to the LORD.

Lamentations 3:40

ASKING

Personalize for missionaries what Job says of the Lord.

I know that you can do all things; no plan of yours can be thwarted.

Job 42:2

_____

_____

_____

_____

_____

_____

_____

YIELDING

Personalize and pray this same Scripture for yourself.

_____

_____

_____

_____

_____

_____

_____

Pray for missionary work in ANDORRA
(Southwestern Europe, between France and Spain)

Week 1
Thoughts and Prayers

_____

_____

_____

_____

_____

_____

_____

_____

_____

_____

_____

_____

_____

_____

_____

_____

_____

_____

_____

_____

_____

Week 2

BREASTPLATE OF RIGHTEOUSNESS

Never forget that the evil one cannot touch a hair on your head without God's permission. Seldom do we realize the times our Lord has protected us when we find ourselves in a dangerous environment. I remember one such time when my family and I served in Venezuela.

Two elderly women were making their way to Sunday evening worship. The church was located in a high crime area of the city. Two thieves jumped out from hiding and shouted at the women, "Stop where you are! Give us all your money or we will kill you!"

Both women were filled with fear. One of them did as many of us would do. She became so nervous that it seemed like she was playing a tune with her knees as her entire body trembled. The other, however, decided to turn her fear over to the Lord. She lifted a prayer to the Father. Then she looked at the thieves and said, "All that I am is because of who Jesus is, and all that I have belongs to Him. So in the name of the Lord Jesus Christ, leave us alone."

Witnesses to the attempted robbery reported that the two thieves immediately became fearful and fled the scene.

The two ladies continued on to church. At the conclusion of the worship service, one of the thieves was waiting outside the church. He stopped one of the men and said, "You know who I am, and you know my partner and I have killed people for looking at us the wrong way. But tonight something happened that I cannot explain. See those two women over there? We tried to rob them, but that one woman said, 'In the name of the Lord Jesus Christ, leave us alone.' Please explain to me where those four huge men with flaming swords came from after she said that."

No one but the two thieves saw the men with flaming swords. But I believe when we get to heaven, we will be surprised to learn of all the times our Lord's holy angels protected us during times we trusted Him, obeyed His voice, went wherever He sent us, and remained faithful to our call.

Bill—South America

> Each time you intercede, be quiet first and worship God in His glory.
> Think of what He can do, of how He delights to hear Christ,
> of your place in Christ, and expect great things.
> *Andrew Murray*

PRAISE & THANKSGIVING

Worship by using the characteristic of God mentioned in
this Scripture—"faithful."

But the Lord is faithful, and He will strengthen and protect you from the evil one.

2 Thessalonians 3:3 (NASB)

REPENTANCE

Search your heart as you meditate on this Scripture.
What is the Holy Spirit revealing to you?

Create in me a pure heart, O God, and renew a steadfast spirit within me.

Psalm 51:10

ASKING

Read the following Scripture. Rewrite it, personalizing
it for missionaries, asking that they would have the
"breastplate of righteousness" in place.

Righteousness will be his belt and faithfulness the sash around his waist.

Isaiah 11:5

_____

_____

YIELDING

Now meditate on the Scripture again. Rewrite it below,
personalizing and praying it for yourself. How can you
respond to what God is saying to you in this Scripture?

_____

_____

_____

_____

_____

Pray for missionary work in ANGOLA
(Southern Africa, bordering the South Atlantic Ocean)

Prayer is lifting up empty hands to an abundant God.
Harvey Kneisel, missionary

PRAISE & THANKSGIVING
Worship the "faithful" One.
But the Lord is faithful, and He will strengthen and protect you from the evil one.
2 Thessalonians 3:3 (NASB)

REPENTANCE
Search your heart as you meditate on this Scripture.
Create in me a pure heart, O God, and renew a steadfast spirit within me.
Psalm 51:10

ASKING
Rewrite this Scripture, personalizing it for missionaries, asking for the "breastplate of righteousness" to be in place.
My prayer is not that you take them out of the world but that you protect them from the evil one. They are not of the world, even as I am not of it. Sanctify them by the truth; your word is truth. As you sent me into the world, I have sent them into the world.
John 17:15–18

_____

_____

_____

_____

YIELDING
Rewrite it again, personalizing and praying it for yourself. Respond to what God is saying to you in this Scripture.

_____

_____

_____

_____

_____

_____

Pray for missionary work in ANGUILLA
(Caribbean islands east of Puerto Rico)

> Avail yourself of the greatest privilege this side of heaven.
> Jesus Christ died to make this communion
> and communication with the Father possible.
> *Billy Graham*

PRAISE & THANKSGIVING

But the Lord is faithful, and He will strengthen and protect you from the evil one.
2 Thessalonians 3:3 (NASB)

REPENTANCE

Create in me a pure heart, O God, and renew a steadfast spirit within me.
Psalm 51:10

ASKING

Personalize this Scripture for missionaries, asking that they would have the "breastplate of righteousness" in place.

You intended to harm me, but God intended it for good to accomplish what is now being done, the saving of many lives.
Genesis 50:20

_____

_____

_____

_____

_____

YIELDING

Now personalize and pray it for yourself. How can you respond to what God is saying to you?

_____

_____

_____

_____

_____

_____

Pray for missionary work in
ANTIGUA and BARBUDA
(Caribbean islands east-southeast of Puerto Rico)

> Walking with God down the avenue of prayer,
> we acquire something of His likeness, and unconsciously
> we become witnesses to others of His beauty and His grace.
> *E. M. Bounds*

PRAISE & THANKSGIVING

But the Lord is faithful, and He will strengthen and protect you from the evil one.
        2 Thessalonians 3:3 (NASB)

REPENTANCE

Create in me a pure heart, O God, and renew a steadfast spirit within me.
        Psalm 51:10

ASKING

Rewrite this Scripture, personalizing it for missionaries.

*Rescue us from the hand of our enemies, and . . . enable us to serve him
without fear in holiness and righteousness before him all our days.*
        Luke 1:74–75

_____

_____

_____

_____

_____

YIELDING

What is God saying to you in this Scripture?

_____

_____

_____

_____

_____

_____

_____

_____

Pray for missionary work in ARGENTINA
(Southern South America, between Chile and Uruguay)

I have been driven many times to my knees by the overwhelming
conviction that I had nowhere else to go. My own wisdom,
and that of all about me, seemed insufficient for the day.
Abraham Lincoln

PRAISE & THANKSGIVING
But the Lord is faithful, and He will strengthen and protect you from the evil one.
2 Thessalonians 3:3 (NASB)

REPENTANCE
Create in me a pure heart, O God, and renew a steadfast spirit within me.
Psalm 51:10

ASKING
Personalize this Scripture today for missionaries.
*Though I walk in the midst of trouble, you preserve my life; you stretch out
your hand against the anger of my foes, with your right hand you save me.*
Psalm 138:7

_____

_____

_____

YIELDING
Personalize and pray this same Scripture for yourself.

_____

_____

_____

_____

_____

_____

_____

_____

Pray for missionary work in ARMENIA
(Southwestern Asia, east of Turkey)

Week 2
Thoughts and Prayers

_____

_____

_____

_____

_____

_____

_____

_____

_____

_____

_____

_____

_____

_____

_____

_____

_____

_____

_____

_____

_____

_____

_____

_____

_____

_____

Week 3

GOSPEL OF PEACE

We know God's timing is perfect, but we don't always realize how often God is at work around us as we go about our daily life.

I was serving as a missionary in South America. On one trip into the jungle, I arrived in a small village in Peru and went to the local inn where I would be staying for a few days. After making my greetings around town, I ate lunch, then headed back to the inn to "hit the hammock" and relax.

After just a few minutes, I noticed a man in one of the hammocks watching me. He saw that I was reading and asked the name of my book. I told him it was a Bible. Our conversation continued and he asked if I lived in the area. I told him about my work as a missionary in a nearby town and among the Ashéninka people in Peru. Surprised by my response, the man responded in Spanish, "I am Ashéninka."

This surprised me because in my work with Ashéninka people, I had discovered that most of them only speak the indigenous language. So I asked the man where he lived. To my amazement he responded, "New Jersey." I nearly fell out of my hammock! The man worked as a chef in a Peruvian restaurant in New Jersey and was here on vacation in Peru.

I was full of questions about his life, of course, and eventually the conversation led to his religious beliefs. He did not have a personal relationship with Christ, so I began to share Bible stories with him. I was learning Bible stories in Spanish at the time, so I was able to tell him the first five stories from the Bible: God's creation of the angels, God the Creator of all things, the sin of Adam and Eve, God's punishment of sin, and the promise of God through Adam.

When I would struggle to find the correct Spanish word, this man understood enough English to know what I was saying. After two hours, the Holy Spirit softened his heart and he understood the truth about Jesus. Tears welled up in his eyes and trickled down his face as he accepted Christ.

God placed me in the right place, at the right time, so an Ashéninka man living in New Jersey could receive forgiveness and eternal life. God has perfect timing!

Marshall—SOUTH AMERICA

> Of all the duties enjoined by Christianity,
> none is more essential and yet more neglected than prayer.
> *François Fénelon*

PRAISE & THANKSGIVING

Worship by using the name of God mentioned in this
Scripture—"peace."

*For He Himself is our peace, who made both groups into one and
broke down the barrier of the dividing wall.*

Ephesians 2:14 (NASB)

REPENTANCE

Search your heart as you meditate on this Scripture.
What is the Holy Spirit revealing to you?

*I acknowledged my sin to You, and my iniquity I have not hidden. I said, "I will
confess my transgressions to the LORD," and You forgave the iniquity of my sin.*

Psalm 32:5 (NKJV)

ASKING

Read the following Scripture. Rewrite it, personalizing it
for missionaries, asking that they would have "feet fitted
with the gospel of peace."

*Conduct yourselves in a manner worthy of the gospel of Christ. Then, whether I
come and see you or only hear about you in my absence, I will know that you stand
firm in one spirit, contending as one man for the faith of the gospel.*

Philippians 1:27–28

_____

_____

_____

YIELDING

Now meditate on the Scripture again. Rewrite it below,
personalizing and praying it for yourself. How can you
respond to what God is saying to you in this Scripture?

_____

_____

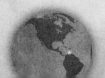

Pray for missionary work in ARUBA
(Caribbean island north of Venezuela)

It is far better to pray in a private room, be unseen by man,
and have the approval of God than to give a public display
of prayer and have a heart full of pride.

Anonymous

PRAISE & THANKSGIVING

Worship Him, the God of "peace."

*For He Himself is our peace, who made both groups into one and
broke down the barrier of the dividing wall.*

Ephesians 2:14 (NASB)

REPENTANCE

Search your heart as you meditate on this Scripture.

*I acknowledged my sin to You, and my iniquity I have not hidden. I said, "I will
confess my transgressions to the LORD," and You forgave the iniquity of my sin.*

Psalm 32:5 (NKJV)

ASKING

Rewrite this Scripture, personalizing it for missionaries,
asking for their feet to be "fitted with the gospel of peace."

*Therefore, my dear brothers, stand firm. Let nothing move you. Always give
yourselves fully to the work of the Lord, because you know that your labor
in the Lord is not in vain.*

1 Corinthians 15:58

_____

_____

_____

_____

YIELDING

Rewrite it again, personalizing and praying it for yourself.
Respond to what God is saying to you in this Scripture.

_____

_____

_____

_____

> The prayer of the feeblest saint who lives in the Spirit
> and keeps right with God is a terror to Satan.
> *John Bunyan*

PRAISE & THANKSGIVING

*For He Himself is our peace, who made both groups into one and broke down
the barrier of the dividing wall.*

Ephesians 2:14 (NASB)

REPENTANCE

*I acknowledged my sin to You, and my iniquity I have not hidden. I said, "I will
confess my transgressions to the LORD," and You forgave the iniquity of my sin.*

Psalm 32:5 (NKJV)

ASKING

Personalize this Scripture for missionaries, asking that
they would have "feet fitted with the gospel of peace."

*How beautiful on the mountains are the feet of those who bring good news
of peace and salvation, the news that the God of Israel reigns!*

Isaiah 52:7 (NLT)

_____

_____

_____

_____

_____

YIELDING

Now personalize and pray it for yourself. How can you
respond to what God is saying to you?

_____

_____

_____

_____

_____

Pray for missionary work in AUSTRIA
(Central Europe, north of Italy and Slovenia)

> Anyone who has ever been used mightily by the Lord
> was a person of the Word and prayer.
> *Rick Warren*

PRAISE & THANKSGIVING

For He Himself is our peace, who made both groups into one and broke down the barrier of the dividing wall.

Ephesians 2:14 (NASB)

REPENTANCE

I acknowledged my sin to You, and my iniquity I have not hidden. I said, "I will confess my transgressions to the LORD," and You forgave the iniquity of my sin.

Psalm 32:5 (NKJV)

ASKING

Rewrite this Scripture, personalizing it for missionaries.

For in the gospel a righteousness from God is revealed, a righteousness that is by faith from first to last, just as it is written: "The righteous will live by faith."

Romans 1:17

_____

_____

_____

_____

_____

YIELDING

What is God saying to you in this Scripture?

_____

_____

_____

_____

_____

_____

_____

_____

Pray for missionary work in AZERBAIJAN
(Southwestern Asia, between Iran and Russia)

No wonder Satan tries to keep our minds fussy
in active work till we cannot think in prayer.
Oswald Chambers

PRAISE & THANKSGIVING

*For He Himself is our peace, who made both groups into one and broke down
the barrier of the dividing wall.*
Ephesians 2:14 (NASB)

REPENTANCE

*I acknowledged my sin to You, and my iniquity I have not hidden. I said, "I will
confess my transgressions to the LORD," and You forgave the iniquity of my sin.*
Psalm 32:5 (NKJV)

ASKING

Personalize this Scripture today for missionaries.
*All men will hate you because of me, but he who stands firm to the end
will be saved.*
Matthew 10:22

_____

_____

_____

_____

_____

YIELDING

Personalize and pray this same Scripture for yourself.

_____

_____

_____

_____

_____

_____

_____

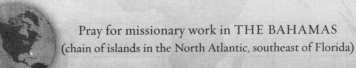

Pray for missionary work in THE BAHAMAS
(chain of islands in the North Atlantic, southeast of Florida)

Week 3
Thoughts and Prayers

Week 4

SHIELD OF FAITH

In the fall of 1999, a missionary walked the streets of a market town taking pictures and buying small items. She happened upon an old man and his wife and was taken by the old man's smile. She asked them to pose, took their picture, and copied down their address so she could send them a copy. After developing the picture, she gave one copy to friends, Jason and Katherine, and sent the other copy to the home of the old man.

In the fall of 2001, my coworker and I met Jason and Katherine prior to our arrival in China. During our time together, they gave us several pictures of the people we'd be working with, including one of the old man and his wife. I took these pictures and made presentations in PowerPoint® format with them, as well as prayer calendars and other materials.

In the fall of 2002, we asked our supporters in America to join us in seeking God for a great awakening among our people group. I also launched a Web site during that time which included the picture of the old man and his wife.

In December, a team of Asian youth came to work with us for a week. One morning we divided up into four teams and began looking for different villages. One team asked a truck driver if he knew the way to a particular village. He answered, "Yes, hop on." Thirty minutes later, he stopped the truck and said, "Climb up that mountain and you'll be there."

Five young women hiked up the steep mountainside, wondering if they would ever reach the top. Nearly an hour later, they finally caught sight of a rooftop. They entered the village and met a young man who said, "I don't live here, but I can translate for you since none of the people in this village can speak Chinese." When the travelers learned the name of the village, they discovered they were in the wrong place. This was not the village they were looking for.

Regardless of their "misfortune," at least one couple in the village was happy to see them. They invited the five ladies into their home and prepared a meal for them. Before long, the visitors were sharing the gospel, first telling the young man and then waiting for him to translate for the older couple to hear.

God opened the ears of the young *and* old man that day, and both prayed to receive Christ. The old man was more than excited that day, and he took joy in showing the guests around his humble village home. In fact, he brought out a frame that held several family photos—and among them was the photo taken by the missionary nearly three years prior! The women were astonished!

Out of 100,000 people in this particular people group, the missionaries had only one photograph of an older man. And out of over 100 villages, they had traveled to less than ten of them. We call this man, "Simeon," for it seems that the Lord had willed that he not see death before he had seen Christ (Luke 2:26).

Second Samuel 14:14 says, "But God does not take away a life; but He devises means, so that His banished ones are not expelled from Him" (NKJV). God used a camera, a postage stamp, a Web site, a prayer calendar, the prayers of countless people, faulty traveling directions, and the mouths of young women and a young man. And He ordered them all so that this 71-year-old man would not be expelled from His presence. Every time we visited Simeon and his wife, we found him to be growing in the knowledge of the Lord and being further changed into His likeness.

—*A Christian worker in Asia*

Prayer is not getting things from God. That is the most initial stage.
Prayer is getting into perfect communion with God; I tell Him what
I know He knows in order that I may get to know it as He does.
Oswald Chambers

PRAISE & THANKSGIVING

Worship by using the description of God mentioned
in this Scripture—"my shield."

You are my refuge and my shield;
I have put my hope in your word.

Psalm 119:114

REPENTANCE

Search your heart as you meditate on this Scripture.
What is the Holy Spirit revealing to you?

Those who live according to the sinful nature
have their minds set on what that nature desires.

Romans 8:5

ASKING

Read the following Scripture. Rewrite it, personalizing
it for missionaries, asking that they would "take up the
shield of faith."

For everyone born of God overcomes the world. This is the victory that has
overcome the world, even our faith.

1 John 5:4

_____

_____

YIELDING

Now meditate on the Scripture again. Rewrite it below,
personalizing and praying it for yourself. How can you
respond to what God is saying to you in this Scripture?

_____

_____

_____

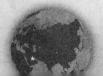

Pray for missionary work in BAHRAIN
(archipelago in the Persian Gulf, east of Saudi Arabia)

> Prayer girds human weakness with divine strength,
> turns human folly into heavenly wisdom, and gives to troubled
> mortals the peace of God. We know not what prayer can do.
> *Charles Spurgeon*

PRAISE & THANKSGIVING

Worship the One who is the "shield" around you.

> *You are my refuge and my shield;*
> *I have put my hope in your word.*
>> Psalm 119:114

REPENTANCE

Search your heart as you meditate on this Scripture.

> *Those who live in accordance with the Spirit have their minds set*
> *on what the Spirit desires.*
>> Romans 8:5

ASKING

Rewrite this Scripture, personalizing it for missionaries,
asking that they would "take up the shield of faith."

> *Now faith is being sure of what we hope for and certain of what we do not see.*
>> Hebrews 11:1

_____

_____

_____

_____

YIELDING

Rewrite it again, personalizing and praying it for yourself.
Respond to what God is saying to you in this Scripture.

_____

_____

_____

_____

_____

Pray for missionary work in BANGLADESH
(Southern Asia, between Burma and India)

Prayer is life passionately wanting, wishing, desiring God's triumph. Prayer is life striving and toiling everywhere and always for that ultimate victory.
G. Campbell Morgan

PRAISE & THANKSGIVING

You are my refuge and my shield;
I have put my hope in your word.

Psalm 119:114

REPENTANCE

Those who live in accordance with the Spirit have their minds set
on what the Spirit desires.

Romans 8:5

ASKING

Personalize this Scripture for missionaries, asking that they would "take up the shield of faith."

The weapons we fight with are not the weapons of the world. On the contrary, they have divine power to demolish strongholds.

2 Corinthians 10:4

_____

_____

_____

_____

YIELDING

Now personalize and pray it for yourself. How can you respond to what God is saying to you?

_____

_____

_____

_____

_____

_____

_____

Pray for missionary work in BARBADOS
(Caribbean island northeast of Venezuela)

If God sees that my spiritual life will be furthered by giving the things
for which I ask, then He will give them, but that is not the end of prayer.
The end of prayer is that I come to know God Himself.
Oswald Chambers

PRAISE & THANKSGIVING

You are my refuge and my shield;
I have put my hope in your word.

Psalm 119:114

REPENTANCE

Those who live in accordance with the Spirit have their minds set
on what the Spirit desires.

Romans 8:5

ASKING

Rewrite this Scripture, personalizing it for missionaries.

Consider it pure joy, my brothers, whenever you face trials of many kinds,
because you know that the testing of your faith develops perseverance.

James 1:2–3

_____

_____

_____

_____

YIELDING

What is God saying to you in this Scripture?

_____

_____

_____

_____

_____

_____

_____

Pray for missionary work in BELARUS
(Eastern Europe, east of Poland)

> We must alter our lives in order to alter our hearts,
> for it is impossible to live one way and pray another.
> *William Law*

PRAISE & THANKSGIVING

You are my refuge and my shield;
I have put my hope in your word.
Psalm 119:114

REPENTANCE

Those who live in accordance with the Spirit have their minds set
on what the Spirit desires.
Romans 8:5

ASKING

Personalize this Scripture today for missionaries.

If you make the Most High your dwelling— even the LORD, who is my refuge—
then no harm will befall you, no disaster will come near your tent. For he will
command his angels concerning you to guard you in all your ways; they will lift
you up in their hands, so that you will not strike your foot against a stone.
Psalm 91:9–12

_____

_____

_____

_____

YIELDING

Personalize and pray this same Scripture for yourself.

_____

_____

_____

_____

_____

Pray for missionary work in BELGIUM
(Western Europe, between France and the Netherlands)

Week 4
Thoughts and Prayers

Week 5

HELMET OF SALVATION

"I am torn between the two: I desire to depart and be with Christ, which is better by far; but it is more necessary for you that I remain in the body." (Phil. 1:23–24)

In 1978, I saw a glimpse of what Paul meant in this passage from Philippians 1 while serving on my first mission trip overseas. On the streets of Niteroi, Brazil, I worked side by side with a missionary who was a very bold witness. Each evening in our hotel room, I drank in his love for the Lord and for the lost.

As we arrived at our hotel the first day, a woman on the hotel staff was still cleaning our room. My missionary friend immediately began sharing the gospel with her. The woman was already a believer, but she wept as she asked us to pray for her 22-year-old son who did not know Christ personally. So we prayed. The next two weeks we saw many people trust their lives to Christ as we shared God's message of hope.

When it was time to return, seventy-two short-term mission workers from the United States climbed aboard the bus that would take us to the airplane and eventually take us home.

Home! I couldn't wait to see it, not to mention those I loved. But suddenly, I remembered that my passport and tickets were still in the strongbox in the hotel room. The missionary yelled to the bus driver to stop. We ran back to our room and discovered a hotel employee refurbishing the little refrigerator with soft drinks. I grabbed my tickets and passport. I was ready to get back to the bus that would take me to the plane that would take me home. But my missionary friend hesitated. "Wait, Bill! Share your testimony with this man." I thought to myself, "But the bus to the plane that will get me home is waiting." I did share my testimony; then the missionary shared the gospel. The young hotel employee bowed his head in prayer and gave his life to the Lord Jesus.

As he prayed, I heard sobs coming from someone in the doorway. When the "amen" was said, the woman standing at the door rushed in, took the young man in her arms and began shouting with joy. Yes, this was the son we had prayed for two weeks earlier. His mother's prayer for his salvation had been answered.

My missionary friend taught me a lifelong lesson. There are times when I can't wait to get home to heaven, but as long as one person needs to hear of the merits of our Savior, my heavenly home can wait.

Bill—SOUTH AMERICA

Prayer, in every care and anxiety and need of life, with thanksgiving, is the
means God has appointed for our obtaining freedom from all anxiety.
R. A. Torrey

PRAISE & THANKSGIVING

Worship by using the name of God mentioned in this
Scripture—"salvation."

The LORD is my light and my salvation—whom shall I fear?
The LORD is the stronghold of my life—of whom shall I be afraid?
Psalm 27:1

REPENTANCE

Search your heart as you meditate on this Scripture.
What is the Holy Spirit revealing to you?

Trust in him at all times, O people; pour out your hearts to him, for God
is our refuge.
Psalm 62:8

ASKING

Read the following Scripture. Rewrite it, personalizing it
for missionaries, asking that they would take the "helmet
of salvation."

But since we belong to the day, let us be self-controlled, putting on faith and love
as a breastplate, and the hope of salvation as a helmet.
1 Thessalonians 5:8

_____

_____

YIELDING

Now meditate on the Scripture again. Rewrite it below,
personalizing and praying it for yourself. How can you
respond to what God is saying to you in this Scripture?

_____

_____

_____

_____

Pray for missionary work in BELIZE
(Central America, between Guatemala and Mexico)

> Prayer is an offering up of our desires unto God for things
> agreeable to His will, in the name of Christ, with confession
> of our sins and thankful acknowledgment of His mercies.
> *The Kneeling Christian*

PRAISE & THANKSGIVING

Worship God, for He is your "salvation."

The LORD is my light and my salvation—whom shall I fear?
The LORD is the stronghold of my life—of whom shall I be afraid?
Psalm 27:1

REPENTANCE

Search your heart as you meditate on this Scripture.

Trust in him at all times, O people; pour out your hearts to him, for God
is our refuge.
Psalm 62:8

ASKING

Rewrite this Scripture, personalizing it for missionaries,
asking that they would "take the helmet of salvation."

I pray also that the eyes of your heart may be enlightened in order that you may
know the hope to which he has called you, the riches of his glorious inheritance
in the saints, and his incomparably great power for us who believe.
Ephesians 1:18–19

_____

_____

_____

YIELDING

Rewrite it again, personalizing and praying it for yourself.
Respond to what God is saying to you in this Scripture.

_____

_____

_____

_____

_____

Pray for missionary work in BENIN
(Western Africa, between Nigeria and Togo)

> Obedience in prayer unleashes the limitless power of our God.
> *Charlene Kneisel, missionary*

PRAISE & THANKSGIVING

> *The LORD is my light and my salvation—whom shall I fear?*
> *The LORD is the stronghold of my life—of whom shall I be afraid?*
>   Psalm 27:1

REPENTANCE

> *Trust in him at all times, O people; pour out your hearts to him, for God*
> *is our refuge.*
>   Psalm 62:8

ASKING

Personalize this Scripture for missionaries, asking
that they would take the "helmet of salvation."

> *We have this hope as an anchor for the soul, firm and secure.*
> *It enters the inner sanctuary behind the curtain.*
>   Hebrews 6:19

_____

_____

_____

_____

YIELDING

Now personalize and pray it for yourself. How can you
respond to what God is saying to you?

_____

_____

_____

_____

_____

_____

_____

_____

Pray for missionary work in BERMUDA
(group of islands in the North Atlantic,
east of South Carolina)

> The ministry of prayer, if it be anything worthy of the Name,
> is a ministry of ardor, a ministry of unwearied and
> intense longing after God and His holiness.
> *E. M. Bounds*

PRAISE & THANKSGIVING

The LORD is my light and my salvation—whom shall I fear?
The LORD is the stronghold of my life—of whom shall I be afraid?
> Psalm 27:1

REPENTANCE

Trust in him at all times, O people; pour out your hearts to him, for God
is our refuge.
> Psalm 62:8

ASKING

Rewrite this Scripture, personalizing it for missionaries.

We are more than conquerors through him who loved us. For I am convinced
that neither death nor life, neither angels nor demons, neither the present nor the
future, nor any powers, neither height nor depth, nor anything else in all creation,
will be able to separate us from the love of God that is in Christ Jesus our Lord.
> Romans 8:37–39

_____

_____

_____

_____

YIELDING

What is God saying to you in this Scripture?

_____

_____

_____

_____

_____

Pray for missionary work in BHUTAN
(Southern Asia, between China and India)

> The purpose of prayer is the maintenance of fitness
> in an ideal relationship with God amid conditions
> which ought not to be merely ideal but really actual.
> *Oswald Chambers*

PRAISE & THANKSGIVING

The LORD is my light and my salvation—whom shall I fear?
The LORD is the stronghold of my life—of whom shall I be afraid?
   Psalm 27:1

REPENTANCE

Trust in him at all times, O people; pour out your hearts to him, for God is
our refuge.
   Psalm 62:8

ASKING

Personalize this Scripture today for missionaries.

May he be enthroned in God's presence forever;
appoint your love and faithfulness to protect him.
   Psalm 61:7

_____

_____

_____

_____

YIELDING

Personalize and pray this same Scripture for yourself.

_____

_____

_____

_____

_____

_____

_____

_____

Pray for missionary work in BOLIVIA
(Central South America, southwest of Brazil)

Week 5
Thoughts and Prayers

Week 6

SWORD OF THE SPIRIT

It began like any other Saturday morning, hearing my husband, Glynn, putting on more firewood to keep us warm on a wintry day in November. Glynn was leaving to take his nephew hunting, so he came back into the bedroom to see if I was awake. I was—already up doing my usual early morning study in the Word. That month God had impressed me to go through the Psalms and make notes of all the places that reminded me of His presence, recording what He *had been* doing, *was* doing, and *would be* doing in my life.

Because I was already up and reading that morning, Glynn kissed me goodbye and we laughed about the frog in my throat! (Maybe the frog-turned-prince had just kissed me!) But the ordinary Saturday morning fell apart three hours later when I received a call that Glynn had been accidentally shot while deer hunting.

I stood beside the window of the home we'd built together and prayed, "Lord, if Glynn can be helped, I'm asking You to help him now. If he is already with You, then I ask You to give me peace." And God's peace—the peace He poured into my heart throughout that month, preparing me day by day to know His presence in my life—was poured over me like a refreshing fountain. I literally *felt* God's peace, and I knew Glynn was with the

Lord. The peace in my heart confirmed that God's Word would prepare me and sustain me every step of the way.

In the years since my husband's death, God has proven His daily guidance in my life, using six short-term overseas mission trips to prepare my heart and mind for the seventh trip, going as a missionary to Argentina. God continues to use what He planted in me—a growing love for His Word and His chosen people—to bring about the call He put in my heart as a child to be a missionary! God is never late. Although we think He has given up on His plan for our life, He has not. No matter how busy you are, how tired you are, wherever you are, I would say, "Stay in the Word!"

Jeannie—SOUTH AMERICA

My husband, Charles, and I were working with the youth in a small community north of the city of Santa Cruz, Bolivia. After a baseball clinic, Charles shared the story of the widow's mite with the boys. The following weekend we showed them the "Jesus" film while the story of the widow was still fresh on their minds.

During the film, Charles sat with about thirty boys between the ages of six and twelve. When the widow made her appearance in the film and gave her offering, Charles felt a slight tug on his shirtsleeve. He glanced down to see who so desperately needed his attention. Ricardo, a seven-year-old boy, whispered, "Hey Charlie, that story is in your book!"

Charles grinned and explained, "Yes, that story is in my book. But it is not just *my* book, it is *our* book from God, the Bible."

Ask the Heavenly Father to provide Christian workers who will teach children to grow in their knowledge of the Bible and to become faithful followers of Christ. Ask God to prepare generations of godly parents, teachers, and leaders of nations. Pray for God to reveal Himself as the one true God to those who have never heard the name of Jesus.

Amy—SOUTH AMERICA

> We have to pray with our eyes on God, not on the difficulties.
> *Oswald Chambers*

PRAISE & THANKSGIVING

Worship by using the name of God mentioned in this Scripture—"the Word."

> *In the beginning was the Word, and the Word was with God, and the Word was God. He was with God in the beginning.*
>
> John 1:1–2

REPENTANCE

Search your heart as you meditate on this Scripture. What is the Holy Spirit revealing to you?

> *I have kept my feet from every evil path so that I might obey your word.*
>
> Psalm 119:101

ASKING

Read the following Scripture. Rewrite it, personalizing it for missionaries, asking that they would "take the sword of the Spirit, which is the word of God."

> *For the word of God is living and active. Sharper than any double-edged sword, it penetrates even to dividing soul and spirit, joints and marrow; it judges the thoughts and attitudes of the heart.*
>
> Hebrews 4:12

_____

_____

_____

_____

YIELDING

Now meditate on the Scripture again. Rewrite it below, personalizing and praying it for yourself. How can you respond to what God is saying to you in this Scripture?

_____

_____

_____

Pray for missionary work in
BOSNIA and HERZOGOVINA
(Southeastern Europe, bordering the Adriatic Sea)

Faith in a prayer-hearing God will make a prayer-loving Christian.
Andrew Murray

PRAISE & THANKSGIVING

Worship the Lord, for He is "the Word."

In the beginning was the Word, and the Word was with God, and the Word was God. He was with God in the beginning.

John 1:1–2

REPENTANCE

Search your heart as you meditate on this Scripture.

I have kept my feet from every evil path so that I might obey your word.

Psalm 119:101

ASKING

Rewrite this Scripture, personalizing it for missionaries, asking that they would "take the sword of the Spirit, which is the word of God."

I have hidden your word in my heart that I might not sin against you.

Psalm 119:11

_____

_____

_____

_____

YIELDING

Rewrite it again, personalizing and praying it for yourself. Respond to what God is saying to you in this Scripture.

_____

_____

_____

_____

_____

_____

_____

Pray for missionary work in BOTSWANA
(Southern Africa, north of South Africa)

Oh, how strenuous is life! I know a little of it. Men "ought always
to pray, and not to faint." How fierce the battle! I know something
of the conflict, but I ought not to faint, because I can pray.
G. Campbell Morgan

PRAISE & THANKSGIVING

*In the beginning was the Word, and the Word was with God, and the Word
was God. He was with God in the beginning.*

Lohn 1:1–2

REPENTANCE

I have kept my feet from every evil path so that I might obey your word.

Psalm 119:101

ASKING

Personalize this Scripture for missionaries, asking that they
would "take the sword of the Spirit"—the Word of God.

As for God, his way is perfect; the word of the LORD is flawless.
He is a shield for all who take refuge in him.

Psalm 18:30

_____

_____

_____

_____

YIELDING

Now personalize and pray it for yourself. How can you
respond to what God is saying to you?

_____

_____

_____

_____

_____

_____

_____

Pray for missionary work in BRAZIL
(Eastern South America, bordering the Atlantic Ocean)

> Let none expect to have the mastery over his inward
> corruption in any degree, without going in weakness
> again and again to the Lord for strength.
> *George Mueller*

PRAISE & THANKSGIVING

*In the beginning was the Word, and the Word was with God, and the Word
was God. He was with God in the beginning.*

John 1:1–2

REPENTANCE

I have kept my feet from every evil path so that I might obey your word.

Psalm 119:101

ASKING

Rewrite this Scripture, personalizing it for missionaries.

*Praise the LORD. Blessed is the man who fears the LORD, who finds great delight
in his commands. His children will be mighty in the land; the generation of the
upright will be blessed. Wealth and riches are in his house, and his righteousness
endures forever. Even in darkness light dawns for the upright, for the gracious
and compassionate and righteous man.*

Psalm 112:1–4

_____

_____

_____

_____

_____

YIELDING

What is God saying to you in this Scripture?

_____

_____

_____

_____

_____

Pray for missionary work in
THE BRITISH VIRGIN ISLANDS
(between the Caribbean and the North Atlantic)

> Have you any days of fasting and prayer? Storm the throne of grace
> and persevere therein, and mercy will come down.
> *John Wesley*

PRAISE & THANKSGIVING

> *In the beginning was the Word, and the Word was with God, and the Word*
> *was God. He was with God in the beginning.*
>
>   John 1:1–2

REPENTANCE

> *I have kept my feet from every evil path so that I might obey your word.*
>
>   Psalm 119:101

ASKING

Personalize this Scripture today for missionaries.

> *I will bow down toward your holy temple and will praise your name for*
> *your love and your faithfulness, for you have exalted above all things your*
> *name and your word.*
>
>   Psalm 138:2

_____

_____

_____

_____

_____

YIELDING

Personalize and pray this same Scripture for yourself.

_____

_____

_____

_____

_____

_____

_____

Pray for missionary work in BRUNEI
(Southeastern Asia, bordering the South China Sea)

Week 6
Thoughts and Prayers

_____

_____

_____

_____

_____

_____

_____

_____

_____

_____

_____

_____

_____

_____

_____

_____

_____

_____

_____

_____

_____

_____

_____

_____

_____

_____

_____

_____

Week 7

PRAYER

Regional women's retreats were always the highlight of the year. Missionary women gathered from different mission organizations for encouragement, teaching, renewal, and rest. The power of prayer became very real for me the year I was asked to facilitate a workshop. My only role was to show a video and then generate a question-and-answer time. I didn't need much preparation to do that, I thought.

But the night before the scheduled workshop, God woke me up in the middle of the night. I felt Him leading me to study the book that accompanied the video. I clearly felt his direction to "get prepared!" I didn't really understand why at the time, but I obeyed. I made a few chicken-scratch notes on a piece of paper, folded it, and put it in my pocket.

It was a hot, humid afternoon in Southeast Asia with no air conditioning, but the room was packed with eighty women, each of them eager, excited, and hopeful to glean new insights on love and marriage! The moment of truth arrived when we sat down to watch the video, and the electronic equipment did not work! This was a common occurrence in this third-world country, but I thought to myself, "Why me? Why today, Lord?"

Several hotel staff worked and worked, but they could not get the VCR/TV to work. I had an hour-and-a-half long session staring me in the face, eighty disappointed women, and only a scrap paper of notes in my pocket. We prayed together for God to redeem the time. With an anointing of the Holy Spirit like I had never experienced before, I spoke and taught the entire content of the book with illustrations, humor, tears, and truth. God was certainly faithful to me that day, giving me a spirit of wisdom and knowledge. He equipped me to minister to the women in a miraculous and powerful way.

Later as I retold this story to my mother by telephone, she asked me the exact date I was speaking. With great excitement and praise, she declared: "Sandy, you were speaking on your birthday. That means that people all over the world were praying for you that day!" Hallelujah! I had not realized the connection of my speaking, my birthday, and the printed prayer calendar that revealed my name to so many.

Specific, bold, personal and powerful prayers do make a difference! I believe with all of my heart that somewhere on that day, people were praying for me by name and using God's Word to stand in the gap for me! Maybe someone was praying, "Father, enable Sandy to be strong in the Lord and in his mighty power" (Eph. 6:10) or perhaps, "Jesus, help Sandy to be anxious for nothing, and may Your peace guard her heart and mind in Christ Jesus" (Phil. 4:6–7).

Another might have prayed, "Father, I pray that in Sandy's life today, You are able to do exceedingly abundantly above all that she asks or thinks, according to the power that works in her" (Eph. 3:20). I am sure that someone was praying Hebrews 13:21: "Lord, equip Sandy with everything good for doing Your will. Do a work in her that is pleasing to You."

Thank You, Lord, for Your Word and for Your knowledge to know what I would need on that day, in that moment. Thank You, Lord, for stirring the hearts of faithful prayer warriors to lift me up on that day. Thank You, Lord, for it is You who is at work in us, both to will and to act for Your good pleasure!" (Phil 2:13).

Sandy—EAST ASIA

> If you want the kingdom speeded, go out and
> speed it yourselves. Only obedience rationalizes prayer.
> Only missions can redeem your intercessions from insincerity.
> *William Carey*

PRAISE & THANKSGIVING

Worship by using the characteristic of God mentioned in this Scripture—"worthy."

I call upon the LORD, who is worthy to be praised, and I am saved from my enemies.

2 Samuel 22:4 (NASB)

REPENTANCE

Search your heart as you meditate on this Scripture. What is the Holy Spirit revealing to you?

After Job had prayed for his friends, the LORD made him prosperous again and gave him twice as much as he had before.

Job 42:10

ASKING

Read the following Scripture. Rewrite it, personalizing it for missionaries, asking that they would "pray in the Spirit on all occasions."

Devote yourselves to prayer, being watchful and thankful.

Colossians 4:2

_____

_____

YIELDING

Now meditate on the Scripture again. Rewrite it below, personalizing and praying it for yourself. How can you respond to what God is saying to you in this Scripture?

_____

_____

_____

_____

Pray for missionary work in BULGARIA
(Southeastern Europe, between Romania and Turkey)

> Pray that we may enter into that travail of soul with Him.
> Nothing less is any good. Spiritual children mean
> travail of soul-spiritual agony.
> *Amy Carmichael*

PRAISE & THANKSGIVING

Worship the Lord, for He is "worthy."

I call upon the LORD, who is worthy to be praised, and I am saved from my enemies.

> 2 Samuel 22:4 (NASB)

REPENTANCE

Search your heart as you meditate on this Scripture.

After Job had prayed for his friends, the LORD made him prosperous again and gave him twice as much as he had before.

> Job 42:10

ASKING

Rewrite this Scripture, personalizing it for missionaries, asking that they would "pray in the Spirit on all occasions."

The end of all things is near. Therefore be clear minded and self-controlled so that you can pray.

> 1 Peter 4:7

_____

_____

_____

_____

YIELDING

Rewrite it again, personalizing and praying it for yourself. Respond to what God is saying to you in this Scripture.

_____

_____

_____

_____

Pray for missionary work in BURKINA FASO
(Western Africa, north of Ghana)

> Prayer is self-discipline. The effort to realize the presence and power
> of God stretches the sinews of the soul and hardens its muscles.
> *Samuel M. Zwemer*

PRAISE & THANKSGIVING

> *I call upon the LORD, who is worthy to be praised, and I am saved
> from my enemies.*
>> 2 Samuel 22:4 (NASB)

REPENTANCE

> *After Job had prayed for his friends, the LORD made him prosperous again
> and gave him twice as much as he had before.*
>> Job 42:10

ASKING

Personalize this Scripture for missionaries, asking that
they would "pray in the Spirit on all occasions."

> *Watch and pray so that you will not fall into temptation. The spirit is willing,
> but the body is weak.*
>> Mark 14:38

_____

_____

_____

_____

YIELDING

Now personalize and pray it for yourself. How can you
respond to what God is saying to you?

_____

_____

_____

_____

_____

_____

_____

Pray for missionary work in BURMA (MYANMAR)
(Southeastern Asia, between Bangladesh and Thailand)

> Prayer—secret, fervent, believing prayer—
> lies at the root of all personal godliness.
> *William Carey*

PRAISE & THANKSGIVING

*I call upon the LORD, who is worthy to be praised, and I am saved
from my enemies.*

> 2 Samuel 22:4 (NASB)

REPENTANCE

*After Job had prayed for his friends, the LORD made him prosperous again
and gave him twice as much as he had before.*

> Job 42:10

ASKING

Rewrite this Scripture, personalizing it for missionaries.

*If my people, who are called by my name, will humble themselves and pray and
seek my face and turn from their wicked ways, then will I hear from heaven
and will forgive their sin and will heal their land.*

> 2 Chronicles 7:14

_____

_____

_____

_____

_____

YIELDING

What is God saying to you in this Scripture?

_____

_____

_____

_____

_____

_____

Pray for missionary work in BURUNDI
(Central Africa, east of the Democratic Republic of the Congo)

> Groanings which cannot be uttered are often
> prayers which cannot be refused.
> *Charles Spurgeon*

PRAISE & THANKSGIVING

*I call upon the LORD, who is worthy to be praised, and I am saved
from my enemies.*
> 2 Samuel 22:4 (NASB)

REPENTANCE

*After Job had prayed for his friends, the LORD made him prosperous again
and gave him twice as much as he had before.*
> Job 42:10

ASKING

Personalize this Scripture today for missionaries.

*Hear my voice when I call, O LORD; be merciful to me and answer me.
My heart says of you, "Seek his face!" Your face, LORD, I will seek.*
> Psalm 27:7–8

_____

_____

_____

_____

_____

YIELDING

Personalize and pray this same Scripture for yourself.

_____

_____

_____

_____

_____

_____

_____

Pray for missionary work in CAMBODIA
(Southeastern Asia, between Thailand, Vietnam, and Laos)

Week 7
Thoughts and Prayers

This I say, therefore, and testify in the Lord,

that you should no longer walk as the rest of the Gentiles walk,

in the futility of their mind, having their understanding darkened,

being alienated from the life of God, because of the ignorance that is in them,

because of the blindness of their heart; who, being past feeling,

have given themselves over to lewdness, to work all uncleanness with greediness.

But you have not so learned Christ, if indeed you have heard Him

and have been taught by Him, as the truth is in Jesus: that you put off,

concerning your former conduct, the old man which grows corrupt

according to the deceitful lusts, and be renewed in the spirit of your mind,

and that you put on the new man which was created according to God,

in true righteousness and holiness.

EPHESIANS 4:17–24 (NKJV)

WALKING
IN
CHRIST

Week 8

AUTHORITY AND ACCOUNTABILITY

When I took responsibility as leader for my mission board's work in Western Europe, I had every intention of walking in a close, daily relationship with God and glorifying Him with my life and my ministry. Yet just three short years later, I found myself at the point of burnout. I could barely concentrate more than a few minutes at a time on what God was trying to say to me.

I often sat down for my morning time of prayer and Bible study and, after reading just a few short verses, my mind tripped off into another world—problem solving, attacking my daily agenda, and dealing with personnel issues. At times, I actually found myself on my way to the office without any memory of having completed my quiet time. Maybe you're wondering how this could happen, especially to a missionary. I'm embarrassed to admit that it did.

All I can say is this: Gradually, I had begun to focus on my work and not on the One who called me to my task. My relationship with Jesus Christ was no longer my first priority. The Sabbath was no longer holy. I often checked e-mail even on my day of "rest." I was traveling about 80 percent of the time, and had no physical or emotional energy left for Him. I felt that everything I was doing was for the cause of the kingdom. I truly believed that the harder I worked, the closer I would come to reaching my goal of seeing all the peoples of Western Europe come to saving faith in Jesus Christ. Of course, Satan wanted me to believe that. I was focusing on good things, but not on the "best" things.

After it became evident that I could no longer continue in this manner, my wife and I took some time off in California. Alone in the desert, both literally and figuratively, I was honest before God. During days of silence and solitude, moments of meditation in the Word, and times of petition before the throne, He spoke clearly into my heart and life.

He told me many things I needed to do in order to have balance in my life. And with His help, I have had victory in these areas. I now have accountability partners who care enough about my well-being to ask me hard questions on a regular basis. During that difficult period of my life, the Lord convicted me that I had been negligent in garnering adequate prayer support for my personal, family, and ministry needs. I've sought and found intercessors who commit to uphold me and my needs.

You might be wondering if this is a problem experienced only by those in leadership. The answer, unfortunately, is no. A number of missionaries involved in direct ministry around the world are overworked and undernourished. I don't mean physical nourishment. I'm talking about nourishment through God's Word, prayer, and fellowship with other believers. If, through neglect of our spiritual feeding, we operate in our own strength rather than allowing the Holy Spirit to work through us, we will all fall miserably short of our goal, and will fail to accomplish the task to which God has called us.

Intercessors often think that we missionaries are exempt from normal, everyday temptations and problems. Please know that we struggle in all the same areas in which you struggle. We desperately need your intercessions! Partner with us in prayer, and see what God can do through the lives of ordinary people when they are covered in extraordinary prayer!

Ed— Western Europe

Nothing is ever done by the truth, used ever so zealously, unless there is a spirit of prayer somewhere in connection with the presentation of truth.
Charles G. Finney

PRAISE & THANKSGIVING

Worship by using the name of God mentioned in this Scripture—"our judge."

For the LORD is our judge, the LORD is our lawgiver,
the LORD is our King; He will save us.

Isaiah 33:22 (NASB)

REPENTANCE

Search your heart as you meditate on this Scripture. What is the Holy Spirit revealing to you?

And this is love: that we walk in obedience to his commands. As you have heard from the beginning, his command is that you walk in love.

2 John 6

ASKING

Read the following Scripture. Rewrite it, personalizing it for missionaries, seeking the Lord in prayer on their behalf regarding accountability.

Obey your spiritual leaders and do what they say. Their work is to watch over your souls, and they know they are accountable to God. Give them reason to do this joyfully and not with sorrow. That would certainly not be for your benefit.

Hebrews 13:17 (NLT)

_____

_____

YIELDING

Now meditate on the Scripture again. Rewrite it below, personalizing and praying it for yourself. How can you respond to what God is saying to you in this Scripture?

_____

_____

_____

Pray for missionary work in CAMEROON
(Western Africa, between Equatorial Guinea and Nigeria)

> The devil is not terribly frightened of our human efforts
> and credentials. But he knows his kingdom will be
> damaged when we begin to lift up our hearts to God.
> *Jim Cymbala*

PRAISE & THANKSGIVING

Worship Him in awe today, He who is "our Judge."

For the LORD is our judge, the LORD is our lawgiver,
the LORD is our King; He will save us.

Isaiah 33:22 (NASB)

REPENTANCE

Search your heart as you meditate on this Scripture.

And this is love: that we walk in obedience to his commands. As you have
heard from the beginning, his command is that you walk in love.

2 John 6

ASKING

Rewrite this Scripture, personalizing it for missionaries,
asking God to grow in them a desire for accountability.

Nothing in all creation is hidden from God's sight. Everything is uncovered
and laid bare before the eyes of him to whom we must give account.

Hebrews 4:13

_____

_____

_____

_____

YIELDING

Rewrite it again, personalizing and praying it for yourself.
Respond to what God is saying to you in this Scripture.

_____

_____

_____

_____

Pray for missionary work in CANADA

> There is not in the world a kind of life more sweet and delightful
> than that of a continual conversation with God.
> *Brother Lawrence*

PRAISE & THANKSGIVING

For the LORD is our judge, the LORD is our lawgiver,
the LORD is our King; He will save us.

> Isaiah 33:22 (NASB)

REPENTANCE

There is an appointed time for everything,
And there is a time for every event under heaven.

> Ecclesiastes 3:1 (NASB)

ASKING

Personalize this Scripture for missionaries, rewriting Jesus'
words on their behalf regarding authority.

All authority in heaven and on earth has been given to me. Therefore go and make
disciples of all nations, baptizing them in the name of the Father and of the Son
and of the Holy Spirit, and teaching them to obey everything I have commanded
you. And surely I am with you always, to the very end of the age.

> Matthew 28:18–20

_____

_____

_____

_____

YIELDING

Now personalize and pray it for yourself. How can you
respond to what God is saying to you?

_____

_____

_____

_____

_____

Pray for missionary work in CAPE VERDE
(Western African islands in the North Atlantic)

> Never make the blunder of trying to forecast
> the way God is going to answer your prayer.
> *Oswald Chambers*

PRAISE & THANKSGIVING

For the LORD is our judge, the LORD is our lawgiver,
the LORD is our King; He will save us.
     Isaiah 33:22 (NASB)

REPENTANCE

There is an appointed time for everything.
And there is a time for every event under heaven.
     Ecclesiastes 3:1 (NASB)

ASKING

Rewrite this Scripture, personalizing it for missionaries.

Each one should retain the place in life that the Lord assigned to him and to
which God has called him. This is the rule I lay down in all the churches.
     1 Corinthians 7:17

_____

_____

_____

_____

_____

YIELDING

What is God saying to you in this Scripture?

_____

_____

_____

_____

_____

_____

Pray for missionary work in
THE CAYMAN ISLANDS
(Caribbean island group south of Cuba, northwest of Jamaica)

Prayer is simple, prayer is supernatural, and to anyone not related
to our Lord Jesus Christ, prayer is apt to look stupid.
Oswald Chambers

PRAISE & THANKSGIVING

For the LORD is our judge, the LORD is our lawgiver,
the LORD is our King; He will save us.
Isaiah 33:22 (NASB)

REPENTANCE

There is an appointed time for everything.
And there is a time for every event under heaven.
Ecclesiastes 3:1 (NASB)

ASKING

Personalize this Scripture today for missionaries.

Teach us to make the most of our time, so that we may grow in wisdom.
Psalm 90:12 (NLT)

_____
_____
_____
_____
_____

YIELDING

Personalize and pray this same Scripture for yourself.

_____
_____
_____
_____
_____
_____

Pray for missionary work in
THE CENTRAL AFRICAN REPUBLIC
(north of the Democratic Republic of the Congo)

Week 8
Thoughts and Prayers

_____

_____

_____

_____

_____

_____

_____

_____

_____

_____

_____

_____

_____

_____

_____

_____

_____

_____

_____

_____

_____

_____

_____

_____

_____

Week 9

EVANGELISM

Sam* has often traveled to the Middle East. On several of these trips, a female worker would be waiting for him to arrive, having already been witnessing to a man in the meantime whom she felt was ready to accept Christ. Each time, she would pass the individual off to Sam, feeling it better that he talk to the man in Arabic. Sam would then have the honor of praying with the person to receive Jesus. This happened on a number of occasions.

On one trip, Sam met with a military man from an area where the female worker was serving in a hospital. The man came holding a bag. Sam and the female worker took him by vehicle up to the mountain so they could not be overheard. As they talked, Sam realized this man already understood about Christianity. He had already received Jesus into his heart. But after they prayed together, Sam wanted to hear the story of how his new friend had come to faith. The man opened his bag and showed Sam a "Jesus" film and a New Testament. This was his story:

He had been sent by his country's military to another Middle Eastern country for two weeks of training. On the day he arrived, he had bought a local Arabic newspaper. Right on the front page was an advertisement for a free New Testament and the "Jesus" film in Arabic for anyone interested. The ad gave a contact number for someone at a local church. Since the offer was advertised so openly, the man went to the church and received two packets. During his stay in the country, he spent all his free time reading the New Testament.

When it was time to return to his own country, the man put one packet containing the New Testament and the "Jesus" film in his suitcase and the other in his carry-on luggage. Upon arrival at the airport in his country, inspectors opened his suitcase and discovered the first packet. Airport officials scolded him, told him the materials were prohibited, and took them away. Because the officials were so intent in searching his luggage, however, they didn't check his carry-on. So he entered with the New Testament and the "Jesus" film.

The man had heard about Christians at the local hospital, so he went there looking for someone to talk to him about the free materials he had obtained. The female worker answered all his questions about Christianity.

That's not the whole story, though. How did that ad get in the newspaper? The United Nations committee on Human Rights was coming to the Middle Eastern country that very week to investigate human rights practices. A government official had called a pastor affiliated with a Great Commission Christian organization that had the films and New Testaments, asking the pastor to run the advertisement so that the Human Rights committee would see that his country had religious freedom. The pastor told the official he didn't have the money to buy an ad in the paper, so the government paid for the ad. This is the ad that ran the day the military man arrived from his country.

Just imagine the orchestration of this: God used the United Nations, the governments of two Muslim countries, a newspaper, a pastor, a female worker, and Sam to pursue one man who was (and is) precious in God's sight. Only a God of true, extravagant love would use so many resources for just one person.

—*A Christian worker in Northern Africa and the Middle East*
*Name changed for security

> Prayer itself is an art which only the Holy Ghost can teach us.
> He is the giver of all prayer. Pray for prayer—pray till you can pray.
> *Charles Spurgeon*

PRAISE & THANKSGIVING

Worship by using the name of God mentioned in this Scripture—"the life."

> *Jesus said to him, "I am the way, and the truth, and the life;*
> *no one comes to the Father but through Me."*
>
> John 14:6 (NASB)

REPENTANCE

Search your heart as you meditate on this Scripture. What is the Holy Spirit revealing to you?

> *We pray this in order that you may live a life worthy of the Lord*
> *and may please him in every way: bearing fruit in every good work,*
> *growing in the knowledge of God.*
>
> Colossians 1:10

ASKING

Read the following Scripture. Rewrite it, personalizing it for missionaries, seeking the Lord in prayer on their behalf regarding evangelism.

> *The God of our fathers has chosen you to know his will and to see the Righteous*
> *One and to hear words from his mouth. You will be his witness to all men of*
> *what you have seen and heard.*
>
> Acts 22:14–15

_____

_____

YIELDING

Now meditate on the Scripture again. Rewrite it below, personalizing and praying it for yourself. How can you respond to what God is saying to you in this Scripture?

_____

_____

Pray for missionary work in CHAD
(Central Africa, south of Libya)

> The purpose of prayer is to reveal the presence of God,
> equally present at all times and in every condition.
> *Oswald Chambers*

PRAISE & THANKSGIVING

Worship Him today, for He is your "life."

*Jesus said to him, "I am the way, and the truth, and the life;
no one comes to the Father but through Me."*

John 14:6 (NASB)

REPENTANCE

Search your heart as you meditate on this Scripture.

*We pray this in order that you may live a life worthy of the Lord
and may please him in every way: bearing fruit in every good work,
growing in the knowledge of God.*

Colossians 1:10

ASKING

Rewrite this Scripture, personalizing it for missionaries,
seeking the Lord on their behalf regarding evangelism.

*But you, keep your head in all situations, endure hardship, do the work of
an evangelist, discharge all the duties of your ministry.*

2 Timothy 4:5

_____

_____

_____

YIELDING

Rewrite it again, personalizing and praying it for yourself.
Respond to what God is saying to you in this Scripture.

_____

_____

_____

_____

_____

Pray for missionary work in CHILE
(Southern South America, bordering the South Pacific Ocean)

> We can do nothing without prayer. All things can be done
> by importunate prayer. That is the teaching of Jesus Christ.
> *E. M. Bounds*

PRAISE & THANKSGIVING

> *Jesus said to him, "I am the way, and the truth, and the life;*
> *no one comes to the Father but through Me."*
>   John 14:6 (NASB)

REPENTANCE

> *We pray this in order that you may live a life worthy of the Lord*
> *and may please him in every way: bearing fruit in every good work,*
> *growing in the knowledge of God.*
>   Colossians 1:10

ASKING

Personalize this Scripture for missionaries, rewriting it
in prayer on their behalf regarding evangelism.

> *But in your hearts set apart Christ as Lord. Always be prepared to give an answer*
> *to everyone who asks you to give the reason for the hope that you have. But do this*
> *with gentleness and respect.*
>   1 Peter 3:15

_____

_____

_____

_____

YIELDING

Now personalize and pray it for yourself. How can you
respond to what God is saying to you?

_____

_____

_____

_____

Pray for missionary work in CHINA
(Eastern Asia, bordering the East China Sea)

> Only turning God's house into a house of fervent prayer
> will reverse the power of evil so evident in the world today.
> *Jim Cymbala*

PRAISE & THANKSGIVING

> *Jesus said to him, "I am the way, and the truth, and the life;*
> *no one comes to the Father but through Me."*
>
> John 14:6 (NASB)

REPENTANCE

> *We pray this in order that you may live a life worthy of the Lord*
> *and may please him in every way: bearing fruit in every good work,*
> *growing in the knowledge of God.*
>
> Colossians 1:10

ASKING

Rewrite this Scripture, personalizing it for missionaries.

> *Be wise in the way you act toward outsiders; make the most of every opportunity.*
> *Let your conversation be always full of grace, seasoned with salt, so that you may*
> *know how to answer everyone.*
>
> Colossians 4:5–6

_____

_____

_____

_____

YIELDING

What is God saying to you in this Scripture?

_____

_____

_____

_____

_____

Pray for missionary work on CHRISTMAS ISLAND
(Southeastern Asia, in the Indian Ocean, south of Indonesia)

> I never prayed sincerely and earnestly for anything but it came
> at some time; no matter at how distant a day, somehow, in some
> shape, probably the least I would have devised, it came.
>
> *Adoniram Judson*

PRAISE & THANKSGIVING

Jesus said to him, "I am the way, and the truth, and the life;
no one comes to the Father but through Me."

John 14:6 (NASB)

REPENTANCE

We pray this in order that you may live a life worthy of the Lord
and may please him in every way: bearing fruit in every good work,
growing in the knowledge of God.

Colossians 1:10

ASKING

Personalize this Scripture today for missionaries.

Sing to the LORD, praise his name; proclaim his salvation day after day.

Psalm 96:2

_____

_____

_____

_____

_____

YIELDING

Personalize and pray this same Scripture for yourself.

_____

_____

_____

_____

_____

_____

Pray for missionary work in
THE COCOS (KEELING) ISLANDS
(Indian Ocean, halfway between Australia and Sri Lanka)

Week 9
Thoughts and Prayers

Week 10

Faith & Trust

Across the river from Georgetown, Guyana, and miles into the interior, was a small village controlled by communism and the practice of witchcraft. God led my husband and me to begin a new church in the area.

George was a schoolteacher from this village, but his involvement in witchcraft caused him to be so unstable that he lived in constant fear. One day he came seeking help and met Jesus. Immediately he asked to join us in starting a church in his community. This was met with great persecution, however. We faced serious threats everywhere we attempted to start a new church.

After much prayer and waiting, a young man invited us to meet in the space under his house. But a very evil man owned the house and had no sympathy for believers in Jesus. This man created a great deal of trouble for us. Yet we continued to meet each week, sitting on small benches lined by rows under the home.

One Sunday the owner lashed out his final threat: "By five o'clock this afternoon, this area will be cleared or I will personally remove everything and burn it!" As five o'clock approached, a villager came running to the house to report that the owner of the home had fallen in his field and hit his head. He was dead.

The persecution stopped immediately. The church began to grow, and soon the people were able to build their own building.

Today, several young men and women from that same village church are serving in Christian leadership around the world. One young convert served as ambassador for Guyana in Washington D.C. after finishing his education.

Charlene—SOUTH AMERICA

The road into the jungle from the city of La Paz, Bolivia, descends from 17,000 to 6,000 feet above sea level in a matter of minutes. Hundreds die each year as buses and automobiles maneuver the narrow road—identified as the most dangerous road in the world—often falling off the mountainous cliffs that drop nearly one-mile into the jungle.

The first time my family traveled this road, I faced my fear of heights. Many places along the road are too narrow for two vehicles to pass, so those going up the mountain pull to the edge of the cliff that allows those descending to travel close to the mountain. Halfway through our three-hour trek, we saw a man standing on the edge of a cliff directing traffic. A small lean-to shack was precariously perched on a wider portion of the road, so we stopped to hear his story.

Several years earlier, the man's family was traveling at exactly this location when their vehicle was hit by a truck and forced over the edge of the cliff. His wife and children died in the crash. Since that tragic event, he had committed his life to saving other families from the same fate. Every day, he stood at a strategic point where he could see traffic coming from both directions. He safely directed travelers around the mountainous road.

After hearing his story, I reexamined my fear of heights, my fear of bringing my children to this unfamiliar land, and my fear of the unknown. This man's commitment to save lives reminded me why I was here. He daily chose to make a selfless sacrifice to save complete strangers from death. Was I willing to selflessly obey my obedience to a faithful God?

Debbie—SOUTH AMERICA

Faith sees the invisible, believes the unbelievable,
and receives the impossible.
Corrie ten Boom

PRAISE & THANKSGIVING

Worship by using the name of God mentioned in this
Scripture—"your confidence."

> *For the LORD will be your confidence and will keep your foot from being caught.*
>
> Proverbs 3:26 (NASB)

REPENTANCE

Search your heart as you meditate on this Scripture.
What is the Holy Spirit revealing to you?

> *Remember your leaders, who spoke the word of God to you.*
> *Consider the outcome of their way of life and imitate their faith.*
>
> Hebrews 13:7

ASKING

Read the following Scripture. Rewrite it, personalizing it
for missionaries, seeking the Lord in prayer on their behalf
regarding faith.

> *Without faith it is impossible to please God, because anyone who comes to him*
> *must believe that he exists and that he rewards those who earnestly seek him.*
>
> Hebrews 11:6

_____

_____

_____

_____

YIELDING

Now meditate on the Scripture again. Rewrite it below,
personalizing and praying it for yourself. How can you
respond to what God is saying to you in this Scripture?

_____

_____

_____

Pray for missionary work in COLOMBIA
(Northern South America, between Panama and Venezuela)

> When God intends great mercy for His people,
> the first thing He does is set them a-praying.
> *Matthew Henry*

PRAISE & THANKSGIVING
Worship Him today, putting all your "confidence" in Him.
> *For the LORD will be your confidence and will keep your foot from being caught.*
> Proverbs 3:26 (NASB)

REPENTANCE
Search your heart as you meditate on this Scripture.
> *Trust in the LORD and do good; dwell in the land and enjoy safe pasture.*
> *Delight yourself in the LORD and he will give you the desires of your heart.*
> Psalm 37:3–4

ASKING
Rewrite this Scripture, personalizing it for missionaries, seeking the Lord on their behalf regarding trust.
> *I am like an olive tree flourishing in the house of God; I trust in God's*
> *unfailing love for ever and ever. I will praise you forever for what you*
> *have done; in your name I will hope, for your name is good. I will praise*
> *you in the presence of your saints.*
> Psalm 52:8–9

_____

_____

_____

_____

YIELDING
Rewrite it again, personalizing and praying it for yourself. Respond to what God is saying to you in this Scripture.

_____

_____

_____

_____

Pray for missionary work in COMOROS
(Southern Africa, at the northern mouth of
the Mozambique Channel)

Prayer is the highest order of business, for it links a powerless human
to the creative force of God's sovereign power.
Anonymous

PRAISE & THANKSGIVING

For the LORD will be your confidence and will keep your foot from being caught.
Proverbs 3:26 (NASB)

REPENTANCE

Trust in the LORD and do good; dwell in the land and enjoy safe pasture.
Delight yourself in the LORD and he will give you the desires of your heart.
Psalm 37:3–4

ASKING

Personalize this Scripture for missionaries, rewriting it
in prayer on their behalf regarding trust.

When I am afraid, I will trust in you. In God, whose word I praise,
in God I trust; I will not be afraid. What can mortal man do to me?
Psalm 56:3–4

_____

_____

_____

_____

_____

_____

YIELDING

Now personalize and pray it for yourself. How can you
respond to what God is saying to you?

_____

_____

_____

_____

_____

Pray for missionary work in THE COOK ISLANDS
(South Pacific Ocean, halfway between
Hawaii and New Zealand)

> The prayer of the saints is never self-important,
> but always God-important.
> *Oswald Chambers*

PRAISE & THANKSGIVING

For the LORD will be your confidence and will keep your foot from being caught.

Proverbs 3:26 (NASB)

REPENTANCE

Observe the commands of the LORD your God,
walking in his ways and revering him.

Deuteronomy 8:6

ASKING

Rewrite this Scripture, personalizing it for missionaries.

The angel of the LORD encamps around those who fear him, and he delivers them.

Psalm 34:7

_____

_____

_____

_____

_____

_____

_____

YIELDING

What is God saying to you in this Scripture?

_____

_____

_____

_____

_____

_____

Pray for missionary work in COSTA RICA
(Central America, between Nicaragua and Panama)

> God will hear His people at the beginning of their prayers
> if the condition of their heart is ready for it.
> *Charles Spurgeon*

PRAISE & THANKSGIVING
> *For the LORD will be your confidence and will keep your foot from being caught.*
> Proverbs 3:26 (NASB)

REPENTANCE
> *Observe the commands of the LORD your God,*
> *walking in his ways and revering him.*
> Deuteronomy 8:6

ASKING
Personalize these Scriptures today for missionaries.
> *The fear of the LORD adds length to life, but the years of the wicked are cut short.*
> Proverbs 10:27

> *The fear of the LORD is the beginning of wisdom, and knowledge of the Holy One is understanding.*
> Proverbs 9:10

_____

_____

_____

_____

_____

YIELDING
Personalize and pray this same Scripture for yourself.

_____

_____

_____

_____

_____

Pray for missionary work in COTE D'IVOIRE
(Western Africa, between Ghana and Liberia)

Week 10
Thoughts and Prayers

Week 11

HOLINESS
& PURITY

Often it seems like every day on the mission field is a realization of how much deeper the Lord wants to relate to us. Through trials, challenges, loneliness, and daily warfare waged for our affections, our trust, and our steadfastness, the Lord shows how little we understand Him.

Often suffering allows us to know God in ways we would not otherwise have known Him. Through these times God shows us His love, His consistency, and His sustaining grace. It was all there before, but sometimes we must be backed into a corner to open our eyes to see His marvelous grace.

But what am I talking about? Sure, there are daily challenges, frustrations, tests, and pain, but there are too many joys and victories to dwell on the negative. Yet it is through the former that God is stretching and showing Himself to us as we depend on Him.

Many of the struggles are internal and have nothing to do with the work itself. We have learned that the filling of our hearts with God's Word increases our faith and causes us to rejoice in Him.

Every prayer you offer for us has counted for our benefit and the Lord's glory. One example was a twelve-day visit into the jungle. My trip had been delayed for one month. It was an especially difficult time to leave my wife and son at home alone. But the work needed to be done, so it was necessary to go.

You may wonder (as I do) why there must be obstacles that seem to slow us down. When I arrived at my destination, it became easier to see what God had in mind. One delay meant my national coworker would not be able to accompany me on the river. In his absence, God provided two other believers. This change in plans allowed me time to attend a conference led by a leader from another evangelical denomination. The speaker taught on the Person and work of the Holy Spirit. The teaching spoke directly to many things going on in my own heart, my family, and my ministry. At times I could only weep as the Lord spoke to me. The Holy Spirit used this man to affirm me and assure me that God is with my family and me. God had not left us alone!

I was convinced the delays in travel were designed to place me under the teaching of God's Word and in position to receive affirmation from the Lord. "How precious also are Your thoughts to me, O God! How vast is the sum of them!" (Ps. 139:17, NASB)

Marty—SOUTH AMERICA

Always respond to every impulse to pray. The impulse to pray may come
when you are reading or when you are battling with a text. I would
make an absolute law of this—always obey such an impulse.
Martyn Lloyd-Jones

PRAISE & THANKSGIVING

Worship by using the characteristic of God mentioned
in this Scripture—"holy."

Thus you are to be holy to Me, for I the LORD am holy;
and I have set you apart from the peoples to be Mine.

Leviticus 20:26 (NASB)

REPENTANCE

Search your heart as you meditate on this Scripture.
What is the Holy Spirit revealing to you?

Test me, O LORD, and try me, examine my heart and my mind.

Psalm 26:2

ASKING

Read the following Scripture. Rewrite it, personalizing
it for missionaries, seeking the Lord in prayer on their
behalf regarding holiness.

Consecrate yourselves and be holy, because I am the LORD your God.
Keep my decrees and follow them. I am the LORD, who makes you holy.

Leviticus 20:7–8

_____

_____

_____

YIELDING

Now meditate on the Scripture again. Rewrite it below,
personalizing and praying it for yourself. How can you
respond to what God is saying to you in this Scripture?

_____

_____

_____

Pray for missionary work in CROATIA
(Southeastern Europe, between
Bosnia/Herzogovina and Slovenia)

> The greatest and best talent that God gives to any man
> or woman in this world is the talent of prayer.
> *Alexander Whyte*

PRAISE & THANKSGIVING
Worship Him today as the "holy" One.

> *Thus you are to be holy to Me, for I the LORD am holy;*
> *and I have set you apart from the peoples to be Mine.*
>
> Leviticus 20:26 (NASB)

REPENTANCE
Search your heart as you meditate on this Scripture.

> *Test me, O LORD, and try me, examine my heart and my mind.*
>
> Psalm 26:2

ASKING
Rewrite this Scripture, personalizing it for missionaries,
seeking the Lord on their behalf regarding holiness.

> *You were taught, with regard to your former way of life, to put off your*
> *old self, which is being corrupted by its deceitful desires; to be made new*
> *in the attitude of your minds; and to put on the new self, created to be like*
> *God in true righteousness and holiness.*
>
> Ephesians 4:22–24

_____

_____

_____

_____

YIELDING
Rewrite it again, personalizing and praying it for yourself.
Respond to what God is saying to you in this Scripture.

_____

_____

_____

_____

Pray for missionary work in CUBA
(Caribbean island, south of Key West, Florida)

Prayer is the root, the fountain, the mother of a thousand blessings.
John Chrysostom

PRAISE & THANKSGIVING

Thus you are to be holy to Me, for I the LORD am holy;
and I have set you apart from the peoples to be Mine.

Leviticus 20:26 (NASB)

REPENTANCE

Do not offer the parts of your body to sin, as instruments of wickedness, but
rather offer yourselves to God, as those who have been brought from death
to life; and offer the parts of your body to him as instruments of righteousness.

Romans 6:13

ASKING

Personalize this Scripture for missionaries, rewriting it
in prayer on their behalf regarding purity.

Religion that God our Father accepts as pure and faultless is this:
to look after orphans and widows in their distress and to keep oneself
from being polluted by the world.

James 1:27

_____

_____

_____

_____

YIELDING

Now personalize and pray it for yourself. How can you
respond to what God is saying to you?

_____

_____

_____

_____

_____

Pray for missionary work in CYPRUS
(Middle Eastern island in the Mediterranean Sea)

Prayer is the supreme way to be workers together with God.
Wesley L. Duewel

PRAISE & THANKSGIVING

*Thus you are to be holy to Me, for I the LORD am holy;
and I have set you apart from the peoples to be Mine.*
Leviticus 20:26 (NASB)

REPENTANCE

*Do not offer the parts of your body to sin, as instruments of wickedness, but
rather offer yourselves to God, as those who have been brought from death
to life; and offer the parts of your body to him as instruments of righteousness.*
Romans 6:13

ASKING

Rewrite this Scripture, personalizing it for missionaries.
Even a child is known by his actions, by whether his conduct is pure and right.
Proverbs 20:11

_____

_____

_____

_____

_____

YIELDING

What is God saying to you in this Scripture?

_____

_____

_____

_____

_____

_____

_____

Pray for missionary work in THE CZECH REPUBLIC
(Central Europe, southeast of Germany)

> The concern of the devil is to keep Christians from praying.
> He fears nothing from prayerless studies, prayerless work,
> and prayerless religion . . . but trembles when we pray.
> *Samuel Chadwick*

PRAISE & THANKSGIVING

Thus you are to be holy to Me, for I the LORD am holy;
and I have set you apart from the peoples to be Mine.

Leviticus 20:26 (NASB)

REPENTANCE

Do not offer the parts of your body to sin, as instruments of wickedness, but
rather offer yourselves to God, as those who have been brought from death
to life; and offer the parts of your body to him as instruments of righteousness.

Romans 6:13

ASKING

Personalize this Scripture today for missionaries.

Dear friends, now we are children of God, and what we will be has not yet
been made known. But we know that when he appears, we shall be like him,
for we shall see him as he is. Everyone who has this hope in him purifies himself,
just as he is pure.

1 John 3:2–3

_____

_____

_____

_____

YIELDING

Personalize and pray this same Scripture for yourself.

_____

_____

_____

_____

_____

Pray for missionary work in the
Democratic Republic of THE CONGO
(Central Africa, northeast of Angola)

Week 11
Thoughts and Prayers

_____

_____

_____

_____

_____

_____

_____

_____

_____

_____

_____

_____

_____

_____

_____

_____

_____

_____

_____

_____

_____

_____

_____

_____

_____

_____

_____

Week 12

JOY & ENCOURAGEMENT

Rosario and I worked together in a refugee camp for Nicaraguans who fled their homeland during civil war. He was one of the most joyful people I have ever known. Every moment of his life was a display of sincere, genuine joy.

One day I asked Rosario why he chose to leave his country and bring his wife and seven children to live in a wretched refugee camp. He told his story of the day soldiers came to the farming valley where he lived. They were looking for enemy rebels. Rosario's eighteen-year-old son was visiting neighbors to invite them to a prayer meeting. The soldiers stopped the son and told him to identify any known rebels and deny Jesus Christ. The boy denied knowledge of any rebels and refused to speak against the King who died for him.

In the hours that followed, the soldiers subjected the young boy to unspeakable torture. Witnesses to the horror said that in spite of his pain, the boy continued to sing, "Oh, How I Love Jesus," as the soldiers slowly took his life.

I now understood why Rosario left his homeland behind, but his story was not over.

"We did not leave at that time," Rosario continued. "We decided to stay, but two weeks later the soldiers returned. They gathered the entire community in front of my married son's home. They shouted, 'We will give you an example of what happens to any family helping the enemy.' The soldiers put my two-year-old grandson in a potato sack, threw him in the house, doused it with gasoline, and put a match to it. All we could do was weep and pray above the death cries of my grandson as the burning inferno engulfed him. That is when we decided to leave."

I began to weep, but I still could not understand the day-by-day, hour-by-hour, moment-by-moment joy so real in his life. I had to ask, "Rosario, what is it that sustains you?"

"Bill," he replied, "Even though the soldiers took something precious from me that day, what they did not know is that I have something more precious that no one can take away. Even though my son and grandson cannot return to me, I will one day go to be with them because of the precious blood of Jesus. On that day, together with all the peoples, nations, and tribes, we will stand around the throne of the Lamb. At the right moment I will say to my son, 'Now is the time.' With my son on one side and my grandson on the other, we will join hands with everyone around the throne and sing for all eternity, 'Oh, How I Love Jesus.' That blessed assurance can never be taken from me."

Bill—SOUTH AMERICA

> Little acquaintance with God, and strangeness and
> coldness to Him, make prayer a rare and feeble thing.
> *E. M. Bounds*

PRAISE & THANKSGIVING

Worship by using the name of God mentioned in this
Scripture—our "exceeding joy."

> *Then I will go to the altar of God, to God my exceeding joy;*
> *and upon the lyre I shall praise You, O God, my God.*
>
> Psalm 43:4 (NASB)

REPENTANCE

Search your heart as you meditate on this Scripture.
What is the Holy Spirit revealing to you?

> *So then, just as you received Christ Jesus as Lord, continue to live in him,*
> *rooted and built up in him, strengthened in the faith as you were taught,*
> *and overflowing with thankfulness.*
>
> Colossians 2:6–7

ASKING

Read the following Scripture. Rewrite it, personalizing it
for missionaries, seeking the Lord in prayer on their behalf
regarding joy.

> *Those who sow in tears will reap with songs of joy. He who goes out weeping,*
> *carrying seed to sow, will return with songs of joy, carrying sheaves with him.*
>
> Psalm 126:5–6

_____

_____

YIELDING

Now meditate on the Scripture again. Rewrite it below,
personalizing and praying it for yourself. How can you
respond to what God is saying to you in this Scripture?

_____

_____

_____

Pray for missionary work in DENMARK
(Northern Europe, a peninsula north of Germany)

> The only power that God will yield to is that of prayer.
> *Leonard Ravenhill*

PRAISE & THANKSGIVING

Make Him your "joy" as you worship Him today.

> *Then I will go to the altar of God, to God my exceeding joy;*
> *and upon the lyre I shall praise You, O God, my God.*
>
> Psalm 43:4 (NASB)

REPENTANCE

Search your heart as you meditate on this Scripture.

> *So then, just as you received Christ Jesus as Lord, continue to live in him,*
> *rooted and built up in him, strengthened in the faith as you were taught,*
> *and overflowing with thankfulness.*
>
> Colossians 2:6—7

ASKING

Rewrite this Scripture, personalizing it for missionaries, seeking the Lord on their behalf regarding joy.

> *We are praying, too, that you will be filled with his mighty, glorious*
> *strength so that you can keep going no matter what happens—*
> *always full of the joy of the Lord.*
>
> Colossians 1:11 (TLB)

_____

_____

_____

_____

YIELDING

Rewrite it again, personalizing and praying it for yourself. Respond to what God is saying to you in this Scripture.

_____

_____

_____

_____

Pray for missionary work in DJIBOUTI
(Eastern Africa, on the Gulf of Aden, between
Eritrea and Somalia)

> Prayerlessness is disobedience, for God's command
> is that men ought always to pray and not faint.
> To be prayerless is to fail God, for He says, "Ask of me."
> *Leonard Ravenhill*

PRAISE & THANKSGIVING

Then I will go to the altar of God, to God my exceeding joy;
and upon the lyre I shall praise You, O God, my God.

Psalm 43:4 (NASB)

REPENTANCE

For we are God's workmanship, created in Christ Jesus to do good works,
which God prepared in advance for us to do.

Ephesians 2:10

ASKING

Personalize this Scripture for missionaries, rewriting it
in prayer on their behalf regarding encouragement.

I thank my God every time I remember you. In all my prayers for all of you,
I always pray with joy because of your partnership in the gospel from the
first day until now, being confident of this, that he who began a good work
in you will carry it on to completion until the day of Christ Jesus.

Philippians 1:3–6

_____

_____

_____

YIELDING

Now personalize and pray it for yourself. How can you
respond to what God is saying to you?

_____

_____

_____

_____

_____

Pray for missionary work in DOMINICA
(Caribbean island, halfway between
Puerto Rico and Trinidad)

> The prayer life does not consist of perpetual repetition
> of petitions. The prayer life consists of life that is
> always upward and onward and Godward.
> *G. Campbell Morgan*

PRAISE & THANKSGIVING

Then I will go to the altar of God, to God my exceeding joy;
and upon the lyre I shall praise You, O God, my God.
Psalm 43:4 (NASB)

REPENTANCE

For we are God's workmanship, created in Christ Jesus to do good works,
which God prepared in advance for us to do.
Ephesians 2:10

ASKING

Rewrite this Scripture, personalizing it for missionaries.

For everything that was written in the past was written to teach us, so that
through endurance and the encouragement of the Scriptures we might have hope.
Romans 15:4

_____

_____

_____

_____

_____

YIELDING

What is God saying to you in this Scripture?

_____

_____

_____

_____

_____

_____

Pray for missionary work in
THE DOMINICAN REPUBLIC
(eastern two-thirds of the island of Hispaniola, east of Haiti)

> The true church lives and moves and has its being in prayer.
> *Leonard Ravenhill*

PRAISE & THANKSGIVING

> *Then I will go to the altar of God, to God my exceeding joy;*
> *and upon the lyre I shall praise You, O God, my God.*
>> Psalm 43:4 (NASB)

REPENTANCE

> *Do not be anxious about anything, but in everything, by prayer and petition,*
> *with thanksgiving, present your requests to God.*
>> Philippians 4:6

ASKING

Personalize this Scripture today for missionaries.

> *May the righteous be glad and rejoice before God; may they be happy and joyful.*
> *Sing to God, sing praise to his name, extol him who rides on the clouds—*
> *his name is the LORD—and rejoice before him.*
>> Psalm 68:3–4

_____

_____

_____

_____

_____

YIELDING

Personalize and pray this same Scripture for yourself.

_____

_____

_____

_____

_____

_____

Pray for missionary work in ECUADOR
(Western South America, between Colombia and Peru)

Week 12
Thoughts and Prayers

_____

_____

_____

_____

_____

_____

_____

_____

_____

_____

_____

_____

_____

_____

_____

_____

_____

_____

_____

_____

_____

_____

_____

_____

_____

_____

_____

Week 13

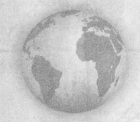

MISSIONARIES IN TRAINING

My first weeks as a new missionary put me in a position of being vulnerable. The mission term for this is "learner," which describes a mind-set more than a state of being. The position of the learner is to admit, "I don't know how you do things here and I need someone to help me learn." This definitely goes against my North American culture where it is humiliating to be the weaker, needy person in a relationship. I truly believe that God uses this status to build bridges to people in order to share the gospel.

My natural tendency when someone asks me a question is to answer and then ask the same question back to him or her. This way I am not sharing any more than the other person. It is a defensive mechanism to keep me from being weaker than the other person. During language study, my teacher would ask me questions left and right to get me to practice talking. She knows me a whole lot better than I know her. I just pray that in seeing who I am, she will also see Jesus in me.

Debra—SOUTH AMERICA

My world is different now. I am the richest man in my village. My possessions include a lamp, a cot, a mosquito net, four t-shirts, one pair of pants, two African outfits, two pairs of sandals (one which cost a dollar at Wal-Mart in the United States, yet my African friends marveled at the quality of the rubber and said, "Certainly, these will last forever"), a pair of hiking shoes, three containers to hold water, a flashlight, six or seven books, a case filled with medicine, a few American food items, another American-made battery-operated light, and a few other things I haven't dug out of the case yet. I am a rich man, and I am keenly aware of the things I possess in my little mud hut.

Things have been great so far. There is definitely a lot of starting over in this work—establishing relationships, not only continuing language learning but re-learning what I learned in a different dialect. There is the adjustment to not having anyone to speak English with, and living in a world where privacy faintly exists. I get sleep, but there is definitely an exhaustion that comes from the onslaught of all these variables.

Father (God) has definitely been drawing people to Himself, and things are happening so quickly that I don't have time to even think about acting like I know what I'm doing. So I'm taking things day by day, just trying to be obedient and "be" light among the people. Though I desire to spend almost all of my time the next few months just learning about the people, area, and culture, two people have come to me personally saying they want to be Christians. Five or so others have said they want me to teach them about Christ, and the village chief's two older brothers have been telling people that there are many wanting to become Christians. This is a people with very little exposure to the "good news."

Pray as your heart is led. Pray that I will always abide in Father's wings, allowing Him to be my strength, hope, and encourager. Pray for Father to establish His church among these people. There are over 571 villages among these people and no known churches. Thank you for being people of prayer.

Chris—WEST AFRICA

People may spurn our appeals, reject our messages, oppose our arguments,
despise our persons; but they are helpless against our prayers.
Thomas Lindberg

PRAISE & THANKSGIVING

Worship by using the aspect of God mentioned in this
Scripture—"understanding."

> *Counsel is mine and sound wisdom; I am understanding, power is mine.*
>
> Proverbs 8:14 (NASB)

REPENTANCE

Search your heart as you meditate on this Scripture.
What is the Holy Spirit revealing to you?

> *Like newborn babies, crave pure spiritual milk, so that by it you may grow
> up in your salvation, now that you have tasted that the Lord is good.*
>
> 1 Peter 2:2–3

ASKING

Read the following Scripture. Rewrite it, personalizing
it for learners and missionaries in training, seeking the
Lord in prayer on their behalf.

> *Don't let anyone look down on you because you are young, but set an example
> for the believers in speech, in life, in love, in faith and in purity.*
>
> 1 Timothy 4:12

_____

_____

_____

YIELDING

Now meditate on the Scripture again. Rewrite it below,
personalizing and praying it for yourself. How can you
respond to what God is saying to you in this Scripture?

_____

_____

_____

_____

Pray for missionary work in EGYPT
(Northern Africa, between Libya, the Red Sea,
and the Gaza Strip)

> Prayer is not given us as a burden to be borne or an irksome duty
> to fulfill, but to be a joy and power to which there is no limit.
> *The Kneeling Christian*

PRAISE & THANKSGIVING

Worship Him today as the giver of "understanding."

Counsel is mine and sound wisdom; I am understanding, power is mine.

Proverbs 8:14 (NASB)

REPENTANCE

Search your heart as you meditate on this Scripture.

*Like newborn babies, crave pure spiritual milk, so that by it you may grow
up in your salvation, now that you have tasted that the Lord is good.*

1 Peter 2:2–3

ASKING

Rewrite this Scripture, personalizing it for learners and
missionaries in training, seeking the Lord on their behalf.

*In a large house there are articles not only of gold and silver, but also of wood
and clay; some are for noble purposes and some for ignoble. If a man cleanses
himself from the latter, he will be an instrument for noble purposes, made holy,
useful to the Master and prepared to do any good work.*

2 Timothy 2:20–21

_____

_____

_____

YIELDING

Rewrite it again, personalizing and praying it for yourself.
Respond to what God is saying to you in this Scripture.

_____

_____

_____

_____

Pray for missionary work in EL SALVADOR
(Central America, between Guatemala and Honduras)

> The coming revival must begin with a great revival of prayer. It is in the closet, with the door shut, that the sound of abundance of rain will first be heard. An increase of secret prayer will be the sure harbinger of blessing.
> *Andrew Murray*

Praise & Thanksgiving

> *Counsel is mine and sound wisdom; I am understanding, power is mine.*
>> Proverbs 8:14 (NASB)

Repentance

> *Like newborn babies, crave pure spiritual milk, so that by it you may grow up in your salvation, now that you have tasted that the Lord is good.*
>> 1 Peter 2:2–3

Asking

Personalize this Scripture for learners and missionaries in training, rewriting it in prayer on their behalf.

> *Do you not know that in a race all the runners run, but only one gets the prize? Run in such a way as to get the prize. Everyone who competes in the games goes into strict training. They do it to get a crown that will not last; but we do it to get a crown that will last forever.*
>> 1 Corinthians 9:24–25

_____

_____

_____

_____

Yielding

Now personalize and pray it for yourself. How can you respond to what God is saying to you?

_____

_____

_____

_____

_____

Pray for missionary work in
EQUATORIAL GUINEA
(Western Africa, between Cameroon and Gabon)

> Prayer is the only adequate way to multiply our efforts
> fast enough to reap the harvest God desires.
> *Wesley L. Duewel*

PRAISE & THANKSGIVING

Counsel is mine and sound wisdom; I am understanding, power is mine.
Proverbs 8:14 (NASB)

REPENTANCE

*Like newborn babies, crave pure spiritual milk, so that by it you may grow up
in your salvation, now that you have tasted that the Lord is good.*
1 Peter 2:2–3

ASKING

Rewrite this Scripture, personalizing it for learners
and missionaries in training.

*Teach me your way, O LORD, and I will walk in your truth;
give me an undivided heart, that I may fear your name*
Psalm 86:11

_____

_____

_____

_____

_____

YIELDING

What is God saying to you in this Scripture?

_____

_____

_____

_____

_____

Pray for missionary work in ERITREA
(Eastern Africa, on the Red Sea, north of Ethiopia)

Prayer is the Christian's first line of defense against demonic influence.
Fervent, sincere prayer thwarts Satan's activity like nothing else.
Neil Anderson

PRAISE & THANKSGIVING

Counsel is mine and sound wisdom; I am understanding, power is mine.

Proverbs 8:14 (NASB)

REPENTANCE

*Like newborn babies, crave pure spiritual milk, so that by it you may grow up
in your salvation, now that you have tasted that the Lord is good.*

1 Peter 2:2–3

ASKING

Personalize this for learners and missionaries in training.

*The LORD said to him, "Who gave man his mouth? Who makes him deaf or
mute? Who gives him sight or makes him blind? Is it not I, the LORD?
Now go; I will help you speak and will teach you what to say."*

Exodus 4:11–12

_____

_____

_____

_____

_____

_____

YIELDING

Personalize and pray this same Scripture for yourself.

_____

_____

_____

_____

_____

Pray for missionary work in ESTONIA
(Eastern Europe, between Latvia and Russia)

Week 13
Thoughts and Prayers

Week 14

LOVE FOR PEOPLE

I was serving as interim pastor of a small church in Brazil. The small congregation was growing in the Lord, new Christians were being baptized, and the Lord was calling young people into the ministry. I personally felt good about what the Lord was doing in my life as shepherd to His sheep.

One night, one of the deacons came to me just before the preaching service. He told me that there was a man outside the church who wanted to speak with me. He warned me that the man was "embriagado" or "drunk." I went outside to find the man sitting on the sidewalk. His clothes were notably less than clean, he smelled strongly of alcohol and related odors, and seemed to be dejected.

As I sat down beside him, he poured out his anguish. "No one loves me," he lamented. "I just went home, and my wife and kids told me they hated me and threw me out of the house." He proceeded to pull up his pant leg to show me a bloody spot and said, "Even my dog bit me as I was leaving. I've decided to just kill myself."

I explained that there was someone who really loved him, and I opened my Bible to John 3:16. As I read the Scripture, he sparked his lighter and put it over my Bible. I was sure he was about to burn it, but he just wanted to see if those words were really there. As many people do in other cultures, he put his face very close to mine. The smell of alcohol was overwhelming. Then he asked, "Does God really love me that much?"

I responded with affirmation, "Yes! God really does love you that much!"

"Do you?" he asked. As I sorted through his drunkenness, the smells, and my response, he quickly replied, "No! You don't!" I hurried to affirm that I really did love him. But he retorted, "No, you don't, because you had to think about it!"

That night I learned that my love for all the people of the world must be unconditional and without hesitation.

As you pray, the depth of love that reaches out even to the Osama Bin-ladens of the world must impel us. May we be reminded that Saul of Tarsus, the original Bin-laden, became Paul the apostle because of that kind of unreserved depth of love.

> *"And I, if I be lifted up from the earth,*
> *will draw all men unto me"* (John 12:32, KJV).

Orman—SOUTH AMERICA

> Holiness is as indispensable for a spiritual warrior
> as is eyesight for a military fighter pilot.
> *C. Peter Wagner*

PRAISE & THANKSGIVING

Worship by using the name of God mentioned in this Scripture—"love."

> *We know and rely on the love God has for us. God is love.*
> *Whoever lives in love lives in God, and God in him.*
>
>> 1 John 4:16

REPENTANCE

Search your heart as you meditate on this Scripture. What is the Holy Spirit revealing to you?

> *Finally, all of you, live in harmony with one another; be sympathetic,*
> *love as brothers, be compassionate and humble.*
>
>> 1 Peter 3:8

ASKING

Read the following Scripture. Rewrite it, personalizing it for missionaries, asking the Lord to give them His love for people.

> *May the Lord make your love increase and overflow for each other and for*
> *everyone else, just as ours does for you. May he strengthen your hearts so that*
> *you will be blameless and holy in the presence of our God and Father when*
> *our Lord Jesus comes with all his holy ones.*
>
>> 1 Thessalonians 3:12–13

_____

_____

YIELDING

Now meditate on the Scripture again. Rewrite it below, personalizing and praying it for yourself. How can you respond to what God is saying to you in this Scripture?

_____

_____

Pray for missionary work in ETHIOPIA
(Eastern Africa, west of Somalia)

> The stream of praying cannot rise higher
> than the fountain of living.
> *E. M. Bounds*

PRAISE & THANKSGIVING
Worship Him today, for He is "love."

We know and rely on the love God has for us. God is love.
Whoever lives in love lives in God, and God in him.

1 John 4:16

REPENTANCE
Search your heart as you meditate on this Scripture.

Finally, all of you, live in harmony with one another; be sympathetic,
love as brothers, be compassionate and humble.

1 Peter 3:8

ASKING
Rewrite this Scripture, personalizing it for missionaries,
asking the Lord to give them love for people.

My purpose is that they may be encouraged in heart and united in love, so that
they may have the full riches of complete understanding, in order that they may
know the mystery of God, namely, Christ, in whom are hidden all the treasures
of wisdom and knowledge.

Colossians 2:2–3

_____

_____

_____

_____

YIELDING
Rewrite it again, personalizing and praying it for yourself.
Respond to what God is saying to you in this Scripture.

_____

_____

_____

_____

Pray for missionary work in
THE FALKLAND ISLANDS
(near the tip of Southern South America, east of Argentina)

God's command to "pray without ceasing" is founded on the necessity
we have of His grace to preserve the life of God in the soul, which can
no more subsist one moment without it than the body can without air.
John Wesley

PRAISE & THANKSGIVING

We know and rely on the love God has for us. God is love.
Whoever lives in love lives in God, and God in him.
1 John 4:16

REPENTANCE

Finally, all of you, live in harmony with one another; be
sympathetic, love as brothers, be compassionate and humble.
1 Peter 3:8

ASKING

Personalize this Scripture for missionaries, rewriting it
in prayer that they would have love for people.

If I speak in the tongues of men and of angels, but have not love, I am only
a resounding gong or a clanging cymbal. If I have the gift of prophecy
and can fathom all mysteries and all knowledge, and if I have a faith
that can move mountains, but have not love, I am nothing.
1 Corinthians 13:1–2

_____

_____

_____

YIELDING

Now personalize and pray it for yourself. How can you
respond to what God is saying to you?

_____

_____

_____

_____

_____

Pray for missionary work in THE FAROE ISLANDS
(in the Norwegian Sea, halfway between Iceland and Norway)

> Prayer is the vital breath of the Christian; not the thing
> that makes him alive, but the evidence that he is alive.
> *Oswald Chambers*

PRAISE & THANKSGIVING

> *We know and rely on the love God has for us. God is love.*
> *Whoever lives in love lives in God, and God in him.*
>> 1 John 4:16

REPENTANCE

> *Finally, all of you, live in harmony with one another; be sympathetic,*
> *love as brothers, be compassionate and humble.*
>> 1 Peter 3:8

ASKING

Rewrite this Scripture, personalizing it for missionaries.

> *As apostles of Christ we could have been a burden to you, but we were gentle*
> *among you, like a mother caring for her little children. We loved you so much*
> *that we were delighted to share with you not only the gospel of God but our*
> *lives as well, because you had become so dear to us.*
>> 1 Thessalonians 2:6–8

_____

_____

_____

_____

YIELDING

What is God saying to you in this Scripture?

_____

_____

_____

_____

_____

Pray for missionary work in the
Federated States of MICRONESIA
(island group in the North Pacific)

Four things let us ever keep in mind: God hears prayer, God heeds prayer,
God answers prayer, and God delivers by prayer.
E. M. Bounds

PRAISE & THANKSGIVING

We know and rely on the love God has for us. God is love.
Whoever lives in love lives in God, and God in him.

     1 John 4:16

REPENTANCE

Finally, all of you, live in harmony with one another; be sympathetic,
love as brothers, be compassionate and humble.

     1 Peter 3:8

ASKING

Personalize this Scripture today for missionaries.

For you know that we dealt with each of you as a father deals with his own
children, encouraging, comforting and urging you to live lives worthy of God,
who calls you into his kingdom and glory.

     1 Thessalonians 2:11−12

_____

_____

_____

_____

_____

YIELDING

Personalize and pray this same Scripture for yourself.

_____

_____

_____

_____

_____

_____

Pray for missionary work in FIJI
(island group in the South Pacific, between Hawaii
and New Zealand)

Week 14
Thoughts and Prayers

_____

_____

_____

_____

_____

_____

_____

_____

_____

_____

_____

_____

_____

_____

_____

_____

_____

_____

_____

_____

_____

_____

_____

_____

_____

_____

_____

Week 15

MINISTRY &
SERVANTHOOD

For days I had tried to find the village chief. I was nearing the end of an exploration trip into the jungle, and I hoped he could furnish me with demographic information, such as population on the local communities. My hope was to learn if each community had a church. But the chief was nowhere to be found.

I arranged my travel and boarded a river taxi boat on a Friday to visit a friend in another community. The boat was delayed two hours. We waited on a few teachers to show up who were traveling to a large meeting. By that time my seat was growing very uncomfortable and I was facing a three-hour trip. We finally pushed off, reached the middle of the river, and the driver turned back to shore. One more passenger and his family had shown up. "Who is it?" I thought. "Why can't we go on, for crying out loud?!"

The unexpected passenger was the village chief and his family. With God's timing, my boat had been delayed long enough to be the last one available, and the village chief had been delayed just long enough to catch it. I was on this particular boat because it belonged to my friend's brother.

I was amazed and convinced that this was the Lord's work. I confirmed a meeting with the chief, but this was not enough. The Lord made it better. As I sat on a deck below my friend's house on Sunday (it's a raised house), the village chief came walking through the community to visit my friend. I was able to talk with him about my needs and the information I needed. He asked me to visit him on Monday to provide everything I needed.

The prayers of friends and the details which fell into place revealed to me that the Lord was guiding this trip, ordering my steps, and coordinating each detail. I felt very unworthy. I also realized that the Lord was working overtime to lift me up and show me His presence.

"Those who love Your law have great peace, and nothing causes them to stumble." (Ps. 119:165, NASB)

"For I am the Lord your God, who upholds your right hand, who says to you, 'Do not fear, I will help you.'" (Isa. 41:13, NASB)

Marty—SOUTH AMERICA

Notice, we never pray for folks we gossip about, and we never gossip about the folk for whom we pray! For prayer is a great detergent.
Leonard Ravenhill

PRAISE & THANKSGIVING

Worship by using the name of God mentioned in this Scripture—our "exceedingly great reward."

I am your shield, your exceedingly great reward.

Genesis 15:1 (NKJV)

REPENTANCE

Search your heart as you meditate on this Scripture. What is the Holy Spirit revealing to you?

Each one should use whatever gift he has received to serve others, faithfully administering God's grace in its various forms.

1 Peter 4:10

ASKING

Read the following Scripture. Rewrite it, personalizing it for missionaries, seeking the Lord in prayer for their ministry.

Preach the Word; be prepared in season and out of season; correct, rebuke and encourage—with great patience and careful instruction.

2 Timothy 4:2

_____

_____

_____

YIELDING

Now meditate on the Scripture again. Rewrite it below, personalizing and praying it for yourself. How can you respond to what God is saying to you in this Scripture?

_____

_____

_____

_____

Pray for missionary work in FINLAND
(Northern Europe, between Sweden and Russia)

> Prayer wonderfully clears the vision; steadies the nerves; defines duty;
> stiffens the purpose; sweetens and strengthens the spirit.
> *S. D. Gordon*

PRAISE & THANKSGIVING

Worship Him today, your "exceedingly great reward."

I am your shield, your exceedingly great reward."

Genesis 15:1 (NKJV)

REPENTANCE

Search your heart as you meditate on this Scripture.

Each one should use whatever gift he has received to serve others,
faithfully administering God's grace in its various forms.

1 Peter 4:10

ASKING

Rewrite this Scripture, personalizing it for missionaries,
seeking the Lord in prayer for their ministry.

As long as it is day, we must do the work of him who sent me.
Night is coming, when no one can work.

John 9:4

_____

_____

_____

_____

YIELDING

Rewrite it again, personalizing and praying it for yourself.
Respond to what God is saying to you in this Scripture.

_____

_____

_____

_____

Pray for missionary work in FRANCE
(Western Europe, between Italy and Spain)

We must bear in mind that mere resolutions to take more time for prayer
and to conquer reluctance to pray will not prove lastingly effective unless
there is a wholehearted and absolute surrender to the Lord Jesus Christ.
The Kneeling Christian

PRAISE & THANKSGIVING

> I am your shield, your exceedingly great reward."
>
> Genesis 15:1 (NKJV)

REPENTANCE

> Each one should use whatever gift he has received to serve others,
> faithfully administering God's grace in its various forms.
>
> 1 Peter 4:10

ASKING

Personalize this Scripture for missionaries, seeking
the Lord in prayer for their ministry.

> Pray for us, too, that God may open a door for our message, so that
> we may proclaim the mystery of Christ, for which I am in chains.
> Pray that I may proclaim it clearly, as I should.
>
> Colossians 4:3–4

_____

_____

_____

_____

YIELDING

Now personalize and pray it for yourself. How can
you respond to what God is saying to you?

_____

_____

_____

_____

_____

Pray for missionary work in FRENCH GUIANA
(Northern South America, on the Atlantic coast,
east of Suriname)

God's greatest agency, man's greatest agency, for defeating
the enemy and winning men back is intercession.
S. D. Gordon

PRAISE & THANKSGIVING

I am your shield, your exceedingly great reward."
Genesis 15:1 (NKJV)

REPENTANCE

*Do nothing out of selfish ambition or vain conceit, but in humility consider
others better than yourselves.*
Philippians 2:3

ASKING

Rewrite this Scripture, personalizing it for missionaries.

*Jesus called them together and said, "You know that the rulers of the Gentiles lord
it over them, and their high officials exercise authority over them. Not so with you.
Instead, whoever wants to become great among you must be your servant, and
whoever wants to be first must be your slave— just as the Son of Man did not come
to be served, but to serve, and to give his life as a ransom for many."*
Matthew 20:25–28

_____

_____

_____

_____

YIELDING

What is God saying to you in this Scripture?

_____

_____

_____

_____

_____

Pray for missionary work in FRENCH POLYNESIA
(South Pacific islands, halfway between
South America and Australia)

> The man who, despite the teaching of Scripture,
> tries to pray without a Savior, insults the deity.
> *Charles Spurgeon*

PRAISE & THANKSGIVING

I am your shield, your exceedingly great reward."

Genesis 15:1 (NKJV)

REPENTANCE

Do nothing out of selfish ambition or vain conceit, but in humility consider others better than yourselves.

Philippians 2:3

ASKING

Personalize this Scripture today for missionaries.

The man who loves his life will lose it, while the man who hates his life in this world will keep it for eternal life. Whoever serves me must follow me; and where I am, my servant also will be. My Father will honor the one who serves me.

John 12:25–26

_____

_____

_____

_____

_____

YIELDING

Personalize and pray this same Scripture for yourself.

_____

_____

_____

_____

_____

_____

_____

Pray for missionary work in GABON
(Western Africa, at the equator, west of the
Republic of the Congo)

Week 15
Thoughts and Prayers

Week 16

OBEDIENCE

We were on stateside assignment after our first four-year term of service in the Pacific Rim. Though our work was going well, we were having second thoughts about returning to the Philippines. The reason for our concern was that our blonde, fair-complected, eight-year-old son was beginning to develop moles on his body where he had been exposed to the tropical sun.

Two years earlier, I'd had surgery to remove two malignant melanoma lesions from my chest and forearm. One well-meaning doctor had gone so far as to say, "If you go back to the Philippines, you will die within two years." His concern was that this form of cancer is usually caused by excessive exposure to the sun. The Philippines is located just above the equator.

Many people prayed for us as we went through this difficult time. In spite of this doctor's counsel, we returned to the Philippines to finish out our first term, placing higher trust in God's leadership than in medical opinion and expertise. But now we were facing a new challenge. It was one thing to trust God for my own life. It was quite another to trust Him for my son's life. Were we carelessly placing his life in danger by raising him in the tropics? Could it be that God would have us to serve Him somewhere else? We asked others to join us in prayer about this.

One January morning, while staying at a missionary residence in Houston, Texas, I read the Genesis 22 account of Abraham's obedience to God's command to offer his son as a sacrifice. Having come to the place to which God had sent him, Abraham discovered that God was there as the Great Provider—*Jehovah Jireh.* "Abraham called the name of that place The LORD Will Provide, as it is said to this day, 'In the mount of the LORD it will be provided'" (Gen. 22:14, NASB). It seemed to me that "the mount of the Lord" to which He had called us was the Philippines. And what we needed God to provide was protection from the sun. If we obeyed Him, going to the place to which He had called us, He would be there to provide what was needed. I wrote down my thoughts in my journal and titled it, "A word from the Lord; re: Returning to the Philippines."

Four days later, I received a phone call from my mother-in-law. She said she had been trying to get in touch with me for several days. Her words: "I read Genesis 22 in my quiet time a few days ago, and I believe you need to read it. I think God may be saying something to you through that passage about returning to the Philippines." Overwhelmed, I replied, "Yes! God has spoken to me through that passage!" It was as if God wanted it to be unmistakably clear: "Trust and obey."

So we returned to the Philippines in the summer, armed with a clear word from God (and an ample supply of sunscreen). Our son graduated from high school in the Philippines and is now living in the United States. To this date, he has had no problem with melanoma, and I have had no recurrence myself. The Lord will provide when we go to "the mount of the Lord!"

Robert—PACIFIC RIM

> True prayer is measured by weight, not by length.
> A single groan before God may have more fullness
> of prayer in it than a fine oration of great length.
>
> *Charles Spurgeon*

PRAISE & THANKSGIVING

Worship by using the characteristic of God mentioned
in this Scripture—"upright and just."

> *He is the Rock, his works are perfect, and all his ways are just.*
> *A faithful God who does no wrong, upright and just is he.*
>
> Deuteronomy 32:4

REPENTANCE

Search your heart as you meditate on this Scripture.
What is the Holy Spirit revealing to you?

> *If anyone obeys his word, God's love is truly made complete in him. This is how*
> *we know we are in him: Whoever claims to live in him must walk as Jesus did.*
>
> 1 John 2:5–6

ASKING

Read the following Scripture. Rewrite it, personalizing
it for missionaries, seeking the Lord in prayer on their
behalf regarding obedience.

> *So then, brothers, stand firm and hold to the teachings we passed on to you,*
> *whether by word of mouth or by letter.*
>
> 2 Thessalonians 2:15

_____

_____

_____

YIELDING

Now meditate on the Scripture again. Rewrite it below,
personalizing and praying it for yourself. How can you
respond to what God is saying to you in this Scripture?

_____

_____

Pray for missionary work in THE GAMBIA
(Western Africa, bordered by the North Atlantic)

Little praying is a kind of make believe,
a salve for the conscience, a farce and a delusion.
E. M. Bounds

PRAISE & THANKSGIVING

Worship Him today as the One who is "upright and just."

He is the Rock, his works are perfect, and all his ways are just.
A faithful God who does no wrong, upright and just is he.

Deuteronomy 32:4

REPENTANCE

Search your heart as you meditate on this Scripture.

If anyone obeys his word, God's love is truly made complete in him. This is how
we know we are in him: Whoever claims to live in him must walk as Jesus did.

1 John 2:5–6

ASKING

Rewrite this Scripture, personalizing it for missionaries,
seeking the Lord in prayer on their behalf regarding
obedience.

This is how we know that we love the children of God: by loving God and
carrying out his commands. This is love for God: to obey his commands.
And his commands are not burdensome, for everyone born of God overcomes
the world. This is the victory that has overcome the world, even our faith.

1 John 5:2–4

_____

_____

_____

_____

YIELDING

Rewrite it again, personalizing and praying it for yourself.
Respond to what God is saying to you in this Scripture.

_____

_____

_____

Pray for missionary work in THE GAZA STRIP
(Middle East, between Egypt and Israel)

There is nothing to be valued more highly than to have people praying
for us; God links up His power in answer to their prayers.
Oswald Chambers

PRAISE & THANKSGIVING

> *He is the Rock, his works are perfect, and all his ways are just.*
> *A faithful God who does no wrong, upright and just is he.*
>
> Deuteronomy 32:4

REPENTANCE

> *If anyone obeys his word, God's love is truly made complete in him. This is how*
> *we know we are in him: Whoever claims to live in him must walk as Jesus did.*
>
> 1 John 2:5–6

ASKING

Personalize this Scripture for missionaries, rewriting it
in prayer on their behalf regarding obedience.

> *How can a young man keep his way pure? By living according to your word.*
> *I seek you with all my heart; do not let me stray from your commands.*
> *I have hidden your word in my heart that I might not sin against you.*
>
> Psalm 119:9–11

_____

_____

_____

_____

YIELDING

Now personalize and pray it for yourself. How can you
respond to what God is saying to you?

_____

_____

_____

_____

_____

Pray for missionary work in GEORGIA
(Southwestern Asia, on the Black Sea,
between Turkey and Russia)

When we discern that people are not going on spiritually and allow the discernment to turn to criticism, we block our way to God. God never gives us discernment in order that we may criticize, but that we may intercede.
Oswald Chambers

PRAISE & THANKSGIVING

He is the Rock, his works are perfect, and all his ways are just.
A faithful God who does no wrong, upright and just is he.
     Deuteronomy 32:4

REPENTANCE

If anyone obeys his word, God's love is truly made complete in him. This is how we know we are in him: Whoever claims to live in him must walk as Jesus did.
     1 John 2:5–6

ASKING

Rewrite this Scripture, personalizing it for missionaries.

For if we are faithful to the end, trusting God just as firmly as when we first believed, we will share in all that belongs to Christ.
     Hebrews 3:14 (NLT)

_____

_____

_____

_____

_____

YIELDING

What is God saying to you in this Scripture?

_____

_____

_____

_____

_____

_____

Pray for missionary work in GERMANY
(Central Europe, between the Netherlands and Poland)

Scripture calls us to pray for many things: . . . for the sending forth of
laborers; for those who labor in the gospel; for all converts; for believers
who have fallen into sin; for one another in our immediate circles.
Andrew Murray

PRAISE & THANKSGIVING

He is the Rock, his works are perfect, and all his ways are just.
A faithful God who does no wrong, upright and just is he.

Deuteronomy 32:4

REPENTANCE

If anyone obeys his word, God's love is truly made complete in him. This is how
we know we are in him: Whoever claims to live in him must walk as Jesus did.

1 John 2:5–6

ASKING

Personalize this Scripture today for missionaries.

I have kept my feet from every evil path so that I might obey your word.

Psalm 119:101

_____

_____

_____

_____

YIELDING

Personalize and pray this same Scripture for yourself.

_____

_____

_____

_____

_____

_____

_____

Pray for missionary work in GHANA
(Western Africa, between Cote d'Ivoire and Togo)

Week 16
Thoughts and Prayers

Week 17

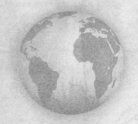

Peace & Contentment

God began doing a work in my heart the moment we landed in our new home overseas. We climbed into a "seatbeltless" taxi careening down the highway within inches of bicyclists, pedestrians, carts, and other vehicles.

Looking back now, I believe one reason God called me to be a missionary was to deal with a lingering problem with fear and worry. Prayer became my daily defense as I walked through streets where sickness, accidents, and injury were much closer realities than in seatbelt-clad, sanitized, modernized, air-bagged America.

Philippians 4:6 became my daily mantra: "Do not be anxious about anything, but in *everything*, by prayer and petition, with thanksgiving, present your requests to God." Anytime I encountered situations that evoked fear, I turned my worry into a prayer.

After one year living overseas, I thought I had this fear problem figured out and under control . . . until I went on a village trip that changed my heart forever, as noted in an excerpt from my journal:

"God has brought me to a point of surrender and peace, replacing fears that used to grip me during these precarious trips across the mountains. But this particular morning it was snowing. The thought of driving on icy, narrow, mountain roads bordered by cliffs was almost more than I could bear. Isn't this more than God should expect from sane people? I remember this thought running through my mind—'You know, Lord, your disciples didn't have to travel on antique buses or along icy roads surrounded by cliffs to do their jobs. Isn't this going above and beyond the call of duty here?'"

At this point I decided to read the Word to get my perspective back in line with His. I just "happened" to turn to Matthew 8:23–27, the story of Jesus calming a storm. As I read this familiar account, I realized for the first time in my life that the disciples thought they were going to die! I grew up thinking the disciples must have been pretty cowardly to be so afraid. But even though the disciples were not traveling on icy mountain roads (like me), they were expecting death at any moment. And what did Jesus say to them when they woke Him up? "Why are you so afraid?"

The words jumped off the pages of my Bible and seared my faithless heart. Why was I so afraid? Yes, from a human standpoint I was in a very precarious position, riding in an old, run-down bus that probably had never been inspected. We were traveling on icy mountain roads with no guardrails and a 500+ foot drop over the edge. But from a spiritual standpoint, I was following Jesus' call on my life. I was in the best place I could be. Peace returned to replace the fears that had overwhelmed my heart.

Just a few minutes later, we heard a thunderous cracking noise. The bus suddenly tilted sideways and veered off to the lefthand side of the road before coming to a screeching halt. All of the passengers piled off to see what had happened. The front steel axle of the bus had snapped in two, and the wheel of the bus was completely broken off. Where did this incident occur? The axle broke along a short stretch of road with level ground extending for several feet on either side of the pavement. This ideal place for a breakdown was nestled between long stretches of narrow mountain roads with sheer cliffs along the edge. Why am I so afraid? Although human odds are against us, our God is in the business of beating the odds!

—A Christian worker in Asia

> Prayer creates hunger for souls; hunger for souls creates prayer.
> The understanding soul prays; the praying soul gets understanding.
> *Leonard Ravenhill*

PRAISE & THANKSGIVING

Worship by using the aspect of God mentioned in this Scripture—"my hiding place."

> *You are my hiding place; you will protect me from trouble and*
> *surround me with songs of deliverance.*
>
> Psalm 32:7

REPENTANCE

Search your heart as you meditate on this Scripture. What is the Holy Spirit revealing to you?

> *But the meek will inherit the land and enjoy great peace.*
>
> Psalm 37:11

ASKING

Read the following Scripture. Rewrite it, personalizing it for missionaries, seeking the Lord in prayer on their behalf regarding peace.

> *May the God of hope fill you with all joy and peace as you trust in him,*
> *so that you may overflow with hope by the power of the Holy Spirit.*
>
> Romans 15:13

_____

_____

YIELDING

Now meditate on the Scripture again. Rewrite it below, personalizing and praying it for yourself. How can you respond to what God is saying to you in this Scripture?

_____

_____

_____

_____

Pray for missionary work in GIBRALTAR
(Southwestern Europe, on the southern coast of Spain)

> The revelation of our spiritual standing is what we ask in prayer;
> sometimes what we ask is an insult to God; we ask with our eyes
> on the possibilities or on ourselves, not on Jesus Christ.
> *Oswald Chambers*

PRAISE & THANKSGIVING
Worship Him today, for He is your "hiding place."
> *You are my hiding place; you will protect me from trouble and*
> *surround me with songs of deliverance.*
> Psalm 32:7

REPENTANCE
Search your heart as you meditate on this Scripture.
> *But the meek will inherit the land and enjoy great peace.*
> Psalm 37:11

ASKING
Rewrite this Scripture, personalizing it for missionaries,
seeking the Lord in prayer on their behalf regarding peace.
> *Don't worry about anything; instead, pray about everything. Tell God what you*
> *need, and thank him for all he has done. If you do this, you will experience God's*
> *peace, which is far more wonderful than the human mind can understand. His*
> *peace will guard your hearts and minds as you live in Christ Jesus.*
> Philippians 4:6–7 (NLT)

_____

_____

_____

YIELDING
Rewrite it again, personalizing and praying it for yourself.
Respond to what God is saying to you in this Scripture.

_____

_____

_____

_____

Pray for missionary work in GREECE
(Southern Europe, between Albania and Turkey)

True prayer is a lonely business.
Samuel Chadwick

PRAISE & THANKSGIVING

*You are my hiding place; you will protect me from trouble and surround
me with songs of deliverance.*

Psalm 32:7

REPENTANCE

*I know what it is to be in need, and I know what it is to have plenty.
I have learned the secret of being content in any and every situation,
whether well fed or hungry, whether living in plenty or in want.
I can do everything through him who gives me strength.*

Philippians 4:12–13

ASKING

Personalize this Scripture for missionaries, rewriting it
in prayer on their behalf regarding contentment.

But godliness with contentment is great gain.

1 Timothy 6:6

_____

_____

_____

YIELDING

Now personalize and pray it for yourself. How can you
respond to what God is saying to you?

_____

_____

_____

_____

_____

_____

Pray for missionary work in GREENLAND
(between the Arctic and North Atlantic Oceans,
northeast of Canada)

A consciousness of personal impotence; faith in the power of prayer; courage to persevere in spite of refusal; and the assurance of an abundant reward; these are the dispositions that constitute a Christian an intercessor.
Andrew Murray

PRAISE & THANKSGIVING

You are my hiding place; you will protect me from trouble and surround me with songs of deliverance.

Psalm 32:7

REPENTANCE

This is what the LORD says: "Stand at the crossroads and look; ask for the ancient paths, ask where the good way is, and walk in it, and you will find rest for your souls."

Jeremiah 6:16

ASKING

Rewrite this Scripture, personalizing it for missionaries.

There remains, then, a Sabbath-rest for the people of God; for anyone who enters God's rest also rests from his own work, just as God did from his. Let us, therefore, make every effort to enter that rest, so that no one will fall by following their example of disobedience.

Hebrews 4:9–11

_____

_____

_____

YIELDING

What is God saying to you in this Scripture?

_____

_____

_____

_____

Pray for missionary work in GRENADA
(Caribbean island, north of Trinidad and Tobago)

> Get a place for prayer where no one imagines that this
> is what you are doing. Shut the door and talk to God.
> *Oswald Chambers*

PRAISE & THANKSGIVING

*You are my hiding place; you will protect me from trouble and surround
me with songs of deliverance.*

Psalm 32:7

REPENTANCE

*This is what the LORD says: "Stand at the crossroads and look; ask for the
ancient paths, ask where the good way is, and walk in it, and you will find
rest for your souls."*

Jeremiah 6:16

ASKING

Personalize this Scripture today for missionaries.

*Come to me, all you who are weary and burdened, and I will give you rest.
Take my yoke upon you and learn from me, for I am gentle and humble
in heart, and you will find rest for your souls.*

Matthew 11:28–29

_____

_____

_____

_____

YIELDING

Personalize and pray this same Scripture for yourself.

_____

_____

_____

_____

_____

_____

Pray for missionary work in THE GRENADINES
(Caribbean islands, north of Trinidad and Tobago)

Week 17
Thoughts and Prayers

_____
_____
_____
_____
_____
_____
_____
_____
_____
_____
_____
_____
_____
_____
_____
_____
_____
_____
_____
_____
_____
_____
_____
_____
_____
_____
_____
_____
_____

Week 18

PROTECTION

While taking time off between ministry commitments, a missionary couple experienced an armed robbery. They were tied and gagged, and three men spent about forty minutes in a small motel room with them, going through everything. The couple said, "It was definitely difficult and scary. We hope not to repeat the experience and don't wish to "spiritualize" it. At the same time, we do want to share that God surrounded us with a genuine sense of His peace, regardless of the outcome. After the incident we were so surrounded with care from friends that we feel we had the advantage before our funeral of knowing we are loved." While reflecting on the robbery they wrote the following:

"They were evil men, with evil intent, and they wished to take all our worldly goods. When thieves broke into our room, they were able to take money, laptop, clothes, shoes, luggage, watches, car, and more. They tied and gagged us, and repeatedly threatened to kill us. I was hit on the back of the head with a gun, and one man put his heel on my lower back and ground it down several times. My husband was gagged so tightly it was quite painful and suffocating. They could have killed us or done us other bodily harm. Praise God, they did not! They could—and did—take our goods. They could not—so did not—take the good in our lives.

"They could take our Bible, hymnal, tracts, and Christian music, but they could not take our relationship to our heavenly Father through our Lord Jesus Christ. They could not take God's love for us, or our love for Him. They could not take our salvation or even one of God's many blessings to us in half a century of life. They could have taken our lives, but that would only have ushered us into God's wonderful presence and eternal life. They could take our passports, but they could not take our United States citizenship. More importantly, they could not take our citizenship to heaven.

"They could take our wedding rings, but not our commitment to one another, our friendship, and our deep and abiding love for one another. This has only allowed us to deepen our relationship, to realize anew that life is finite and we must take full advantage of it. Our love and friendship, because it is based on God, is able through Him to overcome challenges, tragedies, and suffering.

"They could take items given us by Venezuelan friends, colleagues, and family. They could not take our friendship with any of these friends, or the concern and care shown to us by them. They could not take the satisfaction of knowing our three terrific grown kids love and serve the Lord and are married to godly spouses (also terrific) who do likewise. They could not take our darling granddaughter or the two grandbabies on the way. They could not take the inheritance and joy of wonderful Christian parents and family members.

"They could take the camera but none of the lovely memories and experiences through the years. They could take the laptop, with so much of our teaching and administrative materials, but they could not take the ongoing effectiveness of the gospel as it continues to spread. They could not, in fact, take anything of real value.

"Please do pray for the safety of those serving in an increasingly volatile world. Pray also for the thieves that somehow, in some way, they will be able to hear about the love of Christ."

Robin—SOUTH AMERICA

The act that is not prayer in the ultimate, and the word which is not prayer in the last analysis, and the wish that is not prayer in the profoundest depth are to be put away; they do not become the life of faith.

G. *Campbell Morgan*

PRAISE & THANKSGIVING

Worship by using the aspect of God mentioned in this Scripture—"my rock."

The LORD is my rock, my fortress and my deliverer; my God is my rock, in whom I take refuge, my shield and the horn of my salvation. He is my stronghold, my refuge and my savior.

2 Samuel 22:2–3

REPENTANCE

Search your heart as you meditate on this Scripture. What is the Holy Spirit revealing to you?

Fear of man will prove to be a snare, but whoever trusts in the LORD is kept safe.

Proverbs 29:25

ASKING

Read the following Scripture. Rewrite it, personalizing it for missionaries, seeking the Lord in prayer on their behalf for protection.

Whoever listens to me will live in safety and be at ease, without fear of harm.

Proverbs 1:33

_____

_____

_____

YIELDING

Now meditate on the Scripture again. Rewrite it below, personalizing and praying it for yourself. How can you respond to what God is saying to you in this Scripture?

_____

_____

_____

Pray for missionary work on GUADELOUPE
(Caribbean island, between Puerto Rico and Venezuela)

O, let the place of secret prayer become to me
the most beloved spot on earth.
Andrew Murray

PRAISE & THANKSGIVING
Worship Him today—your "rock."

*The LORD is my rock, my fortress and my deliverer; my God is my rock,
in whom I take refuge, my shield and the horn of my salvation. He is
my stronghold, my refuge and my savior.*

2 Samuel 22:2–3

REPENTANCE
Search your heart as you meditate on this Scripture.

Fear of man will prove to be a snare, but whoever trusts in the LORD is kept safe.

Proverbs 29:25

ASKING
Rewrite this Scripture, personalizing it for missionaries,
seeking the Lord in prayer on their behalf for protection.

*Have no fear of sudden disaster or of the ruin that overtakes the wicked, for the
LORD will be your confidence and will keep your foot from being snared.*

Proverbs 3:25–26

_____

_____

_____

_____

YIELDING
Rewrite it again, personalizing and praying it for yourself.
Respond to what God is saying to you in this Scripture.

_____

_____

_____

_____

Pray for missionary work in GUAM
(island in the North Pacific, between Hawaii
and the Philippines)

> The secret of praying is praying in secret.
> *Leonard Ravenhill*

PRAISE & THANKSGIVING

> *The LORD is my rock, my fortress and my deliverer; my God is my rock,*
> *in whom I take refuge, my shield and the horn of my salvation. He is*
> *my stronghold, my refuge and my savior.*
>
> 2 Samuel 22:2–3

REPENTANCE

> *Fear of man will prove to be a snare, but whoever trusts in the LORD is kept safe.*
>
> Proverbs 29:25

ASKING

Personalize this Scripture for missionaries, rewriting it
in prayer on their behalf for protection.

> *Surely God is my help; the Lord is the one who sustains me.*
>
> Psalm 54:4

_____

_____

_____

_____

YIELDING

Now personalize and pray it for yourself. How can you
respond to what God is saying to you?

_____

_____

_____

_____

_____

_____

_____

_____

Pray for missionary work in GUATEMALA
(Central America, between Mexico and El Salvador)

Some people pray just to pray and some people pray to know God.
Andrew Murray

PRAISE & THANKSGIVING

The LORD is my rock, my fortress and my deliverer; my God is my rock,
in whom I take refuge, my shield and the horn of my salvation. He is
my stronghold, my refuge and my savior.

2 Samuel 22:2–3

REPENTANCE

Fear of man will prove to be a snare, but whoever trusts in the LORD is kept safe.

Proverbs 29:25

ASKING

Rewrite this Scripture, personalizing it for missionaries.

There remains, then, a Sabbath-rest for the people of God; for anyone who enters
God's rest also rests from his own work, just as God did from his. Let us, therefore,
make every effort to enter that rest, so that no one will fall by following their
example of disobedience.

Hebrews 4:9–11

_____

_____

_____

_____

YIELDING

What is God saying to you in this Scripture?

_____

_____

_____

_____

_____

_____

Pray for missionary work in GUERNSEY
(islands in the English Channel, northwest of France)

Intercessory prayer for one who is sinning prevails. God says so. The will of the man prayed for does not come into question at all. . . . Prayer on the basis of the Redemption sets the connection working, and God gives life.
Oswald Chambers

PRAISE & THANKSGIVING

The LORD is my rock, my fortress and my deliverer; my God is my rock, in whom I take refuge, my shield and the horn of my salvation. He is my stronghold, my refuge and my savior.

2 Samuel 22:2–3

REPENTANCE

Fear of man will prove to be a snare, but whoever trusts in the LORD is kept safe.

Proverbs 29:25

ASKING

Personalize this Scripture today for missionaries.

In you, O LORD, I have taken refuge; let me never be put to shame. Rescue me and deliver me in your righteousness; turn your ear to me and save me. Be my rock of refuge, to which I can always go; give the command to save me, for you are my rock and my fortress.

Psalm 71:1–3

_____

_____

_____

YIELDING

Personalize and pray this same Scripture for yourself.

_____

_____

_____

_____

_____

Pray for missionary work in GUINEA
(Western Africa, between Guinea-Bissau and Sierra Leone)

Week 18
Thoughts and Prayers

_____

_____

_____

_____

_____

_____

_____

_____

_____

_____

_____

_____

_____

_____

_____

_____

_____

_____

_____

_____

_____

_____

_____

_____

_____

_____

_____

_____

Week 19

RELATIONSHIPS

Imagine being given the task of going to a city of a million and a half people where you do not know anyone and taking the responsibility to plant churches. Added to this challenge of the sheer numbers of people is that you speak very little of their language. How do you begin?

As a strategy coordinator for a city of this size, my husband and I were equipped with many tools for the task. We were given great training within our organization, but along with the training was the constant reminder that the most important preparation comes in the form of prayer.

We could not agree more! We, along with our committed prayer network in the States, began to pray for this city. We presented specific needs to the Lord, and it has been our joy to see God at work.

One of our first requests was for my husband to be able to build relationships with pastors in our city involved in evangelical ministry. The only way to find these men was by word of mouth. Addresses were unavailable and phone numbers unreliable. Within a very short time, however, God enabled my husband to meet several pastors and laymen. One of the pastors, a leader of the largest evangelical congregation in the city, invited my husband to a meeting of pastors in order to present the concept of church planting. God was bringing the potential participants in a church planting movement to us!

A second strategic request was for interested men to emerge from the first meeting to receive further training in church planting methods. My husband shared this need with our prayer network. The conference was successful with a much higher attendance than expected. Two groups of nearly sixty people continued weekly training sessions, and thirteen professions of faith resulted from the group sharing the gospel. Just like the mustard seed, God took a small group of men and gave us many reasons to rejoice. The men have remained faithful and understand the concept of taking what they have learned to teach others. In this way the learning is multiplied and churches can be formed. The newly trained leaders set their own goal of planting 1,000 churches in their city!

All of this happened over a period of only four months because God is creating, nurturing, and strengthening the path. He is doing this as His people pray and seek Him to join God at work in a city of over a million people who do not have a personal relationship with Jesus Christ. God be praised!

—*A Christian worker in South Asia*

> Trouble is one of God's great servants because it
> reminds us how much we continually need the Lord.
> *Jim Cymbala*

PRAISE & THANKSGIVING

Worship by using the aspect of God mentioned in
this Scripture—"compassionate."

> *You, O LORD, are a compassionate and gracious God,*
> *slow to anger, abounding in love and faithfulness.*
>
> Psalm 86:15

REPENTANCE

Search your heart as you meditate on this Scripture.
What is the Holy Spirit revealing to you?

> *Greater love has no one than this, that he lay down his life for his friends.*
>
> John 15:13

ASKING

Read the following Scripture. Rewrite it, personalizing it
for missionaries, praying for their relationships with godly
friends.

> *Do not be yoked together with unbelievers. For what do righteousness and*
> *wickedness have in common? Or what fellowship can light have with darkness?*
> *What harmony is there between Christ and Belial? What does a believer have*
> *in common with an unbeliever?*
>
> 2 Corinthians 6:14–15

_____

_____

YIELDING

Now meditate on the Scripture again. Rewrite it below,
personalizing and praying it for yourself. How can you
respond to what God is saying to you in this Scripture?

_____

_____

Pray for missionary work in GUINEA-BISSAU
(Western Africa, between Guinea and Senegal)

Trouble and perplexity drive me to prayer,
and prayer drives away perplexity and trouble.
Philipp Melanchthon

PRAISE & THANKSGIVING

Come before Him today, for He is "compassionate."

You, O LORD, are a compassionate and gracious God,
slow to anger, abounding in love and faithfulness.
Psalm 86:15

REPENTANCE

Search your heart as you meditate on this Scripture.

I appeal to you, brothers, in the name of our Lord Jesus Christ, that all
of you agree with one another so that there may be no divisions among
you and that you may be perfectly united in mind and thought.
1 Corinthians 1:10

ASKING

Rewrite this Scripture, personalizing it for missionaries,
praying for their relationships among co-laborers.

As a prisoner for the Lord, then, I urge you to live a life worthy of the calling
you have received. Be completely humble and gentle; be patient, bearing with
one another in love. Make every effort to keep the unity of the Spirit through
the bond of peace.
Ephesians 4:1–3

_____

_____

_____

YIELDING

Rewrite it again, personalizing and praying it for yourself.
Respond to what God is saying to you in this Scripture.

_____

_____

_____

Pray for missionary work in GUYANA
(Northern South America, between Suriname and Venezuela)

When the devil sees a whole church on its face before God in prayer,
he trembles' as much as he ever did, for he knows that his day
in that church or community is at an end.
R. A. Torrey

PRAISE & THANKSGIVING

You, O LORD, are a compassionate and gracious God,
slow to anger, abounding in love and faithfulness.
Psalm 86:15

REPENTANCE

I appeal to you, brothers, in the name of our Lord Jesus Christ, that all
of you agree with one another so that there may be no divisions among
you and that you may be perfectly united in mind and thought.
1 Corinthians 1:10

ASKING

Personalize this Scripture for missionaries, rewriting it,
praying for their relationships among co-laborers.

Now the body is not made up of one part but of many. . . . But God has combined
the members of the body and has given greater honor to the parts that lacked it,
so that there should be no division in the body, but that its parts should have
equal concern for each other. If one part suffers, every part suffers with it;
if one part is honored, every part rejoices with it.
1 Corinthians 12:14, 24–26

_____
_____
_____

YIELDING

Now personalize and pray it for yourself. How can you
respond to what God is saying to you?

_____
_____
_____

Pray for missionary work in HAITI
(western third of the island of Hispaniola,
west of the Dominican Republic)

Prayer must be aflame. Its ardor must consume. Prayer without fervor is as a sun without light or heat, or as a flower without beauty or fragrance. A soul devoted to God is a fervent soul, and prayer is the creature of that flame.

E. M. Bounds

PRAISE & THANKSGIVING

You, O LORD, are a compassionate and gracious God,
slow to anger, abounding in love and faithfulness.

Psalm 86:15

REPENTANCE

I appeal to you, brothers, in the name of our Lord Jesus Christ, that all
of you agree with one another so that there may be no divisions among
you and that you may be perfectly united in mind and thought.

1 Corinthians 1:10

ASKING

Rewrite this Scripture, personalizing it for missionaries.

Let us consider how we may spur one another on toward love and good deeds.
Let us not give up meeting together, as some are in the habit of doing, but let us
encourage one another—and all the more as you see the Day approaching.

Hebrews 10:24–25

_____

_____

_____

YIELDING

What is God saying to you in this Scripture?

_____

_____

_____

_____

_____

_____

Pray for missionary work in HONDURAS
(Central America, between Guatemala and Nicaragua)

Prayer is the master strategy that God gives for the defeat and rout of Satan.
Wesley L. Duewel

PRAISE & THANKSGIVING

You, O LORD, are a compassionate and gracious God,
slow to anger, abounding in love and faithfulness.
Psalm 86:15

REPENTANCE

Give everyone what you owe him: If you owe taxes, pay taxes; if revenue,
then revenue; if respect, then respect; if honor, then honor.
Romans 13:7

ASKING

Personalize this Scripture today for missionaries.

Everyone must submit himself to the governing authorities, for there is no
authority except that which God has established. The authorities that exist
have been established by God. Consequently, he who rebels against the authority
is rebelling against what God has instituted, and those who do so will bring
judgment on themselves.
Romans 13:1–2

_____

_____

_____

_____

YIELDING

Personalize and pray this same Scripture for yourself.

_____

_____

_____

_____

_____

_____

Pray for missionary work in HONG KONG
(Eastern Asia, bordering the South China Sea and China)

Week 19
Thoughts and Prayers

_____

_____

_____

_____

_____

_____

_____

_____

_____

_____

_____

_____

_____

_____

_____

_____

_____

_____

_____

_____

_____

_____

_____

_____

_____

_____

_____

Week 20

SPIRITUAL ENRICHMENT

As a young missionary, it was easy to get distracted as we started new churches. Many of the first churches we started met in the lower level of houses built on stilts. The floors were a mixture of cow dung and mud. With four little girls, my mind was cluttered with fear of infection, typhoid, or a dozen other diseases.

The ministry was just beginning and people were so responsive. One part of our ministry included a Christian radio broadcast. Mail came in from around the nation, and we responded with handwritten letters. There was so much for just two missionary couples to accomplish.

In my preoccupied state, I was shocked one Sunday when my husband suddenly stopped his sermon and said, "Isn't that right, Charlene?" He obviously wanted more response from his audience. It certainly roused my attention, as I had no idea what he was talking about. I went home that day thinking, "What in the world am I doing here?" My question was answered almost immediately.

Early in the week, I sat with my daughters on our living room floor. We were cutting stamps off the envelopes coming in from the radio broadcast. Stamp collecting was a family hobby. The long day of household chores left me exhausted. I looked out the front window of our home and noticed one of the new believers coming up the path to our front door.

Mrs. Singh was the mother of nine children. I knew her husband was ill and couldn't work, but in my exhaustion I thought to myself, "Lord, why can't this 'sister' (a term used for believers) come another time? What if I just don't go to the door? Maybe she will leave!"

Sister Singh came in and sat on the floor with the rest of us. She didn't speak. Finally she picked up some scissors and methodically started cutting stamps from the envelopes. We sat in silence for what seemed like a long time. I tried to discover if she had come with a physical need. This was not the case, but she couldn't seem to verbalize why she came.

After some time Sister Singh began to cry, then she blurted out, "I can't go home. I thought I was a Christian, but today, in great anger, I hit my son." The story of her day unfolded as she cried. An argument with her teenage son had become so heated that she picked up an iron skillet and hit the boy in the head. Her neighbor took her son to the hospital and he was going to be fine. Mrs. Singh walked around for hours and finally came to our home.

I knew I could pray for Mrs. Singh, but I couldn't fulfill her need. I simply took the Bible and turned to Proverbs 3:5–6. "Trust in the LORD with all your heart and lean not on your own understanding; in all your ways acknowledge him, and he will make your paths straight."

Mrs. Singh took the Bible from me and read it aloud again. Immediately she stood up and quietly said, "I'm going home now." At that time I didn't know about praying God's Word, but I did know His Word always brought hope and direction. In spite of my weary and distracted heart, God showed me why I was there. His power was sufficient to meet all of her needs—and to answer my questions as well.

Charlene—MIDDLE AMERICA AND THE CARIBBEAN

There come times when I have nothing more to tell God. At such times it is wonderful to say to God, "May I be in Thy presence, Lord? I have nothing more to say to Thee, but I do love to be in Thy presence."

O. Hallesby

PRAISE & THANKSGIVING

Worship by using the aspect of God mentioned in this Scripture—"gracious."

The LORD is gracious and righteous; our God is full of compassion.

Psalm 116:5

REPENTANCE

Search your heart as you meditate on this Scripture. What is the Holy Spirit revealing to you?

Prepare your minds for action; be self-controlled; set your hope fully on the grace to be given you when Jesus Christ is revealed.

1 Peter 1:13

ASKING

Read the following Scripture. Rewrite it, personalizing it for missionaries, seeking the Lord in prayer on their behalf regarding spiritual enrichment.

I pray also that the eyes of your heart may be enlightened in order that you may know the hope to which he has called you, the riches of his glorious inheritance in the saints, and his incomparably great power for us who believe.

Ephesians 1:18–19

_____

_____

YIELDING

Now meditate on the Scripture again. Rewrite it below, personalizing and praying it for yourself. How can you respond to what God is saying to you in this Scripture?

_____

_____

Pray for missionary work in HUNGARY
(Central Europe, northwest of Romania)

> Pray often, for prayer is a shield to the soul,
> a sacrifice to God, and a scourge for Satan.
> *John Bunyan*

PRAISE & THANKSGIVING

Worship God today, and find Him "gracious."

> *The LORD is gracious and righteous; our God is full of compassion.*
>
> Psalm 116:5

REPENTANCE

Search your heart as you meditate on this Scripture.

> *Prepare your minds for action; be self-controlled; set your hope fully on the grace to be given you when Jesus Christ is revealed.*
>
> 1 Peter 1:13

ASKING

Rewrite this Scripture, personalizing it for missionaries, seeking the Lord in prayer on their behalf regarding spiritual enrichment and guidance.

> *The LORD longs to be gracious to you; he rises to show you compassion. For the LORD is a God of justice. Blessed are all who wait for him!*
>
> Isaiah 30:18

_____

_____

_____

YIELDING

Rewrite it again, personalizing and praying it for yourself. Respond to what God is saying to you in this Scripture.

_____

_____

_____

_____

Pray for missionary work in ICELAND
(Northern Europe, in the Greenland Sea, northwest of the UK)

The very powers of darkness are paralyzed by prayer; no spiritualistic
séance can succeed in the presence of a humble, praying saint.
Oswald Chambers

PRAISE & THANKSGIVING

The LORD is gracious and righteous; our God is full of compassion.

Psalm 116:5

REPENTANCE

Prepare your minds for action; be self-controlled; set your hope fully on the
grace to be given you when Jesus Christ is revealed.

1 Peter 1:13

ASKING

Personalize this Scripture for missionaries, rewriting it,
seeking the Lord in prayer on their behalf regarding
spiritual enrichment and guidance.

Seek first his kingdom and his righteousness, and all these things will be given
to you as well.

Matthew 6:33

_____

_____

_____

_____

YIELDING

Now personalize and pray it for yourself. How can you
respond to what God is saying to you?

_____

_____

_____

_____

_____

Pray for missionary work in INDIA
(Southern Asia, between Burma and Pakistan)

Every work of God can be traced to some kneeling form.
Dwight L. Moody

PRAISE & THANKSGIVING

The LORD is gracious and righteous; our God is full of compassion.
Psalm 116:5

REPENTANCE

Prepare your minds for action; be self-controlled; set your hope fully on the grace to be given you when Jesus Christ is revealed.
1 Peter 1:13

ASKING

Rewrite this Scripture, personalizing it for missionaries.
But whatever was to my profit I now consider loss for the sake of Christ. What is more, I consider everything a loss compared to the surpassing greatness of knowing Christ Jesus my Lord, for whose sake I have lost all things. I consider them rubbish, that I may gain Christ.
Philippians 3:7–8

_____

_____

_____

_____

YIELDING

What is God saying to you in this Scripture?

_____

_____

_____

_____

_____

_____

Pray for missionary work in INDONESIA
(Southeastern Asia, islands between the Indian
and Pacific Oceans)

God has chosen to work through His people—and through their prayers.
Ronald Dunn

PRAISE & THANKSGIVING

The LORD is gracious and righteous; our God is full of compassion.
Psalm 116:5

REPENTANCE

Prepare your minds for action; be self-controlled; set your hope fully on the grace to be given you when Jesus Christ is revealed.
1 Peter 1:13

ASKING

Personalize this Scripture today for missionaries.
I will instruct you and teach you in the way you should go; I will counsel you and watch over you.
Psalm 32:8

_____

_____

_____

YIELDING

Personalize and pray this same Scripture for yourself.

_____

_____

_____

_____

_____

_____

_____

_____

Pray for missionary work in IRAN
(Middle East, between Iraq and Pakistan)

Week 20
Thoughts and Prayers

_____
_____
_____
_____
_____
_____
_____
_____
_____
_____
_____
_____
_____
_____
_____
_____
_____
_____
_____
_____
_____
_____

Week 21

STEWARDSHIP

"I am the vine, you are the branches; he who abides in Me and I in him,
he bears much fruit, for apart from Me you can do nothing." (John 15:5, NASB)

Busyness is Satan's greatest tactic of distraction for a missionary. There is busyness with ministry, cultural acquisition, language learning, church activities, and much more. Many things beg for a missionary's attention and energy, but God has called us first and foremost to Himself.

Oh, to truly know Him and to hear His sweet voice; this is my heart's desire. I realize my time with Jesus each morning and night is crucial. No matter how tired I am when I rise, nor how spent my mind and body are as I prepare to sleep, I must guard this time with the Lord. He is the Vine, and I being the branch have no life apart from the abundance He pours into me. When I am distracted from the Most Important One by the many competing activities, my energy, love, vision, and ability are so finite and limited. But when I am truly living in the Spirit and allowing Him to cultivate my walk with Him, I bear His fruit and exuberate with Christ's life in me!

"My Father is glorified by this, that you bear much fruit,
and so prove to be My disciples." (John 15:8, NASB)

Katherine—SOUTH AMERICA

I saw the importance of the body of Christ while serving as a single missionary woman. Each of us plays a vital role, contributing to His church. I worked with volunteer teams from the United States in my first job overseas. Together we visited different people groups in Mali and Cote d'Ivoire. Two times, an American church brought a group to help build a school for the Dogon people of Mali. One volunteer befriended a thirteen-year-old boy named Mark on the first trip. The volunteer was unable to return on the second trip, but he sent Mark a letter and large photo of the two of them with another volunteer. The volunteer also included a letter that explained the simple gospel message.

The last day of the volunteer trip, four of us went on a hunt to search for Mark. We were attempting to find one thirteen-year-old boy in a large Dogon village. This is no easy task! But we did happen upon Mark's good friend, a Christian, who took us right to Mark. We found him sitting on a rock, staring off into the distance, without a smile. Mark's arm was broken and he had been sick for weeks. We explained who we were and that his American friend sent a picture and letter to him. I sat down with Mark and translated the letter, but before I even got to the part about receiving Christ, Mark said, "I want that! I want to accept Jesus!" I was so excited! It was obvious God was at work. We finished the letter together and talked with Mark at length to make sure he understood his decision. He did understand. A Dogon believer prayed with Mark in his heart language to accept Christ as his Savior!

God used the body of Christ, working together, to lead one young man to become a new brother in Christ. Mark now wears a smile on his face because of a volunteer's friendship, the diligence of one who carried the letter, four people trekking through Dogon cliffs, and a Dogon believer who led a new friend to Christ. Mark will spend eternity in heaven because the body of Christ worked together and each one contributed his part. We are one body, with one purpose—to make known His glory among the nations!

Peggy—West Africa

We must either be praying or fainting . . . there is no other alternative.
Ray C. Stedman

PRAISE & THANKSGIVING

Worship by using the name of God mentioned in this
Scripture—the "bread of life."

*Jesus said to them, "I am the bread of life; he who comes to Me will not hunger,
and he who believes in Me will never thirst."*

John 6:35 (NASB)

REPENTANCE

Search your heart as you meditate on this Scripture.
What is the Holy Spirit revealing to you?

*If you have not been trustworthy in handling worldly wealth, who will trust
you with true riches?*

Luke 16:11

ASKING

Read the following Scripture. Rewrite it, personalizing it
for missionaries, seeking the Lord in prayer on their behalf
regarding stewardship.

*I was hungry and you gave me something to eat, I was thirsty and you gave me
something to drink, I was a stranger and you invited me in, I needed clothes
and you clothed me, I was sick and you looked after me, I was in prison and
you came to visit me.*

Matthew 25:35–36

_____

_____

YIELDING

Now meditate on the Scripture again. Rewrite it below,
personalizing and praying it for yourself. How can you
respond to what God is saying to you in this Scripture?

_____

_____

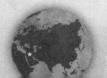

Pray for missionary work in IRAQ
(Middle East, between Iran and Kuwait)

Continue in prayer, and though the blessing tarry, it must come;
in God's own time it must appear to you.
Charles Spurgeon

PRAISE & THANKSGIVING

Worship Him today—the "bread of life."

*Jesus said to them, "I am the bread of life; he who comes to Me will not hunger,
and he who believes in Me will never thirst."*

John 6:35 (NASB)

REPENTANCE

Search your heart as you meditate on this Scripture.

*If you have not been trustworthy in handling worldly wealth, who will trust
you with true riches?*

Luke 16:11

ASKING

Rewrite this Scripture, personalizing it for missionaries,
seeking the Lord in prayer on their behalf regarding
stewardship.

*Remember this: Whoever sows sparingly will also reap sparingly, and whoever
sows generously will also reap generously. Each man should give what he has
decided in his heart to give, not reluctantly or under compulsion, for God loves
a cheerful giver.*

2 Corinthians 9:6–7

_____

_____

_____

YIELDING

Rewrite it again, personalizing and praying it for yourself.
Respond to what God is saying to you in this Scripture.

_____

_____

_____

Pray for missionary work in IRELAND
(Western Europe, island in the Atlantic, west of Great Britain)

The biggest way you can help us is by praying.
Sarah Moses (19-year-old MK)

PRAISE & THANKSGIVING

*Jesus said to them, "I am the bread of life; he who comes to Me will not hunger,
and he who believes in Me will never thirst."*

John 6:35 (NASB)

REPENTANCE

*If you have not been trustworthy in handling worldly wealth, who will trust
you with true riches?*

Luke 16:11

ASKING

Personalize this Scripture for missionaries, rewriting it,
seeking the Lord in prayer on their behalf regarding
stewardship.

*"Bring the whole tithe into the storehouse, that there may be food in my house.
Test me in this," says the LORD Almighty, "and see if I will not throw open the
floodgates of heaven and pour out so much blessing that you will not have room
enough for it."*

Malachi 3:10

_____

_____

_____

_____

YIELDING

Now personalize and pray it for yourself. How can you
respond to what God is saying to you?

_____

_____

_____

_____

Pray for missionary work on THE ISLE OF MAN
(Western Europe, in the Irish Sea, between
Great Britain and Ireland)

> Prayer is God's ordained way to bring
> His miracle power to bear in human need.
> *Wesley L. Duewel*

PRAISE & THANKSGIVING

Jesus said to them, "I am the bread of life; he who comes to Me will not hunger, and he who believes in Me will never thirst."

John 6:35 (NASB)

REPENTANCE

If you have not been trustworthy in handling worldly wealth, who will trust you with true riches?

Luke 16:11

ASKING

Rewrite this Scripture, personalizing it for missionaries.

Give, and it will be given to you. A good measure, pressed down, shaken together and running over, will be poured into your lap. For with the measure you use, it will be measured to you.

Luke 6:38

_____

_____

_____

_____

YIELDING

What is God saying to you in this Scripture?

_____

_____

_____

_____

_____

_____

_____

Pray for missionary work in ISRAEL
(Middle East, between Egypt and Lebanon)

> The conditions of praying are the conditions
> of righteousness, holiness, and salvation.
> *E. M. Bounds*

PRAISE & THANKSGIVING

*Jesus said to them, "I am the bread of life; he who comes to Me will not hunger,
and he who believes in Me will never thirst."*

John 6:35 (NASB)

REPENTANCE

*If you have not been trustworthy in handling worldly wealth, who will trust you
with true riches?*

Luke 16:11

ASKING

Personalize this Scripture today for missionaries.

*One man gives freely, yet gains even more; another withholds unduly,
but comes to poverty. A generous man will prosper; he who refreshes
others will himself be refreshed.*

Proverbs 11:24–25

_____

_____

_____

_____

YIELDING

Personalize and pray this same Scripture for yourself.

_____

_____

_____

_____

_____

_____

_____

Pray for missionary work in ITALY
(Southern Europe, a peninsula extending into
the Mediterranean Sea)

Week 21
Thoughts and Prayers

_____

_____

_____

_____

_____

_____

_____

_____

_____

_____

_____

_____

_____

_____

_____

_____

_____

_____

_____

_____

_____

_____

_____

_____

_____

_____

_____

Week 22

TRANSITION

God is the only constant in a changing world! I have learned this truth in my time as a missionary in West Africa. So far, I have been on the field for eighteen months. I have had two jobs, lived in three countries, four towns, and in seven houses. I have seen my job dissolve and my country go into civil war, so I could no longer safely live there. And yet in all this change, God is there. I have experienced Him in each place.

I have seen Him in the smiles of Ivoirienne, Malian, and Senegalese believers who trust Him with their whole lives. I have seen Him in the rocky cliffs of northern Mali, in the green jungles of Cote d'Ivoire, and in the rolling waves off the coast of Senegal. I have seen people come out from darkness into light as they have learned truth and accepted His Son, Jesus Christ. I've heard them pray in their own heart languages of Bambara, Dogon, Wolof and Jula. I have seen Him in all these places and in all the changes. The Father is moving! And yet He is still and constant, within me.

Peggy—WEST AFRICA

I am beside myself with excitement! I am so ready to be there! When I unpack and get settled into my new home, I can get busy doing what God called me here to do. I know language learning and preparation are necessary, but I can hardly wait to be headed to my assignment. I can hardly contain my joy!

There is a long way to go before I can really communicate in the language, so keep praying. Pray that I will continue to study with effort. Pray for boldness to practice what I know. Pray that I meet new friends when I study the language. Pray that their hearts will be open to the gospel message.

These are the areas where I need you to pray.

That I will press on toward the goal to win the prize for which God has called me.

That I will hold fast to God in all circumstances and hunger for His Word.

That I will lay aside everything that entangles or prevents me from doing everything God has prepared for me.

Ask God to provide a good friend where I am going.

Ask God to continually open doors for the Word so that I may boldly speak forth the mystery of Christ.

Ask God to give endurance and encouragement to my team, and a spirit of unity as we follow Christ Jesus and glorify the Father.

Paige—AFRICA

Let my heart be broken with the things that break the heart of God.
Bob Pierce

PRAISE & THANKSGIVING

Worship by using the name of God mentioned in this Scripture—"my lamp."

You are my lamp, O LORD; the LORD turns my darkness into light.

2 Samuel 22:29

REPENTANCE

Search your heart as you meditate on this Scripture. What is the Holy Spirit revealing to you?

Let us examine our ways and test them, and let us return to the LORD.

Lamentations 3:40

ASKING

Read the following Scripture. Rewrite it, personalizing it for missionaries, seeking the Lord in prayer on their behalf.

We know that in all things God works for the good of those who love him, who have been called according to his purpose.

Romans 8:28

_____

_____

_____

_____

YIELDING

Now meditate on the Scripture again. Rewrite it below, personalizing and praying it for yourself. How can you respond to what God is saying to you in this Scripture?

_____

_____

_____

_____

_____

Pray for missionary work in JAMAICA
(Caribbean island, south of Cuba)

> The greatest hindrance to effective prayer is sin.
> Satan's greatest goal is to keep us from our knees.
> *Dick Eastman*

PRAISE & THANKSGIVING
Worship Him today, for He is your "lamp."

> *You are my lamp, O LORD; the LORD turns my darkness into light.*
> 2 Samuel 22:29

REPENTANCE
Search your heart as you meditate on this Scripture.

> *Let us examine our ways and test them, and let us return to the LORD.*
> Lamentations 3:40

ASKING
Rewrite this Scripture, personalizing it for missionaries, seeking the Lord in prayer on their behalf.

> *He holds victory in store for the upright, he is a shield to those whose walk is blameless, for he guards the course of the just and protects the way of his faithful ones.*
> Proverbs 2:7–8

_____

_____

_____

_____

YIELDING
Rewrite it again, personalizing and praying it for yourself. Respond to what God is saying to you in this Scripture.

_____

_____

_____

_____

_____

_____

Pray for missionary work in JAPAN
(Eastern Asia, island chain east of the Korean peninsula)

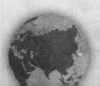

The battle of prayer is against two things in the earthlies: wandering thoughts, and lack of intimacy with God's character as revealed in His Word. Neither can be cured at once, but they can be cured by discipline.
Oswald Chambers

PRAISE & THANKSGIVING

> *You are my lamp, O LORD; the LORD turns my darkness into light.*
> 2 Samuel 22:29

REPENTANCE

> *Let us examine our ways and test them, and let us return to the Lord.*
> Lamentations 3:40

ASKING

Personalize this Scripture for missionaries, rewriting it, seeking the Lord in prayer on their behalf.

> *By faith Abraham, when he was called, obeyed by going out to a place which he was to receive for an inheritance; and he went out, not knowing where he was going.*
> Hebrews 11:8 (NASB)

_____

_____

_____

_____

_____

YIELDING

Now personalize and pray it for yourself. How can you respond to what God is saying to you?

_____

_____

_____

_____

_____

_____

Pray for missionary work in JERSEY
(island in the English Channel, northwest of France)

> He who knows how to overcome with God
> in prayer has heaven and earth at his disposal.
> *Charles Spurgeon*

PRAISE & THANKSGIVING

You are my lamp, O LORD; the LORD turns my darkness into light.

2 Samuel 22:29

REPENTANCE

Let us examine our ways and test them, and let us return to the Lord.

Lamentations 3:40

ASKING

Rewrite this Scripture, personalizing it for missionaries.

Be strong. Take courage. Don't be intimidated. Don't give them a second thought because GOD, your God, is striding ahead of you. He's right there with you. He won't let you down; he won't leave you.

Deuteronomy 31:6 (MSG)

_____

_____

_____

_____

YIELDING

What is God saying to you in this Scripture?

_____

_____

_____

_____

_____

_____

_____

Pray for missionary work in JORDAN
(Middle East, northwest of Saudi Arabia)

All that a Christian does, even in eating and sleeping, is prayer,
when it is done in simplicity, according to the order of God,
without either adding to or diminishing from it by His choice.
John Wesley

PRAISE & THANKSGIVING

You are my lamp, O Lord; the Lord turns my darkness into light.
  2 Samuel 22:29

REPENTANCE

Let us examine our ways and test them, and let us return to the LORD.
  Lamentations 3:40

ASKING

Personalize this Scripture today for missionaries.

*Don't fret or worry. Instead of worrying, pray. Let petitions and praises
shape your worries into prayers, letting God know your concerns. Before
you know it, a sense of God's wholeness, everything coming together for
good, will come and settle you down. It's wonderful what happens when
Christ displaces worry at the center of your life.*

  Philippians 4:6–7 (MSG)

_____

_____

_____

_____

YIELDING

Personalize and pray this same Scripture for yourself.

_____

_____

_____

_____

_____

Pray for missionary work in KAZAKHSTAN
(Central Asia, northwest of China)

Week 22
Thoughts and Prayers

Week 23

TRUTH

It was Thursday night as I sat alone in my hotel room in Asia. God was speaking to me through His Word. I reflected on my eighteen months overseas and the knowledge that I would be returning "home" in five months. I knew the question many people would ask: "What was the most exciting thing you saw?" I didn't think this was a very fair question. I had seen so much, and I knew the months ahead held even more. But the more I thought, the more I realized I already had an answer. The most incredible thing I have seen is the change God has brought about in me.

I have changed from someone weighed down with "junk" to someone in the process of getting rid of it all. No, I'm not free yet, but I am on the path to complete freedom. My heart that was content is now being transformed to pursue God passionately and actively.

When you live overseas, mail is always anticipated with joy. During a morning quiet time, God pulled together many things I had been feeling and reading. These things included a copy of *The Sacred Romance* (by Brent Curtis and John Eldredge) I received in the mail. I had been reading in the Psalms weeks earlier, and Psalm 86:11 came up during a word search on "fear." It really didn't mean much at the time, but this particular morning, it really hit me. David cried out to God, "Teach me your way, O Lord, and I will walk in your truth, give me an undivided heart, that I may fear your name." In Asia, I didn't have fancy Bible tools to pick this verse apart, but the word "undivided" really got my attention. Synonyms for it are "complete, entire, whole, total, full, exclusive, unbroken." Just imagine—a heart that is completely, entirely, wholly, totally, fully, and exclusively His. A quote by Oswald Chambers goes something like this: "The human heart cannot be satisfied until it has been satisfied by God first." That is what I want—for my heart to by satisfied by Him—to be in the "sacred romance," to be pursued by God.

For so long I have known there is something more in this world—something more than religious practices and acts of service that believers use to satisfy their heart's desires. I know there is more than the emptiness of ritual and ordinances. That something more is simply Him—the Great Romancer—the very one who desires an intimate and personal relationship with me. I don't pretend to understand why. Who doesn't want to feel like the princess in the fairy tale rescued by her prince charming?

For years I looked for "something more" in so many different places. I've looked in romantic relationships, only to be disappointed by swaying commitments. Friendships have let me down over petty disagreements and fickleness. Work and ministry have left me feeling unfulfilled by the temporary pleasure of glory and accomplishments. Even my desire to be here in a distant country was fueled by the pursuit for happiness and satisfaction. But in spite of my false motives and empty search, God has used me. More importantly, He continues to pursue me. He delights in me in spite of my imperfections and emotional baggage. I have stolen His heart. I think I finally get it, and the really awesome thing is that He is stealing my heart! I am a work in progress, but He isn't through with me.

A missionary friend said, "We have as much of God as we seek." Over the past months this has been my experience. I want so much of God, and I must seek Him with passion. My question is this, "How hard are you seeking?"

—*A Christian worker in Asia*

To pray with bitterness toward fellowmen nullifies hours on our knees.
Dick Eastman

PRAISE & THANKSGIVING

Worship by using the name of God mentioned in this Scripture—"deliverer."

The LORD is my rock and my fortress and my deliverer, my God, my rock, in whom I take refuge; my shield and the horn of my salvation, my stronghold.

Psalm 18:2 (NASB)

REPENTANCE

Search your heart as you meditate on this Scripture. What is the Holy Spirit revealing to you?

To the Jews who had believed him, Jesus said, "If you hold to my teaching, you are really my disciples. Then you will know the truth, and the truth will set you free."

John 8:31–32

ASKING

Read the following Scripture. Rewrite it, personalizing it for missionaries, seeking the Lord in prayer on their behalf regarding truth in battle.

Though I walk in the midst of trouble, you preserve my life; you stretch out your hand against the anger of my foes, with your right hand you save me.

Psalm 138:7

_____

_____

_____

YIELDING

Now meditate on the Scripture again. Rewrite it below, personalizing and praying it for yourself. How can you respond to what God is saying to you in this Scripture?

_____

_____

_____

Pray for missionary work in KENYA
(Eastern Africa, between Somalia and Tanzania)

Prayer is my chief work, and it is by means of it that I carry on the rest.
Thomas Hooker

PRAISE & THANKSGIVING
Worship Him today as your "deliverer."

The LORD is my rock and my fortress and my deliverer, my God, my rock, in whom I take refuge; my shield and the horn of my salvation, my stronghold.
Psalm 18:2 (NASB)

REPENTANCE
Search your heart as you meditate on this Scripture.

To the Jews who had believed him, Jesus said, "If you hold to my teaching, you are really my disciples. Then you will know the truth, and the truth will set you free."
John 8:31–32

ASKING
Rewrite this Scripture, personalizing it for missionaries, seeking the Lord in prayer on their behalf regarding truth during sickness.

Praise the LORD, O my soul, and forget not all his benefits—who forgives all your sins and heals all your diseases, who redeems your life from the pit and crowns you with love and compassion.
Psalm 103:2–4

_____

_____

_____

YIELDING
Rewrite it again, personalizing and praying it for yourself. Respond to what God is saying to you in this Scripture.

_____

_____

_____

_____

Pray for missionary work in KIRIBATI
(Oceania, group of islands in the Pacific, straddling the equator)

> What breath is to the body, prayer is to the soul.
> *Richard Exley*

PRAISE & THANKSGIVING

> *The LORD is my rock and my fortress and my deliverer, my God, my rock, in whom I take refuge; my shield and the horn of my salvation, my stronghold.*
> Psalm 18:2 (NASB)

REPENTANCE

> *To the Jews who had believed him, Jesus said, "If you hold to my teaching, you are really my disciples. Then you will know the truth, and the truth will set you free."*
> John 8:31–32

ASKING

Personalize this Scripture for missionaries, rewriting it, seeking the Lord in prayer on their behalf regarding truth in times of grief.

> *My soul is weary with sorrow; strengthen me according to your word.*
> Psalm 119:28

_____

_____

_____

_____

YIELDING

Now personalize and pray it for yourself. How can you respond to what God is saying to you?

_____

_____

_____

_____

_____

_____

Pray for missionary work in KOSOVO
(Southeastern Europe, between Serbia and Macedonia)

The word of God is the food by which prayer is nourished and made strong.
E. M. Bounds

Praise & Thanksgiving

The Lord is my rock and my fortress and my deliverer, my God, my rock, in whom I take refuge; my shield and the horn of my salvation, my stronghold.
Psalm 18:2 (nasb)

Repentance

To the Jews who had believed him, Jesus said, "If you hold to my teaching, you are really my disciples. Then you will know the truth, and the truth will set you free."
John 8:31–32

Asking

Rewrite this Scripture, personalizing it for missionaries.

God is able to make all grace abound to you, so that in all things at all times, having all that you need, you will abound in every good work.
2 Corinthians 9:8

_____

_____

_____

Yielding

What is God saying to you in this Scripture?

_____

_____

_____

_____

_____

_____

Pray for missionary work in KUWAIT
(Middle East, between Iraq and Saudi Arabia)

> Prayer is the first thing, the second thing, the third thing necessary
> to a minister. Pray, then, my dear brother; pray, pray, pray.
> *Edward Payson*

PRAISE & THANKSGIVING

> *The LORD is my rock and my fortress and my deliverer, my God, my rock, in*
> *whom I take refuge; my shield and the horn of my salvation, my stronghold.*
> Psalm 18:2 (NASB)

REPENTANCE

> *To the Jews who had believed him, Jesus said, "If you hold to my teaching, you are*
> *really my disciples. Then you will know the truth, and the truth will set you free."*
> John 8:31–32

ASKING

Personalize this Scripture today for missionaries.

> *In this you greatly rejoice, though now for a little while you may have had to suffer*
> *grief in all kinds of trials. These have come so that your faith—of greater worth*
> *than gold, which perishes even though refined by fire—may be proved genuine*
> *and may result in praise, glory and honor when Jesus Christ is revealed.*
> 1 Peter 1:6–7

_____

_____

_____

_____

YIELDING

Personalize and pray this same Scripture for yourself.

_____

_____

_____

_____

_____

_____

Pray for missionary work in KYRGYZSTAN
(Central Asia, west of China)

Week 23
Thoughts and Prayers

Week 24

WISDOM

We were studying the story of creation, so I asked the young student this question: "Who created God?" The young man paused and thoughtfully pondered the question, then he quickly responded, "The Virgin Mary!?!"

I was blown back in my seat by the answer, and I am sure my disbelief was communicated to the student, who quickly changed his answer and responded again, "Nature!?!"

What I thought to be a fairly straightforward question revealed the depth of confusion, deception, and lostness of those living in Southern Ecuador.

Please continue to pray that God's Word will be understood and received as truth—the only way of eternal salvation. Ask God to give missionaries and other Christ-followers wisdom and godliness that reveals Christ through spoken words and holy lives.

As missionaries share the gospel message, they often face difficult questions from seekers of truth who are willing to adapt Christian beliefs while still continuing to believe there are many ways to God. Pray for God's wisdom as they relate to peoples from different cultures in a way that will reveal Jesus as the only Truth.

Dave—SOUTH AMERICA

We live in a world of great diversity, yet the adjustment to a new culture challenges even the most diligent student. It is humbling to discover that the language you have spoken all your life is now strange to the people with whom you must interact every day. Simple daily tasks become great obstacles while struggling to find even one correct vocabulary word to explain your needs. The conveniences of "home" are no longer available. There is excitement in the new surroundings and the joy in following God's call, but the culture, the people, and the worldviews are unfamiliar. Methodologies and training learned in one country may not be acceptable or even applicable in the new culture. Add to this the task of evangelism and church planting, and you begin to understand why missionaries need prayer for wisdom and boldness. Wisdom from God is essential!

God commands us to go and make disciples, yet as my family began language study, I wondered what I could do with such limited language skills. If I looked at the poverty, I was overwhelmed by the need. If I looked at the spiritual condition of the people, the task seemed impossible. If I looked to my ability, well, I came up lacking. My focus had to remain on the only One who can provide the answers—Jesus! There were times when we did not know what to do to reach our people group with the hope of Jesus Christ, but we knew the answers would come from the Lord as we sought His wisdom. We cried out to Him just as King Jehoshaphat cried out in 2 Chronicles 20:12 (HCSB)—"We do not know what to do, but we look to You."

For me, the command was to go; for others, the call is to give or pray and support missionaries and Christians who take the gospel to the world. The fields are white unto harvest, maybe more than ever before in history. We each have a unique role in missions, and we are commanded to be witnesses because God loves people. A very wise three-year-old missionary child said it best when he told his mom, "Jesus loves us, but not everybody knows it yet."

Debbie—SOUTH AMERICA

> The will of God, the name of Jesus, and the glory
> of God are qualifiers of all prayer.
> *Ronald Dunn*

PRAISE & THANKSGIVING

Worship by using the characteristic of God mentioned
in this Scripture—"very great."

> *Praise the LORD, O my soul. O LORD my God, you are very great;*
> *you are clothed with splendor and majesty.*
>
> Psalm 104:1

REPENTANCE

Search your heart as you meditate on this Scripture.
What is the Holy Spirit revealing to you?

> *You spread out our sins before you—our secret sins—and see them all.*
> *No wonder the years are long and heavy here beneath your wrath.*
>
> Psalm 90:8–9 (TLB)

ASKING

Read the following Scripture. Rewrite it, personalizing it
for missionaries, seeking the Lord in prayer on their behalf
regarding wisdom.

> *For this reason, since the day we heard about you, we have not stopped praying for*
> *you and asking God to fill you with the knowledge of his will through all spiritual*
> *wisdom and understanding.*
>
> Colossians 1:9

_____

_____

YIELDING

Now meditate on the Scripture again. Rewrite it below,
personalizing and praying it for yourself. How can you
respond to what God is saying to you in this Scripture?

_____

_____

_____

Pray for missionary work in LAOS
(Southeastern Asia, northeast of Thailand, west of Vietnam)

> The whole field of prayer and praying, as laying
> hold on unlimited power, is unexplored.
> *Peter Marshall*

PRAISE & THANKSGIVING
Worship Him today, for He is "very great."

> *Praise the LORD, O my soul. O LORD my God, you are very great;*
> *you are clothed with splendor and majesty.*
>
> Psalm 104:1

REPENTANCE
Search your heart as you meditate on this Scripture.

> *You spread out our sins before You—our secret sins—and see them all.*
> *No wonder the years are long and heavy here beneath your wrath.*
>
> Psalm 90:8–9 (TLB)

ASKING
Rewrite this Scripture, personalizing it for missionaries, seeking the Lord in prayer on their behalf regarding wisdom.

> *Listen, my son, accept what I say, and the years of your life will be many.*
> *I guide you in the way of wisdom and lead you along straight paths. When*
> *you walk, your steps will not be hampered; when you run, you will not stumble.*
> *Hold on to instruction, do not let it go; guard it well, for it is your life.*
>
> Proverbs 4:10–13

_____

_____

YIELDING
Rewrite it again, personalizing and praying it for yourself. Respond to what God is saying to you in this Scripture.

_____

_____

_____

_____

Pray for missionary work in LEBANON
(Middle East, between Israel and Syria)

The key to a missionary's difficult task is in the hand of God,
and that key is prayer, not work.
Oswald Chambers

PRAISE & THANKSGIVING

Praise the LORD, O my soul. O LORD my God, you are very great;
you are clothed with splendor and majesty.

Psalm 104:1

REPENTANCE

You spread out our sins before You—our secret sins—and see them all.
No wonder the years are long and heavy here beneath your wrath.

Psalm 90:8–9 (TLB)

ASKING

Personalize this Scripture for missionaries, rewriting it,
seeking the Lord in prayer on their behalf regarding
wisdom.

If any of you lacks wisdom, he should ask God, who gives generously to all
without finding fault, and it will be given to him.

James 1:5

_____

_____

_____

_____

YIELDING

Now personalize and pray it for yourself. How can you
respond to what God is saying to you?

_____

_____

_____

_____

_____

Pray for missionary work in LESOTHO
(Southern Africa, an enclave of South Africa)

He that is never on his knees on earth shall
never stand upon his feet in heaven.
Charles Spurgeon

PRAISE & THANKSGIVING

Praise the LORD, O my soul. O LORD my God, you are very great;
you are clothed with splendor and majesty.

Psalm 104:1

REPENTANCE

You spread out our sins before You—our secret sins—and see them all.
No wonder the years are long and heavy here beneath your wrath.

Psalm 90:8–9 (TLB)

ASKING

Rewrite this Scripture, personalizing it for missionaries.

The wisdom that comes from heaven is first of all pure; then peace-loving,
considerate, submissive, full of mercy and good fruit, impartial and sincere.
Peacemakers who sow in peace raise a harvest of righteousness.

James 3:17–18

_____

_____

_____

_____

YIELDING

What is God saying to you in this Scripture?

_____

_____

_____

_____

_____

_____

Pray for missionary work in LIBERIA
(Western Africa, between Cote d"Ivoire and Sierra Leone)

> There is no key to revival. Revival is an answer to prayer.
> *Jonathan Goforth*

PRAISE & THANKSGIVING

Praise the LORD, O my soul. O LORD my God, you are very great;
you are clothed with splendor and majesty.

> Psalm 104:1

REPENTANCE

You spread out our sins before You—our secret sins—and see them all.
No wonder the years are long and heavy here beneath your wrath.

> Psalm 90:8–9 (TLB)

ASKING

Personalize this Scripture today for missionaries.

The fear of the LORD is the beginning of wisdom; all who follow his precepts
have good understanding. To him belongs eternal praise.

> Psalm 111:10

_____

_____

_____

YIELDING

Personalize and pray this same Scripture for yourself.

_____

_____

_____

_____

_____

_____

_____

Pray for missionary work in LIBYA
(Northern Africa, on the Mediterranean,
between Egypt and Tunisia)

Week 24
Thoughts and Prayers

_____

_____

_____

_____

_____

_____

_____

_____

_____

_____

_____

_____

_____

_____

_____

_____

_____

_____

_____

_____

_____

_____

_____

_____

_____

_____

_____

_____

Submit to one another out of reverence for Christ.

Wives, submit to your husbands as to the Lord.

For the husband is the head of the wife as Christ is the

head of the church, his body, of which he is the Savior.

Now as the church submits to Christ, so also wives

should submit to their husbands in everything.

Husbands, love your wives, just as Christ loved

the church and gave himself up for her to make her holy,

cleansing her by the washing with water

through the word, and to present her to himself as a radiant

church, without stain or wrinkle or any other blemish,

but holy and blameless. In this same way, husbands ought

to love their wives as their own bodies. He who loves his wife

loves himself. After all, no one ever hated his own body,

but he feeds and cares for it, just as Christ does the church—

for we are members of his body.

EPHESIANS 5:21–30

THE
MISSIONARY'S
MARRIAGE

Week 25

ACCOUNTABILITY

After many years of ministry, my wife, Elizabeth, and I left a work we deeply loved to transfer to Brazil and assume a leadership role. Our earthly goods arrived with damage that exceeded the value of the entire move. Within the first few months, I had the heartbreaking task of telling three missionary couples they would have to return to the U.S. and resign because of unusual situations in their lives and ministries. Another couple left due to the wife's terminal illness. During this time a couple who had become dear colleagues and friends left our field of service.

New missionaries attended a language school to learn Portuguese, local customs, and adaptation to Brazilian culture and daily life. Administration of the school became a major problem with which I was expected to manage. Problems mounted one after the other until I had almost reached burnout, if not meltdown.

A missionary colleague and I went to Ecuador for a conference. Upon arrival, we entered the elevator to go to our room just as a minor earthquake shook the building and jammed the elevator. People outside were shouting, but neither my friend nor I could understand their Spanish. As we "hung" between floors, I was overwhelmed with a sense of frustration, irritation, and *"I give up!"* We eventually understood enough to get the door open and were freed from the elevator.

That night as I opened my Bible, the Lord led me to verses I did not remember reading before, although I have read the Bible through several times. The words of Psalm 116:7–18 jumped from the pages. I was especially impacted by verses 7 and 8: "Return unto thy rest, O my soul; for the LORD hath dealt bountifully with thee. For thou hast delivered my soul from death, mine eyes from tears, and my feet from falling" (KJV). Immediately I remembered how many times the Lord had literally delivered my soul from death, my eyes from tears of despair and pain, and my feet from falling into foolishness and sinfulness. These verses have become a jumping-off point many times since that day as I "return unto His rest" and commit myself to Him.

As you pray, return unto His rest and allow Him to deliver your soul from death, your eyes from tears, and your feet from falling.

Orman—SOUTH AMERICA

To make a long-lasting difference for God is to learn to pray.
Ronnie Floyd

PRAISE & THANKSGIVING

Worship by using the characteristic of God mentioned
in this Scripture—"altogether lovely."

His mouth is sweetness itself; he is altogether lovely. This is my lover,
this my friend, O daughters of Jerusalem.

Song of Solomon 5:16

REPENTANCE

Search your heart as you meditate on this Scripture.
What is the Holy Spirit revealing to you?

Fear the LORD your God, serve him only and take your oaths in his name.
Do not follow other gods, the gods of the peoples around you; for the LORD
your God, who is among you, is a jealous God.

Deuteronomy 6:13–15

ASKING

Read the following Scripture. Rewrite it, personalizing
it for the missionary's marriage relationship, seeking
the Lord regarding their accountability to God.

Now I want you to realize that the head of every man is Christ, and the head
of the woman is man, and the head of Christ is God.

1 Corinthians 11:3

_____

_____

_____

YIELDING

Now meditate on the Scripture again. Rewrite it below,
personalizing and praying it for yourself. How can you
respond to what God is saying to you in this Scripture?

_____

_____

_____

Pray for missionary work in LIECHTENSTEIN
(Central Europe, between Austria and Switzerland)

Without set times of prayer, the spirit of prayer will be dull and feeble.
Without the continual prayerfulness, the set times will not avail.
Andrew Murray

PRAISE & THANKSGIVING
Worship Him today, for He is "altogether lovely."

*His mouth is sweetness itself; he is altogether lovely. This is my lover,
this my friend, O daughters of Jerusalem.*

Song of Solomon 5:16

REPENTANCE
Search your heart as you meditate on this Scripture.

*Fear the LORD your God, serve him only and take your oaths in his name.
Do not follow other gods, the gods of the peoples around you; for the LORD
your God, who is among you, is a jealous God.*

Deuteronomy 6:13–15

ASKING
Rewrite this Scripture, personalizing it for the missionary's
marriage relationship, seeking the Lord regarding their
accountability to God.

*Each of us will give an account of himself to God. Therefore let us stop passing
judgment on one another. Instead, make up your mind not to put any stumbling
block or obstacle in your brother's way.*

Romans 14:12–13

_____

_____

_____

YIELDING
Rewrite it again, personalizing and praying it for yourself.
Respond to what God is saying to you in this Scripture.

_____

_____

_____

_____

Pray for missionary work in LITHUANIA
(Eastern Europe, between Latvia and Russia)

> The value of consistent prayer is not that He will hear us,
> but that we will hear Him.
> *William McGill*

PRAISE & THANKSGIVING

> *His mouth is sweetness itself; he is altogether lovely. This is my lover,*
> *this my friend, O daughters of Jerusalem.*
> Song of Solomon 5:16

REPENTANCE

> *Above all, love each other deeply, because love covers over a multitude of sins.*
> 1 Peter 4:8

ASKING

Personalize this Scripture for the missionary's marriage,
rewriting it, seeking the Lord regarding their accountability
to each other.

> *Wives, in the same way be submissive to your husbands so that, if any of them do*
> *not believe the word, they may be won over without words by the behavior of their*
> *wives, when they see the purity and reverence of your lives. Your beauty should . . .*
> *be that of your inner self, the unfading beauty of a gentle and quiet spirit, which*
> *is of great worth in God's sight.*
> 1 Peter 3:1–4

_____

_____

_____

YIELDING

Now personalize and pray it for yourself. How can you
respond to what God is saying to you?

_____

_____

_____

_____

Pray for missionary work in LUXEMBOURG
(Western Europe, between France and Germany)

> It takes a tremendous amount of reiteration on
> God's part before we understand what prayer is.
> We do not pray at all until we are at our wits' end.
> *Oswald Chambers*

PRAISE & THANKSGIVING

His mouth is sweetness itself; he is altogether lovely. This is my lover, this my friend, O daughters of Jerusalem.

Song of Solomon 5:16

REPENTANCE

Above all, love each other deeply, because love covers over a multitude of sins.

1 Peter 4:8

ASKING

Rewrite this Scripture, personalizing it for missionaries.

Husbands, in the same way be considerate as you live with your wives, and treat them with respect as the weaker partner and as heirs with you of the gracious gift of life, so that nothing will hinder your prayers.

1 Peter 3:7

_____

_____

_____

_____

YIELDING

What is God saying to you in this Scripture?

_____

_____

_____

_____

_____

_____

_____

Pray for missionary work in MACAU
(Eastern Asia, bordering the South China Sea and China)

The man who has gotten God's word in the prayer closet
neither seeks nor expects encouragement from men for the delivery
of that word. The Spirit himself bears witness of the approval.
Leonard Ravenhill

PRAISE & THANKSGIVING

His mouth is sweetness itself; he is altogether lovely. This is my lover,
this my friend, O daughters of Jerusalem.

Song of Solomon 5:16

REPENTANCE

Train a child in the way he should go, and when he is old he will not turn from it.

Proverbs 22:6

ASKING

Personalize this Scripture today for missionaries.

Fix these words of mine in your hearts and minds; tie them as symbols on your
hands and bind them on your foreheads. Teach them to your children, talking
about them when you sit at home and when you walk along the road, when you
lie down and when you get up.

Deuteronomy 11:18–19

_____

_____

_____

_____

YIELDING

Personalize and pray this same Scripture for yourself.

_____

_____

_____

_____

_____

_____

Pray for missionary work in MACEDONIA
(Southeastern Europe, north of Greece)

Week 25
Thoughts and Prayers

_____
_____
_____
_____
_____
_____
_____
_____
_____
_____
_____
_____
_____
_____
_____
_____
_____
_____
_____
_____
_____
_____
_____
_____
_____
_____
_____

Week 26

COVENANT

"This little light of mine, I'm gonna let it shine, let it shine, let it shine, let it shine." It's a children's song, a commitment to share the love of Jesus in a world of darkness. It was also the closing song at our appointment service to become missionaries. All of us held tiny flashlights—the kind you pinch to keep shining—throughout the chorus. We laughed because it was a real struggle to keep a grip on the flashlight that long. None of us wanted our little lights to go out for even a moment. We certainly had no idea that night what a struggle it would be to keep a grip on our faith and not let the light of our testimony flicker while serving overseas.

My husband and I went to a Last Frontier* people group and faced the same challenges any new couple experiences: culture shock, language acquisition, unexpected role changes, even a couple of major illnesses. But we seemed to be coping reasonably well. Many of our coworkers considered us to be the "perfect" couple. Unfortunately, there were undercurrents that others didn't see. Neither did I.

One day my husband announced that he was leaving. Our marriage of more than twenty-five years was over. As soon as arrangements could be made, we returned to the United States. Despite the love and godly counsel of our sending agency, my husband was determined to go. My world was shattered.

I had lost my husband, my home, my friends, and my job. What was I to do? My fervent prayer was that the Lord would protect me from a root of bitterness. Although I had no idea how He would do it, I trusted God to provide my physical needs; but I also longed to be spiritually whole.

Amazingly, on the very day my husband actually left, I received a phone call. I was offered a job supporting our missionaries. It was as if God had called me personally and said, "I still have a work for you." I laughed and cried and blessed the Lord's name.

It's been several years now, and I am learning to live the abundant life as a single. God has given me a new church family and many friends who love and encourage me.

Sometimes I've wondered if it was a mistake to go to the mission field. Others have said that if we had just stayed in the United States, our marriage would not have failed. But I remain sure of my calling. The Lord knew what was going to happen to our marriage, yet He called me to let my light shine in that distant land anyway. He called me to a Last Frontier people where three women accepted Christ as Savior. In spite of the losses suffered and leaving the field so suddenly, I am grateful that God gave me the privilege of serving Him. And He continues to call me to serve today.

My story is not intended to be seen as a sad tale of loss but rather a tale of victory in spite of loss. And hopefully, it inspires you to pray in a new way for married couples serving on the field. Please pray that their relationships with each other and with the Lord will remain strong.

The Lord is the One who has held me in His grip and sustained my faith. By His grace my little light is still shining—and through the power of the Light of the world, "I'm gonna let it shine, let it shine, let it shine."

—*A missionary worker serving Last Frontier peoples*

*The Last Frontier is a portion of the world's population comprised of unreached people groups (less than 2 percent evangelical Christian) with little or no access to the gospel.

> Prayer for revival will prevail when it is accompanied
> by radical amendment of life; not before.
> *A. W. Tozer*

PRAISE & THANKSGIVING

Worship by using the name of God mentioned in this
Scripture—"Lord Most High."

> *You are the* LORD *Most High over all the earth; You are exalted far above all gods.*
>
> Psalm 97:9 (NASB)

REPENTANCE

Search your heart as you meditate on this Scripture.
What is the Holy Spirit revealing to you?

> *I delight in your decrees; I will not neglect your word.*
>
> Psalm 119:16

ASKING

Read the following Scripture. Rewrite it, personalizing it
for the missionary's marriage relationship, seeking the Lord
regarding their covenant to God.

> *From everlasting to everlasting the* LORD'S *love is with those who fear him,
> and his righteousness with their children's children—with those who keep
> his covenant and remember to obey his precepts.*
>
> Psalm 103:17–18

_____

_____

_____

_____

YIELDING

Now meditate on the Scripture again. Rewrite it below,
personalizing and praying it for yourself. How can you
respond to what God is saying to you in this Scripture?

_____

_____

_____

Pray for missionary work in MADAGASCAR
(Southern Africa, island in the Indian Ocean,
east of Mozambique)

Too busy; O forgive, dear Lord, that I should ever be too much
engrossed in earthly tasks to spend an hour with thee.
A. B. Christiansen

PRAISE & THANKSGIVING
Worship Him today, for He is the "Lord Most High."

You are the LORD Most High over all the earth; You are exalted far above all gods.
Psalm 97:9 (NASB)

REPENTANCE
Search your heart as you meditate on this Scripture.

I delight in your decrees; I will not neglect your word.
Psalm 119:16

ASKING
Rewrite this Scripture, personalizing it for the missionary's
marriage relationship, seeking the Lord regarding their
covenant to God.

*All the ways of the LORD are loving and faithful for those who keep the demands
of his covenant.*
Psalm 25:10

_____

_____

_____

_____

YIELDING
Rewrite it again, personalizing and praying it for yourself.
Respond to what God is saying to you in this Scripture.

_____

_____

_____

_____

_____

Pray for missionary work in MALAWI
(Southern Africa, east of Zambia)

Our true character comes out in the way we pray.
Oswald Chambers

PRAISE & THANKSGIVING

You are the LORD Most High over all the earth; You are exalted far above all gods.
Psalm 97:9 (NASB)

REPENTANCE

Submit to one another out of reverence for Christ.
Ephesians 5:21

ASKING

Personalize this Scripture for the missionary's marriage, rewriting it, seeking the Lord regarding their covenant to each other.

For this reason a man will leave his father and mother and be united to his wife, and the two will become one flesh. So they are no longer two, but one. Therefore what God has joined together, let man not separate.
Matthew 19:5–6

_____

_____

_____

_____

_____

YIELDING

Now personalize and pray it for yourself. How can you respond to what God is saying to you?

_____

_____

_____

_____

_____

Pray for missionary work in MALAYSIA
(Southeastern Asia, a peninsula bordering
Thailand, south of Vietnam)

Prayer has mighty power to move mountains because the Holy Spirit is ready both to encourage our praying and to remove the mountains hindering us. Prayer has the power to change mountains into highways.
Wesley L. Duewel

PRAISE & THANKSGIVING

You are the LORD Most High over all the earth; You are exalted far above all gods.
Psalm 97:9 (NASB)

REPENTANCE

Submit to one another out of reverence for Christ.
Ephesians 5:21

ASKING

Rewrite this Scripture, personalizing it for missionaries.

Has not the LORD made them one? In flesh and spirit they are his. And why one? Because he was seeking godly offspring. So guard yourself in your spirit, and do not break faith with the wife of your youth.
Malachi 2:15

_____

_____

_____

_____

_____

YIELDING

What is God saying to you in this Scripture?

_____

_____

_____

_____

_____

_____

Pray for missionary work in THE MALDIVES
(Southern Asia, group of islands in the Indian Ocean,
southwest of India)

> Prayer is talking with God and telling Him you love Him,
> conversing with God about all the things that are important in life,
> both large and small, and being assured that He is listening.
> *C. Neil Strait*

PRAISE & THANKSGIVING

You are the LORD Most High over all the earth; You are exalted far above all gods.
Psalm 97:9 (NASB)

REPENTANCE

Submit to one another out of reverence for Christ.
Ephesians 5:21

ASKING

Personalize this Scripture today for missionaries.

Place me like a seal over your heart, like a seal on your arm; for love is as strong as death, its jealousy unyielding as the grave. It burns like blazing fire, like a mighty flame.
Song of Solomon 8:6

_____

_____

_____

_____

YIELDING

Personalize and pray this same Scripture for yourself.

_____

_____

_____

_____

_____

_____

_____

Pray for missionary work in MALI
(Western Africa, southwest of Algeria)

Week 26
Thoughts and Prayers

_____

_____

_____

_____

_____

_____

_____

_____

_____

_____

_____

_____

_____

_____

_____

_____

_____

_____

_____

_____

_____

_____

_____

_____

_____

Week 27

COMMUNICATION

Preparation for anything of value and purpose can be long and at times difficult. Prayer and discipline to stick with your calling and goals can grow tiring. During college days, with a poor paying job and a weekend church that paid even less, my husband and I often wanted to quit.

One weekend, tired and discouraged, we drove home discussing the possibility of giving up our church. It was three o'clock in the morning and classes began at eight. As we stepped out of the car, we almost fell backward. A huge cross was suspended in the sky just over the garage. For ten minutes we propped ourselves against the car and just stared. Recovering from the shock, we began to assure each other we were not quitting. The Lord had answered so many prayers for us, and we were certain He had called us into His service. We were also aware of the great prayer support from family and friends.

As we proceeded up the driveway, it became apparent that there was no miraculous cross. It was a miracle for us, however, because of the timing and the need. We could now see past the garage to a telephone pole lighted by a streetlight. It was enough.

Because of the Lord's great love we are not consumed, for his compassions never fail. They are new every morning; great is your faithfulness.
(Lam. 3:22–23)

Charlene—SOUTH AMERICA

*Many Christians are so spiritually frail, sickly, and lacking in spiritual vitality
that they cannot stick to prayer for more than a few minutes at a time.*
Wesley L. Duewel

PRAISE & THANKSGIVING

Worship by using the characteristic of God mentioned
in this Scripture—"goodness."

*My goodness, and my fortress; my high tower, and my deliverer; my shield,
and he in whom I trust; who subdueth my people under me.*

Psalm 144:2 (KJV)

REPENTANCE

Search your heart as you meditate on this Scripture.
What is the Holy Spirit revealing to you?

Set a guard over my mouth, O LORD; keep watch over the door of my lips.

Psalm 141:3

ASKING

Read the following Scripture. Rewrite it, personalizing
it for the missionary's marriage relationship, seeking
the Lord regarding their communication.

*My dear brothers, take note of this: Everyone should be quick to listen,
slow to speak and slow to become angry, for man's anger does not bring
about the righteous life that God desires.*

James 1:19—20

_____

_____

_____

YIELDING

Now meditate on the Scripture again. Rewrite it below,
personalizing and praying it for yourself. How can you
respond to what God is saying to you in this Scripture?

_____

_____

_____

Pray for missionary work on MALTA
(Southern Europe, islands in the Mediterranean)

> The main thing that God asks for is our attention.
> *Jim Cymbala*

PRAISE & THANKSGIVING

Worship Him today as the perfection of "goodness."

*My goodness, and my fortress; my high tower, and my deliverer; my shield,
and he in whom I trust; who subdueth my people under me.*

Psalm 144:2 (KJV)

REPENTANCE

Search your heart as you meditate on this Scripture.

Set a guard over my mouth, O LORD; keep watch over the door of my lips.

Psalm 141:3

ASKING

Rewrite this Scripture, personalizing it for the missionary's
marriage relationship, seeking the Lord regarding their
communication.

*Do not let any unwholesome talk come out of your mouths, but only what
is helpful for building others up according to their needs, that it may benefit
those who listen.*

Ephesians 4:29

_____

_____

_____

YIELDING

Rewrite it again, personalizing and praying it for yourself.
Respond to what God is saying to you in this Scripture.

_____

_____

_____

_____

_____

Pray for missionary work in MALI
(Western Africa, southwest of Algeria)

> A powerful and necessary weapon in the prayer warfare
> is thinking—sharp, discerning thinking. This attitude is a
> manifestation of the kingdom of God in the midst of turmoil.
> *Lars Widerberg*

PRAISE & THANKSGIVING

My goodness, and my fortress; my high tower, and my deliverer; my shield,
and he in whom I trust; who subdueth my people under me.

Psalm 144:2 (KJV)

REPENTANCE

Set a guard over my mouth, O LORD; keep watch over the door of my lips.

Psalm 141:3

ASKING

Personalize this Scripture for the missionary's marriage,
rewriting it, seeking the Lord regarding their communication with each other.

Pleasant words are a honeycomb, sweet to the soul and healing to the bones.

Proverbs 16:24

_____

_____

_____

_____

YIELDING

Now personalize and pray it for yourself. How can you
respond to what God is saying to you?

_____

_____

_____

_____

_____

Pray for missionary work in MARTINIQUE
(Caribbean island, between Puerto Rico and Venezuela)

Prayer thrives in the atmosphere of true devotion.
E. M. Bounds

PRAISE & THANKSGIVING

My goodness, and my fortress; my high tower, and my deliverer; my shield, and he in whom I trust; who subdueth my people under me.

Psalm 144:2 (KJV)

REPENTANCE

Set a guard over my mouth, O LORD; keep watch over the door of my lips.

Psalm 141:3

ASKING

Rewrite this Scripture, personalizing it for missionaries.

They raised their voices together in prayer to God.

Acts 4:24

_____

_____

_____

_____

_____

YIELDING

What is God saying to you in this Scripture?

_____

_____

_____

_____

_____

_____

_____

_____

Pray for missionary work in MAURITANIA
(Northern Africa, between Senegal and Western Sahara)

When we become too glib in prayer, we are most surely talking to ourselves.
A. W. Tozer

PRAISE & THANKSGIVING

> *My goodness, and my fortress; my high tower, and my deliverer; my shield,*
> *and he in whom I trust; who subdueth my people under me.*
>
> Psalm 144:2 (KJV)

REPENTANCE

> *Set a guard over my mouth, O LORD; keep watch over the door of my lips.*
> Psalm 141:3

ASKING

Personalize this Scripture today for missionaries.

> *The wisdom that comes from heaven is first of all pure; then peace-loving,*
> *considerate, submissive, full of mercy and good fruit, impartial and sincere.*
> *Peacemakers who sow in peace raise a harvest of righteousness.*
>
> James 3:17–18

_____

_____

_____

_____

_____

_____

YIELDING

Personalize and pray this same Scripture for yourself.

_____

_____

_____

_____

_____

_____

Pray for missionary work in MAURITIUS
(Southern Africa, island in the Indian Ocean,
east of Madagascar)

Week 27
Thoughts and Prayers

_____
_____
_____
_____
_____
_____
_____
_____
_____
_____
_____
_____
_____
_____
_____
_____
_____
_____
_____
_____
_____
_____
_____
_____
_____
_____

Week 28

LOVE FOR
EACH OTHER

At the beginning of the calendar year, I was an eager music teacher in a rural North Alabama school. My husband, Steve, was senior partner in a well-established veterinary practice. Our three children were happily married, and we enjoyed being only twenty minutes away from our grandchild. We lived in our dream house, sitting on ten acres with a bass-filled pond in front and a refreshing, secluded swimming pool out back. We were debt-free, but I had the layouts of all malls within a fifty-mile radius memorized and in frequent use. We were happy, healthy, in love, and full of hope.

Yet on December 28, we got off a plane in Ecuador, headed to our new home in the Andes Mountains, as newly appointed missionaries. Our house, veterinary practice, boat, car, and most of our furnishings had been sold. Some cherished family belongings were stored, and the remainder of our worldly goods were given away or thrown out. We arrived in our new country with a few suitcases and footlockers. Two wooden crates of household supplies and books were scheduled to arrive in a few months. We celebrated Christmas, said tearful good-byes to family and friends, and arrived in a place with no familiar faces, smells, sounds, or tastes. How in the world did we get from North Alabama to South America?

It was a Thursday night the previous January when Steve and I shared a meal with some dear retired missionary friends. For the first time, we learned about a program where adults of our age and training could become full-time missionaries. After a weekend of soul-searching and praying, we contacted the mission board and began the process toward missionary appointment.

This idea didn't suddenly appear out of nowhere. I had been deeply interested in mission work since I was ten years old. For twelve years, Steve and I participated in seven volunteer mission projects. Each trip deepened our desire to be involved on a more long-term basis. We knew that his veterinary experience and my teaching skills could be useful tools for sharing the love of Christ. We felt God was clearly showing us this was the time to go.

Was it a year of smooth transition? No! We sweated through interviews and medical exams waiting to be approved by the mission board. At the same time, we sorted through every scrap we had accumulated in thirty years of marriage. Steve's widowed mother had serious open-heart surgery, and a daughter filed for divorce. Turmoil, second-guessing, upheaval, stomach churning, sleepless nights, and buckets of tears were regular companions through the year. But God blessed us through words of encouragement, genuine acts of help, and unconditional support from our children.

We were amazed at the ways God protected, guided, and blessed us. Our understanding of the Spanish language increased daily, and Steve helped a group of men improve the milk production of their cows. I was still figuring out how to safely disinfect the fruits and vegetables and learning how to swallow the roasted guinea pig served by generous hosts eagerly watching for our approval. (I still wonder why a country that produces so many bananas doesn't have a single box of vanilla wafers for making banana pudding!) But we are grateful God is allowing us to be used in this place, and we are committed to using these empty-nest years for His honor and glory. We are happy, healthy, in love, and full of hope.

Connie—SOUTH AMERICA

> Prayer will promote our personal holiness
> as nothing else, except the study of the Word of God.
> *R. A. Torrey*

PRAISE & THANKSGIVING

Worship by using the characteristic of God mentioned
in this Scripture—"blessed."

*Blessed be the Lord God of Israel, for He has visited us and accomplished
redemption for His people.*

Luke 1:68 (NASB)

REPENTANCE

Search your heart as you meditate on this Scripture.
What is the Holy Spirit revealing to you?

*Love is as strong as death, its jealousy unyielding as the grave. It burns
like blazing fire, like a mighty flame.*

Song of Solomon 8:6

ASKING

Read the following Scripture. Rewrite it, personalizing it
for the missionary's marriage relationship, seeking the Lord
regarding their love for each other.

*Love is patient, love is kind. It does not envy, it does not boast, it is not proud. It is
not rude, it is not self-seeking, it is not easily angered, it keeps no record of wrongs.
Love does not delight in evil but rejoices with the truth. It always protects, always
trusts, always hopes, always perseveres.*

1 Corinthians 13:4–7

_____

_____

YIELDING

Now meditate on the Scripture again. Rewrite it below,
personalizing and praying it for yourself. How can you
respond to what God is saying to you in this Scripture?

_____

_____

Pray for missionary work in MAYOTTE
(Southern Africa, island in the Mozambique Channel)

> Give me one hundred preachers who fear nothing but sin and
> desire nothing but God . . . such alone will shake the gates
> of hell and set up the kingdom of heaven on earth.
> *John Wesley*

PRAISE & THANKSGIVING

Worship Him today—the "blessed" One.

> *Blessed be the Lord God of Israel, for He has visited us and accomplished
> redemption for His people.*
>> Luke 1:68 (NASB)

REPENTANCE

Search your heart as you meditate on this Scripture.

> *Love is as strong as death, its jealousy unyielding as the grave. It burns
> like blazing fire, like a mighty flame.*
>> Song of Solomon 8:6

ASKING

Rewrite this Scripture, personalizing it for the missionary's
marriage relationship, seeking the Lord regarding their love
for each other.

> *Salute one another with a kiss of love [the symbol of mutual affection.] To all of
> you that are in Christ Jesus (the Messiah), may there be peace (every kind of peace
> and blessing, especially peace with God, and freedom from fears, agitating passions,
> and moral conflicts). Amen (so be it).*
>> 1 Peter 5:14 (AMP)

_____

_____

YIELDING

Rewrite it again, personalizing and praying it for yourself.
Respond to what God is saying to you in this Scripture.

_____

_____

_____

_____

Pray for missionary work in MEXICO

The men who have guided the destiny of the United States have found
the strength for their tasks by going to their knees. This private unity
of public men and their God is an enduring source of reassurance.
Lyndon B. Johnson

PRAISE & THANKSGIVING

Blessed be the Lord God of Israel, for He has visited us and accomplished
redemption for His people.
   Luke 1:68 (NASB)

REPENTANCE

Love is as strong as death, its jealousy unyielding as the grave. It burns
like blazing fire, like a mighty flame.
   Song of Solomon 8:6

ASKING

Personalize this Scripture for the missionary's marriage,
rewriting it, seeking the Lord regarding their love for
each other.

He who finds a wife finds what is good and receives favor from the LORD.
   Proverbs 18:22

_____

_____

_____

_____

YIELDING

Now personalize and pray it for yourself. How can you
respond to what God is saying to you?

_____

_____

_____

_____

_____

Pray for missionary work in MOLDOVA
(Eastern Europe, northeast of Romania)

> To despise the world is the way to enjoy heaven; and blessed
> are they who delight to converse with God by prayer.
> *John Bunyan*

PRAISE & THANKSGIVING

Blessed be the Lord God of Israel, for He has visited us and accomplished
redemption for His people.
> Luke 1:68 (NASB)

REPENTANCE

Love is as strong as death, its jealousy unyielding as the grave. It burns
like blazing fire, like a mighty flame.
> Song of Solomon 8:6

ASKING

Rewrite this Scripture, personalizing it for missionaries.
The husband should fulfill his marital duty to his wife, and likewise the wife to her
husband. The wife's body does not belong to her alone but also to her husband. In
the same way, the husband's body does not belong to him alone but also to his wife.
> 1 Corinthians 7:3–4

_____

_____

_____

_____

YIELDING

What is God saying to you in this Scripture?

_____

_____

_____

_____

_____

_____

Pray for missionary work in MONACO
(Western Europe, on the southern coast of France)

No man—I don't care how colossal his intellect—
no man is greater than his prayer life.
Leonard Ravenhill

PRAISE & THANKSGIVING

Blessed be the Lord God of Israel, for He has visited us and accomplished redemption for His people.
Luke 1:68 (NASB)

REPENTANCE

Love is as strong as death, its jealousy unyielding as the grave. It burns like blazing fire, like a mighty flame.
Song of Solomon 8:6

ASKING

Personalize this Scripture today for missionaries.

Above all, love each other deeply, because love covers over a multitude of sins.
1 Peter 4:8

_____

_____

_____

_____

_____

_____

YIELDING

Personalize and pray this same Scripture for yourself.

_____

_____

_____

_____

_____

_____

Pray for missionary work in MONGOLIA
(Northern Asia, between China and Russia)

Week 28
Thoughts and Prayers

_____
_____
_____
_____
_____
_____
_____
_____
_____
_____
_____
_____
_____
_____
_____
_____
_____
_____
_____
_____
_____
_____
_____
_____
_____
_____
_____
_____
_____

Week 29

PRAYING HUSBANDS

We had struggled to begin a Bible study group in a willing person's home. We lived and worked in a large city of Southeast Asia. There was much communist opposition during this time, with parades right in front of the home where the Bible study met. So, of course, many people were afraid to come. The group had dwindled to two! We asked prayer partners at home to pray with us concerning this matter.

I was very sick in bed with dengue fever on my January 23 birthday. As my husband, John, left for the study, we reminded ourselves that since it was my birthday, perhaps many were praying for us.

We knew God had answered these prayers when John returned to find my fever gone and to happily report that twelve people had been present at Bible study!

Glenn—PACIFIC RIM

While serving in Calcutta, India, my husband, Harvey, and I heard of a desperate need in a small mountain village. A concerned Christian couple had opened an orphanage for young boys, ages three to sixteen. There was no financial assistance and the needs were overwhelming. Each child had one pair of shorts and a tattered shirt. There were no shoes or medical care. Our plan was to go there to assist in resource connections and offer our help.

A long siege of amebic dysentery had depleted my health and almost my hope for recovery as well. Prayer was our only source of strength. Boarding the train for an all-night trip, I faced the prospect of a long miserable night in a filthy bathroom or trying to sleep on a cold metal berth.

Surprisingly, the next thing I knew, it was early morning and we had reached the village. But much more to my surprise—I was well! God had answered our prayers and touched me with His healing hand. It was truly a miracle. I had a very peaceful night of sleep and awakened to wellness in the morning.

As we reached the orphanage, the sound of angelic voices rang through the air. The thin, pitifully dressed boys, covered in infected sores, were singing praise songs! Their faces were beautiful as they sang with such joy. In their great need they had already given to me far more than I had come to share with them.

God had not only met my physical need, but he had taught me a lesson in praise.

*"They raised their voices in praise to the LORD and sang:
'He is good; his love endures forever.'" (2 Chron. 5:13)*

"His praise will always be on my lips." (Ps. 34:1)

Charlene—SOUTH ASIA

> Public prayers are of little worth unless they are
> founded on or followed up by private praying.
> *E. M. Bounds*

PRAISE & THANKSGIVING

Worship by using the name of God mentioned in this
Scripture—"Almighty."

> *The four living creatures . . . do not cease to say, "Holy, holy, holy is the Lord God,
> the Almighty, who was and who is and who is to come.*
>
> Revelation 4:8 (NASB)

REPENTANCE

Search your heart as you meditate on this Scripture.
What is the Holy Spirit revealing to you?

> *Turn to me and have mercy on me, as you always do to those who love your name.
> Direct my footsteps according to your word; let no sin rule over me.*
>
> Psalm 119:132–133

ASKING

Read the following Scripture. Rewrite it, personalizing it
for the missionary husband, as he might pray it for himself.

> *Put to death, therefore, whatever belongs to your earthly nature: sexual immoral-
> ity, impurity, lust, evil desires and greed, which is idolatry. . . . Do not lie to each
> other, since you have taken off your old self with its practices and have put on the
> new self, which is being renewed in knowledge in the image of its Creator.*
>
> Colossians 3:5, 9–10

_____

_____

YIELDING

Now meditate on the Scripture again. Rewrite it below,
personalizing and praying it for yourself. How can you
respond to what God is saying to you in this Scripture?

_____

_____

Pray for missionary work in MONTENEGRO
(Northern Asia, between China and Russia)

Fall on your knees and grow there. There is no burden of the spirit but
is lighter by kneeling under it. Prayer means not always talking to Him,
but waiting before Him till the dust settles and the stream runs clear.

F. B. Meyer

PRAISE & THANKSGIVING

Worship Him today—the "Almighty."

The four living creatures . . . do not cease to say, "Holy, holy, holy is the Lord God,
the Almighty, who was and who is and who is to come.

Revelation 4:8 (NASB)

REPENTANCE

Search your heart as you meditate on this Scripture.

Turn to me and have mercy on me, as you always do to those who love your name.
Direct my footsteps according to your word; let no sin rule over me.

Psalm 119:132–133

ASKING

Rewrite this Scripture, personalizing it for the missionary
husband, as he might pray it for himself.

Let the loveliness of our Lord, our God, rest on us, confirming the work that we do.
Oh, yes. Affirm the work that we do!

Psalm 90:17 (MSG)

_____

_____

_____

_____

YIELDING

Rewrite it again, personalizing and praying it for yourself.
Respond to what God is saying to you in this Scripture.

_____

_____

_____

_____

Pray for missionary work in MONTSERRAT
(Caribbean island, southeast of Puerto Rico)

> All that God is, and all that God has, is at the disposal
> of prayer. Prayer can do anything that God can do,
> and as God can do everything, prayer is omnipotent.
> *R. A. Torrey*

PRAISE & THANKSGIVING

> *The four living creatures . . . do not cease to say, "Holy, holy, holy is the Lord God,
> the Almighty, who was and who is and who is to come.*
>
> Revelation 4:8 (NASB)

REPENTANCE

> *As for me, far be it from me that I should sin against the LORD by failing
> to pray for you.*
>
> 1 Samuel 12:23

ASKING

Personalize this Scripture for the missionary husband,
rewriting it as he might pray it for his wife.

> *I thank my God every time I remember you. In all my prayers for all of you,
> I always pray with joy because of your partnership in the gospel from the first
> day until now.*
>
> Philippians 1:3–5

_____

_____

_____

_____

YIELDING

Now personalize and pray it for yourself. How can you
respond to what God is saying to you?

_____

_____

_____

_____

Pray for missionary work in MOROCCO
(Northern Africa, between Algeria and Western Sahara)

To pray is to let Jesus come into our hearts. It is not our prayer
which moves the Lord Jesus. It is Jesus who moves us to pray.
O. Hallesby

PRAISE & THANKSGIVING

The four living creatures . . . do not cease to say, "Holy, holy, holy is the Lord God,
the Almighty, who was and who is and who is to come.
Revelation 4:8 (NASB)

REPENTANCE

As for me, far be it from me that I should sin against the LORD by failing
to pray for you.
1 Samuel 12:23

ASKING

Rewrite this Scripture, personalizing it for missionaries.
May he give you the desire of your heart and make all your plans succeed.
We will shout for joy when you are victorious and will lift up our banners
in the name of our God. May the LORD grant all your requests.
Psalm 20:4–5

_____

_____

_____

_____

YIELDING

What is God saying to you in this Scripture?

_____

_____

_____

_____

_____

_____

_____

Pray for missionary work in MOZAMBIQUE
(Southeastern Africa, between Tanzania and South Africa)

To stand before men on behalf of God is one thing.
To stand before God on behalf of men is something entirely different.
Leonard Ravenhill

PRAISE & THANKSGIVING

The four living creatures . . . do not cease to say, "Holy, holy, holy is the Lord God,
the Almighty, who was and who is and who is to come.
Revelation 4:8 (NASB)

REPENTANCE

As for me, far be it from me that I should sin against the LORD by failing
to pray for you.
1 Samuel 12:23

ASKING

Personalize this Scripture today for missionaries.

Do not withhold your mercy from me, O LORD; may your love and
your truth always protect me.
Psalm 40:11

_____

_____

_____

_____

YIELDING

Personalize and pray this same Scripture for yourself.

_____

_____

_____

_____

_____

_____

_____

_____

Pray for missionary work in NAMIBIA
(Southern Africa, between Angola and South Africa)

Week 29
Thoughts and Prayers

Week 30

PRAYING WIVES

Living overseas can be difficult for missionaries. The stress can cause us to wonder if we'll be able to make it. Often husbands and wives must be separated for days or weeks at a time. The wife stays at home with ministry obligations she sometimes feels unprepared or unable to handle. For families with children, the wife has full responsibility when her husband is traveling.

She is also concerned for the safety of her husband. He travels frequently into dangerous, even life-threatening situations, often facing unsanitary conditions with little time or place to rest. Availability of food may be limited and the roads can be dangerous to travel.

The husband is concerned with the safety of his family and the added stress on his wife and children while he is away. When he returns home, he may return discouraged, stressed, and exhausted. He looks forward to a long bath, a good meal, and time to rest and relax. But the children have missed Dad, so they want and need his attention.

These circumstances are a fertile field for disharmony between husband and wife, children and parents.

The following verses were Scriptures that I prayed when my husband traveled to dangerous areas with unsanitary conditions and uncomfortable climates that made his work stressful. These verses can be prayed for all missionaries.

> *He holds victory in store for the upright, he is a shield to those whose walk is blameless, for he guards the course of the just and protects the way of his faithful ones. (Prov. 2:7—8)*

> *The LORD gives strength to his people; the LORD blesses his people with peace. (Ps. 29:11)*

> *He who dwells in the shelter of the Most High will rest in the shadow of the Almighty. I will say of the LORD, "He is my refuge and my fortress, my God, in whom I trust." (Ps. 91:1—2)*

Doris —Central, Eastern, and Southern Africa

> Prayer is the greatest of all forces, because it
> honors God and brings Him into active aid.
> *E. M. Bounds*

PRAISE & THANKSGIVING

Worship by using the aspect of God mentioned in this
Scripture—"glory."

> *I have seen you in the sanctuary and beheld your power and your glory.*
>
> Psalm 63:2

REPENTANCE

Search your heart as you meditate on this Scripture.
What is the Holy Spirit revealing to you?

> *Our offenses are many in your sight, and our sins testify against us.*
> *Our offenses are ever with us, and we acknowledge our iniquities.*
>
> Isaiah 59:12

ASKING

Read the following Scripture. Rewrite it, personalizing it
for the missionary wife, as she might pray it for herself.

> *Teach the older women to be reverent in the way they live, not to be slanderers*
> *or addicted to much wine, but to teach what is good. Then they can train the*
> *younger women to love their husbands and children, to be self-controlled and pure,*
> *to be busy at home, to be kind, and to be subject to their husbands, so that no one*
> *will malign the word of God.*
>
> Titus 2:3–5

_____

_____

YIELDING

Now meditate on the Scripture again. Rewrite it below,
personalizing and praying it for yourself. How can you
respond to what God is saying to you in this Scripture?

_____

_____

Pray for missionary work in NAURU
(island in the South Pacific, south of the Marshall Islands)

All that true prayer seeks is God Himself, for with Him we get all we need.
The Kneeling Christian

PRAISE & THANKSGIVING
Worship Him today, the One who is full of "glory."

I have seen you in the sanctuary and beheld your power and your glory.

Psalm 63:2

REPENTANCE
Search your heart as you meditate on this Scripture.

Our offenses are many in your sight, and our sins testify against us.
Our offenses are ever with us, and we acknowledge our iniquities.

Isaiah 59:12

ASKING
Rewrite this Scripture, personalizing it for the missionary wife, as she might pray it for herself.

This is the way the holy women of the past who put their hope in God used to make
themselves beautiful. They were submissive to their own husbands, like Sarah, who
obeyed Abraham and called him her master. You are her daughters if you do what
is right and do not give way to fear.

1 Peter 3:5–6

_____

_____

_____

_____

YIELDING
Rewrite it again, personalizing and praying it for yourself.
Respond to what God is saying to you in this Scripture.

_____

_____

_____

_____

Pray for missionary work in NEPAL
(Southern Asia, between China and India)

Pray for a tough hide and a tender heart.
Ruth Bell Graham

PRAISE & THANKSGIVING

I have seen you in the sanctuary and beheld your power and your glory.
Psalm 63:2

REPENTANCE

Therefore let us leave the elementary teachings about Christ and go on to maturity, not laying again the foundation of repentance from acts that lead to death, and of faith in God.
Hebrews 6:1

ASKING

Personalize this Scripture for the missionary wife, rewriting it as she might pray it for her husband.

We have not stopped praying for you and asking God to fill you with the knowledge of his will through all spiritual wisdom and understanding. And we pray this in order that you may live a life worthy of the Lord and may please him in every way: bearing fruit in every good work, growing in the knowledge of God.
Colossians 1:9–10

_____

_____

_____

_____

YIELDING

Now personalize and pray it for yourself. How can you respond to what God is saying to you?

_____

_____

_____

_____

_____

Pray for missionary work in THE NETHERLANDS
(Western Europe, on the North Sea,
between Belgium and Germany)

> Prayer, real prayer, is lethal to Satan's cause.
> *Anonymous*

PRAISE & THANKSGIVING

I have seen you in the sanctuary and beheld your power and your glory.
Psalm 63:2

REPENTANCE

Therefore let us leave the elementary teachings about Christ and go on to maturity, not laying again the foundation of repentance from acts that lead to death, and of faith in God.
Hebrews 6:1

ASKING

Rewrite this Scripture, personalizing it for missionaries.

We constantly pray for you, that our God may count you worthy of his calling, and that by his power he may fulfill every good purpose of yours and every act prompted by your faith.
2 Thessalonians 1:11

_____

_____

_____

_____

YIELDING

What is God saying to you in this Scripture?

_____

_____

_____

_____

_____

_____

Pray for missionary work in
THE NETHERLANDS ANTILLES
(two island groups in the Caribbean, east of the US Virgin Islands)

> Any concern too small to be turned into a prayer
> is too small to be made into a burden.
> *Corrie ten Boom*

PRAISE & THANKSGIVING

I have seen you in the sanctuary and beheld your power and your glory.

Psalm 63:2

REPENTANCE

Therefore let us leave the elementary teachings about Christ and go on to maturity, not laying again the foundation of repentance from acts that lead to death, and of faith in God.

Hebrews 6:1

ASKING

Personalize this Scripture today for missionaries.

Blessed is the man who does not walk in the counsel of the wicked or stand in the way of sinners or sit in the seat of mockers. But his delight is in the law of the LORD, and on his law he meditates day and night. He is like a tree planted by streams of water, which yields its fruit in season and whose leaf does not wither. Whatever he does prospers.

Psalm 1:1–3

_____

_____

_____

_____

YIELDING

Personalize and pray this same Scripture for yourself.

_____

_____

_____

_____

_____

Pray for missionary work in NEW CALEDONIA
(South Pacific islands, east of Australia)

Week 30
Thoughts and Prayers

_____

_____

_____

_____

_____

_____

_____

_____

_____

_____

_____

_____

_____

_____

_____

_____

_____

_____

_____

_____

_____

_____

_____

_____

_____

_____

_____

_____

Week 31

PURITY

God is stretching us and showing Himself to us as we depend on Him. Many of the struggles are internal and have nothing to do with the work itself. But we have come to learn that it is by filling our hearts with God's Word that we grow in our faith and can rejoice in Him.

Marty —SOUTH AMERICA

We have learned that our primary task as missionaries is to see where God is at work and then join Him. But Jesus tells us that only those who are "pure in heart" will see God.

My parents served as missionaries in a city far from the nearest English school, so I moved to a boarding school at age twelve. My innocence was soon lost in the company of world-wise upper classmen telling off-color jokes, bragging about their exploits, and sharing their pornography. It was all too easy to get hooked on the deceptiveness of sin.

It was after my teenage years that I finally came to know Christ as my Savior and Lord. I experienced dramatic victory over sin. Jesus transformed my life! But even after serving as a pastor and being appointed as a missionary, I found that the enemy continued to tempt me with the old delusion of pornography. I believe it was Satan's attempt to prevent me from seeing where God was at work around me so that I would be unfruitful. During my years growing up as a missionary kid (MK), and now as a missionary, I have seen numbers of missionaries sent home because of sexual sin—a sin that began in the heart and mind and was eventually acted out.

Other missionaries who shared my desire to keep a pure heart agreed to be my accountability partners over the years. What a blessing it is to have a brother to walk with through the battle! "Confess your sins to each other and pray for each other so that you may be healed" (James 5:16).

With the easy accessibility of pornography on the Internet as well as explicit programming on cable television and video, even the mission field is a spiritual minefield! The enemy is unrelenting in his attempts to destroy the work of God. Please pray for missionaries as well as missionary kids to "flee from sin" and to live with moral purity.

—A *missionary serving overseas*

In souls filled with love, the desire to please God is continual prayer.
John Wesley

PRAISE & THANKSGIVING

Worship by using the name of God mentioned in this
Scripture—"the Lord your God."

*I am the LORD your God, who brought you out of the land of Egypt so that
you would not be their slaves.*

Leviticus 26:13 (NASB)

REPENTANCE

Search your heart as you meditate on this Scripture.
What is the Holy Spirit revealing to you?

*For from within, out of men's hearts, come evil thoughts, sexual immorality, theft,
murder, adultery, greed, malice, deceit, lewdness, envy, slander, arrogance and folly.
All these evils come from inside and make a man "unclean."*

Mark 7:21–23

ASKING

Read the following Scripture. Rewrite it, personalizing it
for the missionary's marriage relationship, seeking the Lord
regarding purity and moral integrity.

*Marriage should be honored by all, and the marriage bed kept pure, for God will
judge the adulterer and all the sexually immoral.*

Hebrews 13:4

_____

_____

_____

YIELDING

Now meditate on the Scripture again. Rewrite it below,
personalizing and praying it for yourself. How can you
respond to what God is saying to you in this Scripture?

_____

_____

_____

Pray for missionary work in NEW ZEALAND
(South Pacific islands, southeast of Australia)

The price of prayerlessness far exceeds the price of prayer.
Anonymous

PRAISE & THANKSGIVING

Worship Him today—"the Lord your God."

I am the LORD your God, who brought you out of the land of Egypt so that you would not be their slaves.

Leviticus 26:13 (NASB)

REPENTANCE

Search your heart as you meditate on this Scripture.

For from within, out of men's hearts, come evil thoughts, sexual immorality, theft, murder, adultery, greed, malice, deceit, lewdness, envy, slander, arrogance and folly. All these evils come from inside and make a man "unclean."

Mark 7:21–23

ASKING

Rewrite this Scripture, personalizing it for the missionary's marriage relationship, seeking the Lord regarding purity and moral integrity.

Do you not know that your body is a temple of the Holy Spirit, who is in you, whom you have received from God? You are not your own; you were bought at a price. Therefore honor God with your body.

1 Corinthians 6:19–20

_____

_____

_____

YIELDING

Rewrite it again, personalizing and praying it for yourself. Respond to what God is saying to you in this Scripture.

_____

_____

_____

_____

Pray for missionary work in NICARAGUA
(Central America, between Costa Rica and Honduras)

To pray as a duty and as if obliging God by our prayer is quite ridiculous,
and is certain indication of a backslidden heart.
Charles G. Finney

PRAISE & THANKSGIVING

*I am the LORD your God, who brought you out of the land of Egypt so that
you would not be their slaves.*

> Leviticus 26:13 (NASB)

REPENTANCE

*For from within, out of men's hearts, come evil thoughts, sexual immorality, theft,
murder, adultery, greed, malice, deceit, lewdness, envy, slander, arrogance and folly.
All these evils come from inside and make a man "unclean."*

> Mark 7:21–23

ASKING

Personalize this Scripture for the missionary's marriage
relationship, rewriting it, seeking the Lord regarding purity
and moral integrity.

*If you think you are standing firm, be careful that you don't fall! No temptation
has seized you except what is common to man. And God is faithful; he will not let
you be tempted beyond what you can bear. But when you are tempted, he will also
provide a way out so that you can stand up under it.*

> 1 Corinthians 10:12–13

_____

_____

_____

YIELDING

Now personalize and pray it for yourself. How can you
respond to what God is saying to you?

_____

_____

_____

_____

Pray for missionary work in NIGER
(Western Africa, southeast of Algeria)

> Never say you will pray about a thing; pray about it.
> *Oswald Chambers*

PRAISE & THANKSGIVING

> *I am the LORD your God, who brought you out of the land of Egypt so that you would not be their slaves.*
>
> Leviticus 26:13 (NASB)

REPENTANCE

> *For from within, out of men's hearts, come evil thoughts, sexual immorality, theft, murder, adultery, greed, malice, deceit, lewdness, envy, slander, arrogance and folly. All these evils come from inside and make a man "unclean."*
>
> Mark 7:21–23

ASKING

Rewrite this Scripture, personalizing it for missionaries.

> *"Everything is permissible for me"—but not everything is beneficial. "Everything is permissible for me"—but I will not be mastered by anything.*
>
> 1 Corinthians 6:12

_____

_____

_____

_____

YIELDING

What is God saying to you in this Scripture?

_____

_____

_____

_____

_____

_____

_____

Pray for missionary work in NIGERIA
(Western Africa, between Benin and Cameroon)

There is no greater test to spirituality than prayer. The man who tries
to pray quickly discovers just where he stands in God's sight.
The Kneeling Christian

PRAISE & THANKSGIVING

I am the LORD your God, who brought you out of the land of Egypt so that
you would not be their slaves.

Leviticus 26:13 (NASB)

REPENTANCE

For from within, out of men's hearts, come evil thoughts, sexual immorality, theft,
murder, adultery, greed, malice, deceit, lewdness, envy, slander, arrogance and folly.
All these evils come from inside and make a man "unclean."

Mark 7:21–23

ASKING

Personalize this Scripture today for missionaries.

Clothe yourselves with the Lord Jesus Christ, and do not think about how to
gratify the desires of the sinful nature.

Romans 13:14

_____

_____

_____

_____

YIELDING

Personalize and pray this same Scripture for yourself.

_____

_____

_____

_____

_____

_____

Pray for missionary work on NIUE ISLAND
(South Pacific island, east of Tonga)

Week 31
Thoughts and Prayers

_____

_____

_____

_____

_____

_____

_____

_____

_____

_____

_____

_____

_____

_____

_____

_____

_____

_____

_____

_____

_____

_____

_____

_____

_____

_____

_____

Week 32

UNITY

My wife and I serve in South Asia among a Muslim population in a city of over ten million. We've only been on the field for three weeks as we write this. We're still getting adjusted, but it is obvious God was at work here long before we arrived.

During our orientation and training in the United States, we were in frequent contact with our future team members in this city. One day we received some exciting news! The prayer coordinator for our team shared a conversation she'd had with a man from another Great Commission Christian organization. The man told her he had been praying for some time asking God to send someone to work among a minority group in our city numbering two million. There were few if any believers, and he had been burdened to pray for this people group for quite a while. Our prayer coordinator shared with excitement that a family was moving to this city—(us!)—in a matter of weeks to reach the exact group for which he had been praying!

We had "goose bumps" as we realized our calling to work with the Muslims of this city was partly the direct result of this man's prayers. We were seeing Matthew 9:37–38 played out in our own lives. We were the workers this man prayed God would send to this harvest field—and God was faithful to answer! How humbling, and how awesome, to be part of a living body, divinely fitted together to achieve the Father's plan! As we anticipate three years of service among the Muslims of this city, we do so with increased expectations because of the prayers of this faithful saint.

—*Christian workers in South Asia*

> A true prayer is an inventory of needs, a catalog of necessities,
> an exposure of secret wounds, a revelation of hidden poverty.
> *Charles Spurgeon*

PRAISE & THANKSGIVING

Worship by using the name of God mentioned in this Scripture—"dwelling place."

> *The eternal God is a dwelling place, and underneath are the everlasting arms; and He drove out the enemy from before you, and said, "Destroy!"*
>
> Deuteronomy 33:27 (NASB)

REPENTANCE

Search your heart as you meditate on this Scripture. What is the Holy Spirit revealing to you?

> *Then those who feared the LORD talked with each other, and the LORD listened and heard. A scroll of remembrance was written in his presence concerning those who feared the LORD and honored his name.*
>
> Malachi 3:16

ASKING

Read the following Scripture. Rewrite it, personalizing it for the missionary's marriage relationship, seeking the Lord regarding unity.

> *So they are no longer two, but one. Therefore what God has joined together, let man not separate.*
>
> Matthew 19:6

_____

_____

YIELDING

Now meditate on the Scripture again. Rewrite it below, personalizing and praying it for yourself. How can you respond to what God is saying to you in this Scripture?

_____

_____

Pray for missionary work on NORFOLK ISLAND
(South Pacific island, east of Australia)

> Prevailing prayer must have in it the quality which waits
> and perseveres, the courage that never surrenders, the patience
> which never grows tired, the resolution that never wavers.
>
> *E. M. Bounds*

PRAISE & THANKSGIVING

Worship Him today as your "dwelling place."

The eternal God is a dwelling place, and underneath are the everlasting arms;
and He drove out the enemy from before you, and said, "Destroy!"

Deuteronomy 33:27 (NASB)

REPENTANCE

Search your heart as you meditate on this Scripture.

Then those who feared the LORD talked with each other, and the LORD listened
and heard. A scroll of remembrance was written in his presence concerning those
who feared the LORD and honored his name.

Malachi 3:16

ASKING

Rewrite this Scripture, personalizing it for the missionary's
marriage relationship, seeking the Lord regarding unity.

May the God who gives endurance and encouragement give you a spirit of unity
among yourselves as you follow Christ Jesus, so that with one heart and mouth
you may glorify the God and Father of our Lord Jesus Christ.

Romans 15:5–6

_____

_____

_____

YIELDING

Rewrite it again, personalizing and praying it for yourself.
Respond to what God is saying to you in this Scripture.

_____

_____

_____

Pray for missionary work in NORTH KOREA
(Eastern Asia, between China and South Korea)

Prayer makes the darkened clouds withdraw; prayer climbs the ladder Jacob
saw; gives exercise to faith and love, brings every blessing from above.
Leonard Ravenhill

PRAISE & THANKSGIVING

The eternal God is a dwelling place, and underneath are the everlasting arms;
and He drove out the enemy from before you, and said, "Destroy!"

Deuteronomy 33:27 (NASB)

REPENTANCE

Then those who feared the LORD talked with each other, and the LORD listened
and heard. A scroll of remembrance was written in his presence concerning those
who feared the LORD and honored his name.

Malachi 3:16

ASKING

Personalize this Scripture for the missionary's marriage
relationship, rewriting it, seeking the Lord regarding unity.

I appeal to you, brothers, in the name of our Lord Jesus Christ, that all of you
agree with one another so that there may be no divisions among you and that
you may be perfectly united in mind and thought.

1 Corinthians 1:10

_____

_____

_____

_____

YIELDING

Now personalize and pray it for yourself. How can you
respond to what God is saying to you?

_____

_____

_____

_____

_____

Pray for missionary work in
THE NORTHERN MARIANA ISLANDS
(North Pacific islands, between Hawaii and the Philippines)

> We cannot ask in behalf of Christ what
> Christ would not ask Himself if He were praying.
> *A. B. Simpson*

PRAISE & THANKSGIVING

> *The eternal God is a dwelling place, and underneath are the everlasting arms;*
> *and He drove out the enemy from before you, and said, "Destroy!"*
>
> Deuteronomy 33:27 (NASB)

REPENTANCE

> *Then those who feared the LORD talked with each other, and the LORD listened*
> *and heard. A scroll of remembrance was written in his presence concerning those*
> *who feared the LORD and honored his name.*
>
> Malachi 3:16

ASKING

Rewrite this Scripture, personalizing it for missionaries.

> *Bear with each other and forgive whatever grievances you may have against one*
> *another. Forgive as the Lord forgave you. And over all these virtues put on love,*
> *which binds them all together in perfect unity.*
>
> Colossians 3:13–14

_____

_____

_____

_____

YIELDING

What is God saying to you in this Scripture?

_____

_____

_____

_____

_____

_____

Pray for missionary work in NORWAY
(Northern Europe, west of Sweden)

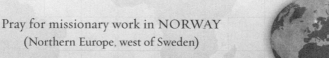

> Prevailing prayer is prayer that not only takes the initiative but
> continues on the offensive for God until spiritual victory is won.
> *Wesley L. Duewel*

PRAISE & THANKSGIVING

The eternal God is a dwelling place, and underneath are the everlasting arms;
and He drove out the enemy from before you, and said, "Destroy!"
Deuteronomy 33:27 (NASB)

REPENTANCE

Then those who feared the LORD talked with each other, and the LORD listened
and heard. A scroll of remembrance was written in his presence concerning those
who feared the LORD and honored his name.
Malachi 3:16

ASKING

Personalize this Scripture today for missionaries.

My purpose is that they may be encouraged in heart and united in love, so that they
may have the full riches of complete understanding, in order that they may know
the mystery of God, namely, Christ, in whom are hidden all the treasures of
wisdom and knowledge.
Colossians 2:2–3

_____

_____

_____

_____

YIELDING

Personalize and pray this same Scripture for yourself.

_____

_____

_____

_____

_____

Pray for missionary work in OMAN
(Middle East, on the Arabian Sea, east of Yemen)

Week 32
Thoughts and Prayers

_____

_____

_____

_____

_____

_____

_____

_____

_____

_____

_____

_____

_____

_____

_____

_____

_____

_____

_____

_____

_____

_____

_____

_____

_____

_____

_____

_____

_____

These are the commands, decrees and laws

the LORD your God directed me to teach you to observe

in the land that you are crossing the Jordan to possess,

so that you, your children and their children after them

may fear the LORD your God as long as you live by keeping

all his decrees and commands that I give you,

and so that you may enjoy long life.

Hear, O Israel, and be careful to obey so that it may go well with you

and that you may increase greatly in a land flowing with milk and honey,

just as the LORD, the God of your fathers, promised you. Hear, O Israel:

The LORD our God, the LORD is one. Love the LORD your God with

all your heart and with all your soul and with all your strength.

These commandments that I give you today are to be upon your hearts.

Impress them on your children. Talk about them when you sit at home

and when you walk along the road, when you lie down and when you get up.

Tie them as symbols on your hands and bind them on your foreheads.

Write them on the doorframes of your houses and on your gates.

DEUTERONOMY 6:1–9

THE
MISSIONARY'S
CHILDREN

Week 33

AUTHORITY

In John 17:13, our Savior prayed this for you: "Now I come to You, and these things I speak in the world, that they may have My joy fulfilled in themselves" (NKJV).

While studying this Scripture, my eleven-year-old and her ten-year-old friend walked into my study on a serious mission. They could not get the lid off of the jar of cheese dip.

Katie, my daughter, was telling Emily, her friend, as they came through the door, "Daddies are special," as she handed me the jar. With a snap of the wrist, I loosened the lid that was more than their strength. I handed the jar to Katie, relishing the joy in their eyes as they left with their treat in hand.

As they walked away down the hall, I heard Katie say again, "See, daddies are special," and Emily replied, "Yes, daddies are magical!" What joy that little incident gave me. Truly, my joy was "fulfilled" in them as I saw the blessing they had received from Daddy's hand.

Do you think that Jesus prayed for your joy to be fulfilled just so He could hear his own voice? Do you know of any prayer of the Savior that has not, cannot, or will not be answered? Why, then, would you be convinced that the present night of trouble you are going through will never see the light of a new morning?

Bill—SOUTH AMERICA

I learned as never before that persistent calling upon the Lord breaks
through every stronghold of the devil, for nothing is impossible with God.
For Christians in these troubled times, there is simply no other way.
Jim Cymbala

PRAISE & THANKSGIVING

Worship by using the name of God mentioned in this
Scripture—"defender."

> *It will be a sign and witness to the LORD Almighty in the land of Egypt.*
> *When they cry out to the LORD because of their oppressors, he will send*
> *them a savior and defender, and he will rescue them.*
>
> Isaiah 19:20

REPENTANCE

Search your heart as you meditate on this Scripture.
What is the Holy Spirit revealing to you?

> *Let us examine our ways and test them, and let us return to the LORD.*
>
> Lamentations 3:40

ASKING

Read the following Scripture. Rewrite it, personalizing it
for the missionary's children, seeking the Lord regarding
authority and honoring their parents.

> *Honor your father and your mother, so that you may live long in the land*
> *the LORD your God is giving you.*
>
> Exodus 20:12

_____

_____

YIELDING

Now meditate on the Scripture again. Rewrite it below,
personalizing and praying it for yourself. How can you
respond to what God is saying to you in this Scripture?

_____

_____

Pray for missionary work in PAKISTAN
(Southern Asia, between India and Afghanistan)

Intercession is cooperation with the Holy Spirit in His work to convict
the world concerning sin, and righteousness, and judgment.
Lars Widerberg

PRAISE & THANKSGIVING

Worship your "savior and defender."

*It will be a sign and witness to the LORD Almighty in the land of Egypt.
When they cry out to the LORD because of their oppressors, he will send
them a savior and defender, and he will rescue them.*

Isaiah 19:20

REPENTANCE

Search your heart as you meditate on this Scripture.

Let us examine our ways and test them, and let us return to the LORD.

Lamentations 3:40

ASKING

Rewrite this Scripture, personalizing it for the missionary's
children, seeking the Lord regarding authority and honoring their parents.

Children, obey your parents in everything, for this pleases the Lord.

Colossians 3:20

_____

_____

_____

_____

YIELDING

Rewrite it again, personalizing and praying it for yourself.
Respond to what God is saying to you in this Scripture.

_____

_____

_____

_____

_____

Pray for missionary work in PALAU
(group of islands in the North Pacific,
southeast of the Philippines)

> He only can truly pray who is all aglow
> for holiness, for God, and for heaven.
> *E. M. Bounds*

PRAISE & THANKSGIVING

> *It will be a sign and witness to the LORD Almighty in the land of Egypt.*
> *When they cry out to the LORD because of their oppressors, he will send*
> *them a savior and defender, and he will rescue them.*
>
> Isaiah 19:20

REPENTANCE

> *Let us examine our ways and test them, and let us return to the LORD.*
>
> Lamentations 3:40

ASKING

Personalize this Scripture for the missionary's children, rewriting it, seeking the Lord regarding authority.

> *Listen, my son, to your father's instruction and do not forsake*
> *your mother's teaching.*
>
> Proverbs 1:8

_____

_____

_____

_____

YIELDING

Now personalize and pray it for yourself. How can you respond to what God is saying to you?

_____

_____

_____

_____

_____

_____

Pray for missionary work in PANAMA
(Central America, between Colombia and Costa Rica)

> You can do more than pray after you've prayed, but you
> cannot do more than pray until you have prayed.
> *John Bunyan*

PRAISE & THANKSGIVING

It will be a sign and witness to the LORD Almighty in the land of Egypt.
When they cry out to the LORD because of their oppressors, he will send
them a savior and defender, and he will rescue them.

    Isaiah 19:20

REPENTANCE

Let us examine our ways and test them, and let us return to the LORD.

    Lamentations 3:40

ASKING

Rewrite this Scripture, personalizing it for missionaries.

Young men, in the same way be submissive to those who are older.
All of you, clothe yourselves with humility toward one another, because,
"God opposes the proud but gives grace to the humble."

    1 Peter 5:5

_____

_____

_____

_____

_____

YIELDING

What is God saying to you in this Scripture?

_____

_____

_____

_____

_____

_____

Pray for missionary work in PAPUA NEW GUINEA
(island group between the Coral Sea and the South Pacific)

O believing brethren! What an instrument is this which God hath
put into your hands! Prayer moves Him that moves the universe.
Robert Murray McCheyne

PRAISE & THANKSGIVING

It will be a sign and witness to the LORD Almighty in the land of Egypt.
When they cry out to the LORD because of their oppressors, he will send
them a savior and defender, and he will rescue them.

Isaiah 19:20

REPENTANCE

Let us examine our ways and test them, and let us return to the LORD.

Lamentations 3:40

ASKING

Personalize this Scripture today for missionaries.

Everyone must submit himself to the governing authorities,
for there is no authority except that which God has established.
The authorities that exist have been established by God.

Romans 13:1

_____

_____

_____

_____

YIELDING

Personalize and pray this same Scripture for yourself.

_____

_____

_____

_____

_____

_____

Pray for missionary work in PARAGUAY
(Central South America, northeast of Argentina)

Week 33
Thoughts and Prayers

Week 34

ENCOURAGEMENT

"What! We're moving again?"

Perhaps you lived in the same house and worshiped with the same church during your childhood, but this statement was often my response growing up as a missionary kid (MK). Today's generation is more mobile than the previous generation, but still, many people never move much farther than a few miles from their childhood home.

For missionary kids, however, "home" is a relative term. If you ask an MK where he or she is from, the response is usually, "Wherever I happen to be at the time."

When my husband and I became missionaries, we lived in nine different places in three countries over a period of nine years. Our daughters perfected the art of packing a box. That's a lot of moving for anyone, but it's especially difficult for children.

My sister, who also serves as a missionary, sent me a timely gift during our first year overseas. Painted on a wooden heart was a simple phrase: "Home is where God sends us." This little phrase became a promise for my family. Every time we packed our belongings, we knew God was sending us, and He would make the next place a home.

I know my three daughters often preferred to stay put. Leah, our oldest child, chose to be homeschooled her last year of high school. The alternative was a move to the United States where she would attend a new school as a senior. Our middle child did start over her senior year—her fourth school in four years—then she went to college. Every new home meant a new school with new friends and a new start. It wasn't easy.

I understood how my daughters felt because I experienced similar transitions growing up as an MK. But I discovered that God always blesses our obedience as we follow Him. I learned the truth of Jeremiah 29:11—"For I know the plans I have for you— this is the LORD's declaration—plans for your welfare, not for disaster, to give you a future and a hope" (HCSB). My parents moved our family *my* senior year of high school, but it placed me in a church where I met my husband. One of my daughters met her husband in the city where we moved her senior year. God has "plans for [our] welfare," and He is forever constant.

God loves us more than we can imagine, and "we know that all things work together for the good of those who love God: those who are called according to His purpose" (Rom. 8:28, HCSB). Living in one house, going to school, and worshiping with the same body of believers from birth to retirement is not a reality for MKs, but obedience to His call allows God to meet our every need according to His great riches. (Phil. 4:19).

Have you given thanks for the place you call home today? Consider how your home can be a haven for a missionary family while they are in the United States. Internationals living in America are separated from family and all that is familiar. How can your home be a blessing to an international student or family?

Ask God to provide protection and contentment for MKs as their families are in transition. Ask God to burden you to pray for MKs living around the world.

Debbie—SOUTH AMERICA

> The Spirit of prayer will help you become an intercessor,
> asking great things of God for those around you.
> *Andrew Murray*

PRAISE & THANKSGIVING

Worship by using the name of God mentioned in this
Scripture—"the One who lifts up my head."

You, O LORD, are a shield for me, my glory and the One who lifts up my head.

Psalm 3:3 (NKJV)

REPENTANCE

Search your heart as you meditate on this Scripture.
What is the Holy Spirit revealing to you?

*I am like an olive tree flourishing in the house of God; I trust in God's
unfailing love for ever and ever.*

Psalm 52:8

ASKING

Read the following Scripture. Rewrite it, personalizing it
for missionary children, seeking the Lord regarding their
encouragement.

*My purpose is that they may be encouraged in heart and united in love,
so that they may have the full riches of complete understanding, in order
that they may know the mystery of God, namely, Christ, in whom are
hidden all the treasures of wisdom and knowledge.*

Colossians 2:2–3

_____

_____

YIELDING

Now meditate on the Scripture again. Rewrite it below,
personalizing and praying it for yourself. How can you
respond to what God is saying to you in this Scripture?

_____

_____

_____

Pray for missionary work in PERU
(Western South America, between Chile and Ecuador)

We should look to the Holy Spirit to really lead us into the presence of God
and should not be hasty in words until He has actually brought us there.
R. A. Torrey

PRAISE & THANKSGIVING
Worship the One who "lifts up" your head.

> *You, O LORD, are a shield for me, my glory and the One who lifts up my head.*
> Psalm 3:3 (NKJV)

REPENTANCE
Search your heart as you meditate on this Scripture.

> *I am like an olive tree flourishing in the house of God; I trust in God's*
> *unfailing love for ever and ever.*
> Psalm 52:8

ASKING
Rewrite this Scripture, personalizing it for missionary
children, seeking the Lord regarding their contentment.

> *The fear of the LORD leads to life: then one rests content, untouched by trouble.*
> Proverbs 19:23

_____

_____

_____

_____

YIELDING
Rewrite it again, personalizing and praying it for yourself.
Respond to what God is saying to you in this Scripture.

_____

_____

_____

_____

_____

_____

Pray for missionary work in THE PHILIPPINES
(Southeastern Asia, island group east of Vietnam)

> Wise is he in the day of trouble who knows his true
> source of strength and who fails not to pray.
> *E. M. Bounds*

PRAISE & THANKSGIVING

> *You, O LORD, are a shield for me, my glory and the One who lifts up my head.*
> Psalm 3:3 (NKJV)

REPENTANCE

> *I am like an olive tree flourishing in the house of God; I trust in God's
> unfailing love for ever and ever.*
> Psalm 52:8

ASKING

Personalize this Scripture for missionary children,
rewriting it, seeking the Lord regarding contentment.

> *Do not be anxious about anything, but in everything, by prayer and petition,
> with thanksgiving, present your requests to God. And the peace of God,
> which transcends all understanding, will guard your hearts and your
> minds in Christ Jesus.*
> Philippians 4:6–7

_____

_____

_____

_____

YIELDING

Now personalize and pray it for yourself. How can you
respond to what God is saying to you?

_____

_____

_____

_____

_____

Pray for missionary work in
THE PITCAIRN ISLANDS
(South Pacific islands, halfway between Peru and New Zealand)

Before a word of petition is offered, we should have the definite and vivid
consciousness that we are talking to God and should believe that He is
listening to our petition and is going to grant the thing that we ask.
R. A. Torrey

PRAISE & THANKSGIVING

You, O LORD, are a shield for me, my glory and the One who lifts up my head.
Psalm 3:3 (NKJV)

REPENTANCE

*I am like an olive tree flourishing in the house of God; I trust in God's
unfailing love for ever and ever.*
Psalm 52:8

ASKING

Rewrite this Scripture, personalizing it for missionaries.
*My eyes are ever on the LORD, for only he will release my feet from the snare.
Turn to me and be gracious to me, for I am lonely and afflicted. The troubles
of my heart have multiplied; free me from my anguish.*
Psalm 25:15–17

_____

_____

_____

_____

YIELDING

What is God saying to you in this Scripture?

_____

_____

_____

_____

_____

_____

_____

Pray for missionary work in POLAND
(Central Europe, east of Germany)

> He who is too busy to pray will be too busy to live
> a holy life. Satan had rather we let the grass grow on
> the path to our prayer chamber than anything else.
> *E. M. Bounds*

PRAISE & THANKSGIVING

You, O LORD, are a shield for me, my glory and the One who lifts up my head.

Psalm 3:3 (NKJV)

REPENTANCE

*I am like an olive tree flourishing in the house of God; I trust in God's
unfailing love for ever and ever.*

Psalm 52:8

ASKING

Personalize this Scripture today for missionaries.

*My soul finds rest in God alone; my salvation comes from him.
He alone is my rock and my salvation; he is my fortress, I will never be shaken.*

Psalm 62:1–2

_____

_____

_____

_____

YIELDING

Personalize and pray this same Scripture for yourself.

_____

_____

_____

_____

_____

_____

_____

Pray for missionary work in PORTUGAL
(Southwestern Europe, bordering the North Atlantic)

Week 34
Thoughts and Prayers

_____
_____
_____
_____
_____
_____
_____
_____
_____
_____
_____
_____
_____
_____
_____
_____
_____
_____
_____
_____
_____
_____
_____
_____
_____
_____
_____
_____
_____

Week 35

FORGIVENESS & RESTORATION

Our friend Bill Hyde was killed in a 2003 bombing in the Philippines. Bill and twenty Filipinos lost their lives outside the Davao City Airport in the southern Philippines. Bill was awaiting the arrival of a missionary couple and their two small children. The missionary mother and her baby received shrapnel wounds but survived the blast. To this day it is not known who was responsible for the bombing, but by God's grace the young missionary couple and their children recovered. They were not deterred by the event and have continued a fruitful ministry while also enabling many others in their work.

For the Hyde family, things were obviously more difficult. But in looking back they saw ways God had prepared them. Bill and his wife, Lyn, had just enjoyed a memorable time with their oldest son who had come to the Philippines on a mission trip from the United States. They had also recently visited their younger son, a Christian worker in another Asian country. This son showed his parents a plot of land he had purchased for the ministry. He told his dad he wanted to retire on this land or, if he died, to be buried on this land. Two days before the bombing, the Filipinos in Bill's Sunday school class were talking about death. Bill shared his son's comment about being buried in his newly-adopted country. Bill said, "My son is willing to die for the people of that country. I had to ask myself if I am willing to die for the Filipino people; and my answer is, 'Yes.' I would die for the Filipino people."

God also used a devotional for a women's retreat Lyn was preparing before the bombing to assure her of His steadfast love and care through her most difficult time. Lyn planned to show the ladies they were in the most secure place possible no matter what the circumstances, as illustrated by Jesus' words in John 14:20 — "On that day you will realize that I am in my Father, and you are in me, and I am in you." Lyn never gave that devotional teaching at the retreat because Bill was killed that week, but she knew that its truth was God's promise to her. She is in Christ, who is in the Father, and Christ is in her.

The year after Bill's death, Lyn joined the team in the northern Philippines with which my family serves. She has been invaluable to the work of mobilizing and preparing Filipinos and other Asians to go out as cross-cultural missionaries and tentmakers. Lyn has been able to share her firsthand knowledge of God's care in difficult circumstances, often using the same visual illustration from that devotional God had given her years before.

Prior to Lyn's coming, my husband and I had searched for a good way to help new disciples and Christian leaders "hear from God." We had not been too successful. When Lyn joined our team, we discovered she had a special way of teaching the new cross-cultural workers how to hear from God. Based on years of personal experience of spending time in the Word, recognizing God's voice, and keeping a record of what she discerns Him saying, Lyn has helped hundreds of new missionaries get a handle on this essential part of knowing the Shepherd's voice and following Him. Though we wish it had been through less difficult circumstances, we believe God brought Lyn to implant this essential element in the lives of the new missionaries.

Diana—PACIFIC RIM

> Jesus taught that perseverance is the essential element in prayer.
> *E. M. Bounds*

PRAISE & THANKSGIVING

Worship by using the name of God mentioned in this Scripture—the "atoning sacrifice."

> *He is the atoning sacrifice for our sins, and not only for ours but also for the sins of the whole world.*
>
> 1 John 2:2

REPENTANCE

Search your heart as you meditate on this Scripture. What is the Holy Spirit revealing to you?

> *Forgive my hidden faults. Keep your servant also from willful sins; may they not rule over me. Then will I be blameless, innocent of great transgression.*
>
> Psalm 19:12–13

ASKING

Read the following Scripture. Rewrite it, personalizing it for missionary children, seeking the Lord regarding forgiveness and restoration.

> *If we walk in the light, as he is in the light, we have fellowship with one another, and the blood of Jesus, his Son, purifies us from all sin. . . . If we confess our sins, he is faithful and just and will forgive us our sins and purify us from all unrighteousness.*
>
> 1 John 1:7, 9

_____

_____

YIELDING

Now meditate on the Scripture again. Rewrite it below, personalizing and praying it for yourself. How can you respond to what God is saying to you in this Scripture?

_____

_____

Pray for missionary work in PUERTO RICO
(Caribbean island, east of the Dominican Republic)

Pray alone. Let prayer be the key of the morning and the bolt at night.
The best way to fight against sin is to fight it on our knees.
Philip Henry

PRAISE & THANKSGIVING

Worship Him as your "atoning sacrifice."

*He is the atoning sacrifice for our sins, and not only for ours but also
for the sins of the whole world.*

1 John 2:2

REPENTANCE

Search your heart as you meditate on this Scripture.

*Forgive my hidden faults. Keep your servant also from willful sins; may they
not rule over me. Then will I be blameless, innocent of great transgression.*

Psalm 19:12–13

ASKING

Rewrite this Scripture, personalizing it for missionary
children, seeking the Lord regarding forgiveness and
restoration.

*Be kind and compassionate to one another, forgiving each other,
just as in Christ God forgave you.*

Ephesians 4:32

_____

_____

_____

_____

YIELDING

Rewrite it again, personalizing and praying it for yourself.
Respond to what God is saying to you in this Scripture.

_____

_____

_____

_____

Pray for missionary work in QATAR
(Middle East, a peninsula bordering the
Persian Gulf and Saudi Arabia)

Holiness is not to love Jesus and do whatever you want.
Holiness is to love God and do what He wants.
C. Peter Wagner

PRAISE & THANKSGIVING

*He is the atoning sacrifice for our sins, and not only for ours but also
for the sins of the whole world.*

1 John 2:2

REPENTANCE

*Forgive my hidden faults. Keep your servant also from willful sins; may they
not rule over me. Then will I be blameless, innocent of great transgression.*

Psalm 19:12–13

ASKING

Personalize this Scripture for missionary children,
rewriting it, seeking the Lord regarding forgiveness.

*If you forgive men when they sin against you, your heavenly Father will
also forgive you. But if you do not forgive men their sins, your Father
will not forgive your sins.*

Matthew 6:14–15

_____

_____

_____

_____

YIELDING

Now personalize and pray it for yourself. How can you
respond to what God is saying to you?

_____

_____

_____

_____

_____

Pray for missionary work in
THE REPUBLIC OF THE CONGO
(Western Africa, between Angola and Gabon)

God uses prayer to educate His people and
to produce holiness of character in them.
Harold Lindsell

PRAISE & THANKSGIVING

He is the atoning sacrifice for our sins, and not only for ours but also
for the sins of the whole world.

1 John 2:2

REPENTANCE

Forgive my hidden faults. Keep your servant also from willful sins; may they
not rule over me. Then will I be blameless, innocent of great transgression.

Psalm 19:12–13

ASKING

Rewrite this Scripture, personalizing it for missionaries.

And the God of all grace, who called you to his eternal glory in Christ,
after you have suffered a little while, will himself restore you and make
you strong, firm and steadfast.

1 Peter 5:10

_____

_____

_____

_____

YIELDING

What is God saying to you in this Scripture?

_____

_____

_____

_____

_____

_____

Pray for missionary work on REUNION
(island in the Indian Ocean, east of Madagascar)

Prayer plumes the wings of God's young eaglets so they may learn to mount above the clouds. Prayer brings inner strength to God's warriors and sends them forth to spiritual battle with their muscles firm and armor in place.
Charles Spurgeon

PRAISE & THANKSGIVING

He is the atoning sacrifice for our sins, and not only for ours but also for the sins of the whole world.
1 John 2:2

REPENTANCE

Forgive my hidden faults. Keep your servant also from willful sins; may they not rule over me. Then will I be blameless, innocent of great transgression.
Psalm 19:12–13

ASKING

Personalize this Scripture today for missionaries.

He restores my soul. He guides me in paths of righteousness for his name's sake.
Psalm 23:3

_____

_____

_____

_____

YIELDING

Personalize and pray this same Scripture for yourself.

_____

_____

_____

_____

_____

_____

_____

Pray for missionary work in ROMANIA
(Southeastern Europe, between Bulgaria and Ukraine)

Week 35
Thoughts and Prayers

Week 36

LOVING GOD

As a missionary kid (MK) in Peru, there are countless fun jobs for kids like me to do year-round. My parents and their team often go on trips to the mountains or to the jungle with volunteer groups from the United States. Peruvian translators are often needed. Taking translators along is good because some of them don't know about Jesus. Every month, missionary teams have English meetings with the translators to help them improve their English.

One opportunity to share Jesus with the translators was an overnight retreat to a mission camp. There were many activities for fellowship among the people who came. There was plenty of work for all the MKs to do, as well. The MKs and their parents used stations to play games such as Simon Says®, Pictionary®, and then an additional station for Bible storying. The MKs ran a snack bar in-between stations and helped aunts and uncles (other missionary adults) lead the games.

In the evening, the MKs helped build a bonfire. As our parents told stories about Jesus Christ, we joined others who were praying that the translators would choose to surrender their life to Jesus. The next morning the group had a time of worship and taught Christian songs and music with tongue twisters to help with English pronunciations.

Soon after the music time, everybody headed home. All in all, it was a rich experience for everyone, and it was a creative way to share a witness with our Peruvian friends.

Rebecca—MISSIONARY KID, SOUTH AMERICA

[Missionary kids are a valuable part of the team as they live out their faith, using their gifts and abilities to share Christ. God will often use the missionary's children to open doors of witness. The children have many unique opportunities and also face many challenges. Pray that they will grow spiritually and trust God to meet their every need.]

Prayer is not a hard requirement—it is the natural duty of a creature to its creator, the simplest homage that human need can pay to divine liberality.
Charles Spurgeon

PRAISE & THANKSGIVING

Worship by using the aspect of God mentioned in this Scripture—"shepherd."

> The LORD is my shepherd, I shall not want.
>> Psalm 23:1 (KJV)

REPENTANCE

Search your heart as you meditate on this Scripture. What is the Holy Spirit revealing to you?

> What does the LORD your God ask of you but to fear the LORD your God, to walk in all his ways, to love him, to serve the LORD your God with all your heart and with all your soul.
>> Deuteronomy 10:12

ASKING

Read the following Scripture. Rewrite it, personalizing it for missionary children, seeking the Lord regarding their love for Him.

> Do not love the world or anything in the world. If anyone loves the world, the love of the Father is not in him. . . . The world and its desires pass away, but the man who does the will of God lives forever.
>> 1 John 2:15, 17

_____

_____

YIELDING

Now meditate on the Scripture again. Rewrite it below, personalizing and praying it for yourself. How can you respond to what God is saying to you in this Scripture?

_____

_____

_____

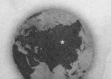

Pray for missionary work in RUSSIA
(Eastern Europe and Northern Asia,
bordering the Arctic Ocean)

> Men ought not to faint because men ought to pray.
> *G. Campbell Morgan*

PRAISE & THANKSGIVING

Worship Him today, for He is your "shepherd."

> *The LORD is my shepherd, I shall not want.*
>
> Psalm 23:1 (KJV)

REPENTANCE

Search your heart as you meditate on this Scripture.

> *What does the LORD your God ask of you but to fear the LORD your God, to walk in all his ways, to love him, to serve the LORD your God with all your heart and with all your soul.*
>
> Deuteronomy 10:12

ASKING

Rewrite this Scripture, personalizing it for missionary children, seeking the Lord regarding their love for Him.

> *This is love for God: to obey his commands. And his commands are not burdensome.*
>
> 1 John 5:3

_____

_____

_____

_____

YIELDING

Rewrite it again, personalizing and praying it for yourself. Respond to what God is saying to you in this Scripture.

_____

_____

_____

_____

_____

Pray for missionary work in RWANDA
(Central Africa, east of the Democratic Republic of the Congo)

Prevailing prayer is prayer that pushes right through all difficulties
and obstacles, drives back all the opposing forces of Satan, and secures
the will of God. Its purpose is to accomplish God's will on earth.
Wesley L. Duewel

PRAISE & THANKSGIVING

The Lord is my shepherd, I shall not want.
   Psalm 23:1 (KJV)

REPENTANCE

What does the Lord your God ask of you but to fear the Lord your God,
to walk in all his ways, to love him, to serve the Lord your God with all
your heart and with all your soul.
   Deuteronomy 10:12

ASKING

Personalize this Scripture for missionary children, rewriting it, seeking the Lord regarding their love for Him.
We, who with unveiled faces all reflect the Lord's glory, are being transformed
into his likeness with ever-increasing glory, which comes from the Lord, who
is the Spirit.
   2 Corinthians 3:18

_____

_____

_____

YIELDING

Now personalize and pray it for yourself. How can you
respond to what God is saying to you?

_____

_____

_____

_____

_____

Pray for missionary work on ST. BARTHELEMY
(Caribbean island, northwest of Guadeloupe)

> I have seen God do more in people's lives during
> ten minutes of real prayer than in ten of my sermons.
> *Jim Cymbala*

PRAISE & THANKSGIVING

The LORD is my shepherd, I shall not want.

Psalm 23:1 (KJV)

REPENTANCE

*What does the LORD your God ask of you but to fear the LORD your God,
to walk in all his ways, to love him, to serve the LORD your God with all
your heart and with all your soul.*

Deuteronomy 10:12

ASKING

Rewrite this Scripture, personalizing it for missionaries.

*I urge you, brothers, in view of God's mercy, to offer your bodies as living sacrifices,
holy and pleasing to God—this is your spiritual act of worship. Do not conform
any longer to the pattern of this world, but be transformed by the renewing of your
mind. Then you will be able to test and approve what God's will is—his good,
pleasing and perfect will.*

Romans 12:1–2

_____

_____

_____

_____

YIELDING

What is God saying to you in this Scripture?

_____

_____

_____

_____

_____

Pray for missionary work on ST. HELENA
(South Atlantic islands, halfway between
South America and Africa)

> No man can do a great and enduring work for God
> who is not a man of prayer, and no man can be a man
> of prayer who does not give much time to praying.
> *E. M. Bounds*

PRAISE & THANKSGIVING

> *The LORD is my shepherd, I shall not want.*
>
> Psalm 23:1 (KJV)

REPENTANCE

> *What does the LORD your God ask of you but to fear the LORD your God,*
> *to walk in all his ways, to love him, to serve the LORD your God with all*
> *your heart and with all your soul.*
>
> Deuteronomy 10:12

ASKING

Personalize this Scripture today for missionaries.

> *I will listen to what God the LORD will say; he promises peace*
> *to his people, his saints.*
>
> Psalm 85:8

_____

_____

_____

_____

YIELDING

Personalize and pray this same Scripture for yourself.

_____

_____

_____

_____

_____

_____

_____

Pray for missionary work on
ST. KITTS and NEVIS
(Caribbean islands, between Puerto Rico and Trinidad)

Week 36
Thoughts and Prayers

Week 37

OBEDIENCE & RESPONSIBILITY

My prayer life has been dramatically changed as a result of something I tried one day while returning home from carpooling kids to school. The drive to or from school takes about twenty minutes when traffic is light, but on normal school mornings in the capital city of Peru, the commute takes at least thirty minutes. On one particular morning, I left the school and immediately was in a long line of slow traffic. Rather than let myself get frustrated, I decided to begin thanking the Lord audibly for everything that came to mind.

Then came an idea: "Why not go through the alphabet praising Him?" I began: "Thank you, Lord . . .

A—for answering my prayers, for Your angels who watch over us, for being Almighty.

B—for always being with me, for being my burden bearer, for Your blessings.

C—for being the Christ, the Anointed One, my Messiah; for Your care; for Your concern for Your people.

D—and so on, and so on . . .

X took me a while, but I began to think about His excellent grace and mercy and His exceeding great love.

Y—that He is Yahweh.

Z—for His zeal on behalf of His people.

By the time I reached home, my heart was overflowing with love and praise for my Lord and the awareness of God's presence. It was such an awesome time with the Savior that I began the "alphabet praise times" often. Soon I began to incorporate them into the beginning moments of my daily devotions.

"Alphabet praise" has transformed my prayer life. It has helped me become much more specific in praising the Lord for who He is and for what He means to me. I am more aware of His presence during the rest of my devotional time and throughout the day. This is one small way I can exalt and glorify His name

Carol—SOUTH AMERICA

> God's children should pray. They should cry day and night
> to Him. God hears every one of your cries in the busy hour
> of the daytime and in the lonely watches of the night.
> *Robert Murray McCheyne*

PRAISE & THANKSGIVING

Worship by using the name of God mentioned in this
Scripture—"my portion."

> *"The LORD is my portion," says my soul, "therefore I have hope in Him.*
> Lamentations 3:24 (NASB)

REPENTANCE

Search your heart as you meditate on this Scripture.
What is the Holy Spirit revealing to you?

> *God is just. . . . He will punish those who do not know God and do not obey*
> *the gospel of our Lord Jesus.*
> 2 Thessalonians 1:6, 8

ASKING

Read the following Scripture. Rewrite it, personalizing
it for missionary children, seeking the Lord regarding
obedience.

> *Children, obey your parents in the Lord, for this is right. "Honor your father*
> *and mother"—which is the first commandment with a promise— "that it may*
> *go well with you and that you may enjoy long life on the earth."*
> Ephesians 6:1–3

_____

_____

_____

YIELDING

Now meditate on the Scripture again. Rewrite it below,
personalizing and praying it for yourself. How can you
respond to what God is saying to you in this Scripture?

_____

_____

Pray for missionary work on ST. LUCIA
(Caribbean island, north of Trinidad and Tobago)

It is not well for a man to pray cream and to live skim milk.
Henry Ward Beecher

PRAISE & THANKSGIVING

Worship Him today—the One who is your "portion."

"The LORD is my portion," says my soul, "therefore I have hope in Him.
Lamentations 3:24 (NASB)

REPENTANCE

Search your heart as you meditate on this Scripture.

God is just. . . . He will punish those who do not know God and do not obey the gospel of our Lord Jesus.
2 Thessalonians 1:6, 8

ASKING

Rewrite this Scripture, personalizing it for missionary children, seeking the Lord regarding obedience.

Whatever we ask we receive from Him, because we keep His commandments and do those things that are pleasing in His sight.
1 John 3:22 (NKJV)

_____

_____

_____

_____

YIELDING

Rewrite it again, personalizing and praying it for yourself. Respond to what God is saying to you in this Scripture.

_____

_____

_____

_____

_____

Pray for missionary work on ST. MARTIN
(Caribbean island, southeast of Puerto Rico)

> God only requires of his adult children, that their hearts be truly purified,
> and that they offer Him continually the wishes and vows that naturally
> spring from perfect love. For these desires . . . are the most perfect prayers.
> *John Wesley*

PRAISE & THANKSGIVING

> *"The LORD is my portion," says my soul, "therefore I have hope in Him.*
> Lamentations 3:24 (NASB)

REPENTANCE

> *God is just. . . . He will punish those who do not know God and do not obey*
> *the gospel of our Lord Jesus.*
> 2 Thessalonians 1:6, 8

ASKING

Personalize this Scripture for missionary children,
rewriting it, seeking the Lord regarding obedience.

> *Teach me, O LORD, to follow your decrees; then I will keep them to the end.*
> *Give me understanding, and I will keep your law and obey it with all my heart.*
> Psalm 119:33–34

_____

_____

_____

_____

YIELDING

Now personalize and pray it for yourself. How can you
respond to what God is saying to you?

_____

_____

_____

_____

_____

Pray for missionary work on
ST. PIERRE and MIQUELON
(Northern North America, south of Newfoundland)

> The prayer of faith is the only power in the universe to which
> the Great Jehovah yields. Prayer is the sovereign remedy.
> *Robert Hall*

PRAISE & THANKSGIVING

"The LORD is my portion," says my soul, "therefore I have hope in Him.
Lamentations 3:24 (NASB)

REPENTANCE

God is just. . . . He will punish those who do not know God and do not obey
the gospel of our Lord Jesus.
2 Thessalonians 1:6, 8

ASKING

Rewrite this Scripture, personalizing it for missionaries.
Whoever claims to live in him must walk as Jesus did.
1 John 2:6

_____

_____

_____

_____

YIELDING

What is God saying to you in this Scripture?

_____

_____

_____

_____

_____

_____

_____

_____

Pray for missionary work on ST. VINCENT
(Caribbean island, north of Trinidad and Tobago)

A prayer meeting is an index to the state of religion in a church.
Charles G. Finney

PRAISE & THANKSGIVING

"The LORD is my portion," says my soul, "therefore I have hope in Him.
Lamentations 3:24 (NASB)

REPENTANCE

God is just. . . . He will punish those who do not know God and do not obey the gospel of our Lord Jesus.
2 Thessalonians 1:6, 8

ASKING

Personalize this Scripture today for missionaries.
Guard my life and rescue me; let me not be put to shame, for I take refuge in you. May integrity and uprightness protect me, because my hope is in you.
Psalm 25:20–21

_____

_____

_____

_____

YIELDING

Personalize and pray this same Scripture for yourself.

_____

_____

_____

_____

_____

_____

_____

_____

Pray for missionary work on SAMOA
(South Pacific islands, halfway between Hawaii
and New Zealand)

Week 37
Thoughts and Prayers

_____

_____

_____

_____

_____

_____

_____

_____

_____

_____

_____

_____

_____

_____

_____

_____

_____

_____

_____

_____

_____

_____

_____

_____

_____

Week 38

PRAYER FOR PARENTS

The more I read, the greater my fears grew. Appointed as a new missionary to Guyana, I had searched the encyclopedia for information about this small South American country. Since we had four little girls, I was anxious about where they would be raised. I read about the tropical rain forest filled with wild animals and snakes. These images brought to mind tropical diseases and the lack of good medical care.

One night when my husband was traveling, I read Isaiah 55:12—"You will go out in joy and be led forth in peace; the mountains and hills will burst into song before you, and all the trees of the field will clap their hands." This love letter was addressed to me, and the promise erased my fear. I realized I was reading the wrong book.

As we moved to Guyana, the joy and peace of Jesus accompanied us. God's promise of a harvest was ever true, and even the clapping of the trees became a reality.

Years into our missionary career, and a continent away, we were beginning work for a new church in a village hostile toward Christians. City officials would not even allow us to rent a building. We began the first service sitting under a large tree. There was a lot of heckling going on. As the noisy service progressed, a woman whispered to me, "Did you hear that clapping?" Suddenly, stillness came over the crowd, and—yes—I distinctly heard soft clapping. As a light breeze blew, the wind caused the leaves on our sheltering tree to sound like soft applause. What an answer to prayer! It was as if we'd experienced the visible presence of the Holy Spirit.

Are we amazed that God keeps every promise? As we "go out in joy," He provides the peace, and even confirms His presence to the ends of the earth.

Charlene—SOUTH AMERICA AND SOUTH ASIA

The spirit of prayer is more precious than treasures of gold and silver.
John Bunyan

PRAISE & THANKSGIVING

Worship by using the characteristic of God mentioned
in this Scripture—"exalted."

> Let them praise the name of the LORD, for His name alone is exalted;
> His glory is above earth and heaven.

Psalm 148:13 (NASB)

REPENTANCE

Search your heart as you meditate on this Scripture.
What is the Holy Spirit revealing to you?

> This is what the Sovereign LORD, the Holy One of Israel, says: "In repentance
> and rest is your salvation, in quietness and trust is your strength."

Isaiah 30:15

ASKING

Read the following Scripture. Rewrite it, personalizing
it for missionary children, the way they might pray it
for their parents.

> Blessed is the man who finds wisdom, the man who gains understanding,
> for she is more profitable than silver and yields better returns than gold.
> She is more precious than rubies; nothing you desire can compare with her.

Proverbs 3:13–15

_____

_____

_____

YIELDING

Now meditate on the Scripture again. Rewrite it below,
personalizing and praying it for yourself. How can you
respond to what God is saying to you in this Scripture?

_____

_____

_____

Pray for missionary work on SAN MARINO
(Southern Europe, an enclave in central Italy)

> As white snowflakes fall quietly and thickly on a winter day, answers to prayer will settle down upon you at every step you take, even to your dying day. The story of your life will be the story of prayer and answers to prayer.
> *O. Hallesby*

PRAISE & THANKSGIVING

Worship Him today—the One who is "exalted."

> *Let them praise the name of the LORD, for His name alone is exalted;*
> *His glory is above earth and heaven.*
> Psalm 148:13 (NASB)

REPENTANCE

Search your heart as you meditate on this Scripture.

> *This is what the Sovereign LORD, the Holy One of Israel, says: "In repentance and rest is your salvation, in quietness and trust is your strength."*
> Isaiah 30:15

ASKING

Rewrite this Scripture, personalizing it for missionary children, the way they might pray it for their parents.

> *Jesus replied: "'Love the Lord your God with all your heart and with all your soul and with all your mind.'"*
> Matthew 22:37

_____
_____
_____
_____

YIELDING

Rewrite it again, personalizing and praying it for yourself. Respond to what God is saying to you in this Scripture.

_____
_____
_____
_____

Pray for missionary work on
SAO TOME AND PRINCIPE
(Western Africa, islands in the Gulf of Guinea, on the equator)

> The prayer that sparks revival begins long before
> the countryside seems to awaken from its slumber in sin.
> It starts when men fall on their knees and cry out to God.
> *Wellington Boone*

PRAISE & THANKSGIVING

Let them praise the name of the LORD, for His name alone is exalted;
His glory is above earth and heaven.

    Psalm 148:13 (NASB)

REPENTANCE

Those who hope in the LORD will renew their strength. They will soar on wings
like eagles; they will run and not grow weary, they will walk and not be faint.

    Isaiah 40:31

ASKING

Personalize this Scripture for missionary children,
rewriting it, the way they might pray it for their parents.

Teach me, O LORD, to follow your decrees; then I will keep them to the end.
Give me understanding, and I will keep your law and obey it with all my heart.

    Psalm 119:33–34

_____

_____

_____

_____

YIELDING

Now personalize and pray it for yourself. How can you
respond to what God is saying to you?

_____

_____

_____

_____

Pray for missionary work in SAUDI ARABIA
(Middle East, bordering the Persian Gulf and the Red Sea)

> The more helpless you are, the better you are fitted to pray,
> and the more answers to prayer you will experience.
> *O. Hallesby*

PRAISE & THANKSGIVING

Let them praise the name of the LORD, for His name alone is exalted;
His glory is above earth and heaven.

Psalm 148:13 (NASB)

REPENTANCE

Those who hope in the LORD will renew their strength. They will soar on wings
like eagles; they will run and not grow weary, they will walk and not be faint.

Isaiah 40:31

ASKING

Rewrite this Scripture, personalizing it for missionaries.

And so we know and rely on the love God has for us.

1 John 4:16

_____

_____

_____

YIELDING

What is God saying to you in this Scripture?

_____

_____

_____

_____

_____

_____

_____

_____

Pray for missionary work in SENEGAL
(Western Africa, between Guinea-Bissau and Mauritania)

> Jesus Christ carries on intercession for us in heaven;
> the Holy Ghost carries on intercession in us on earth;
> and we the saints have to carry on intercession for all men.
> *Oswald Chambers*

PRAISE & THANKSGIVING

> *Let them praise the name of the LORD, for His name alone is exalted;*
> *His glory is above earth and heaven.*
> Psalm 148:13 (NASB)

REPENTANCE

> *Those who hope in the LORD will renew their strength. They will soar on wings*
> *like eagles; they will run and not grow weary, they will walk and not be faint.*
> Isaiah 40:31

ASKING

Personalize this Scripture today for missionaries.

> *May the God of peace, who through the blood of the eternal covenant brought back*
> *from the dead our Lord Jesus, that great Shepherd of the sheep, equip you with*
> *everything good for doing his will, and may he work in us what is pleasing to him,*
> *through Jesus Christ, to whom be glory for ever and ever. Amen.*
> Hebrews 13:20–21

_____

_____

_____

_____

YIELDING

Personalize and pray this same Scripture for yourself.

_____

_____

_____

_____

_____

Pray for missionary work in SERBIA
(Southeastern Europe, between Macedonia and Hungary)

Week 38
Thoughts and Prayers

_____

_____

_____

_____

_____

_____

_____

_____

_____

_____

_____

_____

_____

_____

_____

_____

_____

_____

_____

_____

_____

_____

_____

_____

_____

_____

_____

Week 39

PROTECTION

We were accustomed to the frequent sound of gunshots. Our house faced the naval academy firing range in La Paz, Bolivia. But something about this sound was different.

I sat at my desk working on my Sunday school lesson and praising God for the many blessings of the week. Just the ability to prepare a lesson in Spanish was a reason to rejoice. I was still a language learner.

As I prayed about the upcoming week, I suddenly heard a tremendous "boom." It shook the whole house.

Jumping to my feet, I rushed to the kitchen where my daughter Laura was preparing lunch. When I opened the kitchen door, I immediately smelled the gas fumes. When Laura saw me, she burst into tears. Then she told me what happened. An open gas valve on the oven had gone unnoticed, and the kitchen had filled with fumes. When Laura had hit the ignite switch, all she remembered was a loud "boom." I found her standing several feet across the room from the oven, but she didn't remember how she got there. Amazingly, only a few singed hairs on her eyebrows and arms resulted from the explosion.

I stood in my kitchen praising God for her safety, and I immediately thought of the Father's protection. We pray for God's provision for our children, but we don't always realize how often He answers our prayers. At other times we clearly see His protection, and we breathe a word of "thanks" to God. That day in La Paz was one of those times. I praise God for the many times He surrounds us—and our children—with His angels and His protective hand of love.

Debbie—SOUTH AMERICA

> We don't have praying churches, just praying
> people who make up praying churches.
> *Anonymous*

PRAISE & THANKSGIVING

Worship by using the name of God mentioned in
this Scripture—"your keeper."

> *The LORD is your keeper; the LORD is your shade on your right hand.*
> Psalm 121:5 (NASB)

REPENTANCE

Search your heart as you meditate on this Scripture.
What is the Holy Spirit revealing to you?

> *Do not forsake wisdom, and she will protect you;*
> *love her, and she will watch over you.*
> Proverbs 4:6

ASKING

Read the following Scripture. Rewrite it, personalizing
it for missionary children, seeking the Lord for protection.

> *The LORD watches over you— the LORD is your shade at your right hand;*
> *the sun will not harm you by day, nor the moon by night. The LORD will keep*
> *you from all harm— he will watch over your life; the LORD will watch over*
> *your coming and going both now and forevermore.*
> Psalm 121:5–8

_____

_____

_____

YIELDING

Now meditate on the Scripture again. Rewrite it below,
personalizing and praying it for yourself. How can you
respond to what God is saying to you in this Scripture?

_____

_____

_____

Pray for missionary work in THE SEYCHELLES
(islands in the Indian Ocean, northeast of Madagascar)

It is always too soon to quit praying, even when
praying is the last thing we seem able to do.
Harold Lindsell

PRAISE & THANKSGIVING

Worship Him today, for He is your "keeper."

The LORD is your keeper; the LORD is your shade on your right hand.

Psalm 121:5 (NASB)

REPENTANCE

Search your heart as you meditate on this Scripture.

Do not forsake wisdom, and she will protect you;
love her, and she will watch over you.

Proverbs 4:6

ASKING

Rewrite this Scripture, personalizing it for missionary
children, seeking the Lord for their protection.

The LORD will protect him and preserve his life; he will bless him in the land
and not surrender him to the desire of his foes.

Psalm 41:2

_____

_____

_____

_____

YIELDING

Rewrite it again, personalizing and praying it for yourself.
Respond to what God is saying to you in this Scripture.

_____

_____

_____

_____

_____

Pray for missionary work in SIERRA LEONE
(Western Africa, between Guinea and Liberia)

> Prayer is the answer to every problem there is.
> *Oswald Chambers*

PRAISE & THANKSGIVING

> *The LORD is your keeper; the LORD is your shade on your right hand.*
>
> Psalm 121:5 (NASB)

REPENTANCE

> *Do not forsake wisdom, and she will protect you;*
> *love her, and she will watch over you.*
>
> Proverbs 4:6

ASKING

Personalize this Scripture for missionary children, rewriting it, seeking the Lord for their protection.

> *Teach me, O LORD, to follow your decrees; then I will keep them to the end.*
> *Give me understanding, and I will keep your law and obey it with all my heart.*
>
> Psalm 119:33–34

_____

_____

_____

_____

YIELDING

Now personalize and pray it for yourself. How can you respond to what God is saying to you?

_____

_____

_____

_____

_____

_____

Pray for missionary work in SINGAPORE
(Southeastern Asia, islands between Malaysia and Indonesia)

A life growing in its purity and devotion will be a more prayerful life.
E. M. Bounds

PRAISE & THANKSGIVING

The LORD is your keeper; the LORD is your shade on your right hand.
Psalm 121:5 (NASB)

REPENTANCE

Do not forsake wisdom, and she will protect you;
love her, and she will watch over you.
Proverbs 4:6

ASKING

Rewrite this Scripture, personalizing it for missionaries.
My prayer is not that you take them out of the world but that you protect them
from the evil one.
John 17:15

_____

_____

_____

_____

YIELDING

What is God saying to you in this Scripture?

_____

_____

_____

_____

_____

_____

_____

_____

Pray for missionary work in SLOVAKIA
(Central Europe, south of Poland)

In spite of Satan, pray; spend hours in prayer; rather neglect
friends than not pray; rather fast and lose breakfast,
dinner, tea, and supper—and sleep too—than not pray.
Andrew A. Bonar

PRAISE & THANKSGIVING

The LORD is your keeper; the LORD is your shade on your right hand.
Psalm 121:5 (NASB)

REPENTANCE

Do not forsake wisdom, and she will protect you;
love her, and she will watch over you.

Proverbs 4:6

ASKING

Personalize this Scripture today for missionaries.

Now may the Lord of peace himself give you peace at all times and in every way.
The Lord be with all of you.

2 Thessalonians 3:16

_____

_____

_____

_____

YIELDING

Personalize and pray this same Scripture for yourself.

_____

_____

_____

_____

_____

_____

_____

Pray for missionary work in SLOVENIA
(Central Europe, between Austria and Croatia)

Week 39
Thoughts and Prayers

_____

_____

_____

_____

_____

_____

_____

_____

_____

_____

_____

_____

_____

_____

_____

_____

_____

_____

_____

_____

_____

_____

_____

_____

_____

_____

Week 40

PURITY

Called out to teach among indigenous people in the jungles of South America, I didn't realize all God would teach me. I knew life in the Amazon would be hard, but as a former Marine I had trained to endure tough times. This experience, however, proved to be the greatest test of my life. I soon learned God had many lessons for this young missionary to learn.

The night before boarding a plane to Peru, God prompted me to read Psalm 126:5–6. "Those who sow in tears will reap with songs of joy. He who goes out weeping, carrying seed to sow, will return with songs of joy, carrying sheaves with him."

After fifteen months in the jungle, the words of that psalm took on new meaning. The challenges were great and at times overwhelming. My ministry required learning two languages—neither one was English. I was adapting to a new culture and serving with a team. Teamwork was essential to accomplish the task before me. I had so much to learn. Could I do this?

We all face challenges in life, but the key is in what we will learn from them. Will we stand strong in the face of adversity, or choose anger in our pain? The daily trials were real, but I knew the Lord had called me to this place to serve, in spite of myself—a sinner saved by grace.

One afternoon, I cried out to the Lord in my frustration, "Why don't you just give up on me?" Heading out the door for a game of volleyball, I remember walking across my room to shut down my stereo. And there it was! The view from my window revealed the most magnificent rainbow I had ever seen. But the frame of my window was too small. Running outside, I could see the full array of the rainbow's color and I heard the still, small voice of God say, "I love you, son. I will never give up on you."

How unworthy I was to be loved by such a great God. The Almighty Creator was revealing Himself to a simple servant in the jungles of Peru. His unspoken words were majestically revealed: "I love you, and I am always with you."

Could it be that God brought me here for such a time as this? Did my desperation and loneliness, far away from my busy life in the United States, finally allow me to hear the still, small voice of God? Yes, I would teach among the peoples of Peru, but I would leave the jungle forever changed—touched by the hand of God.

The frame of my window on life is often too small for the unimaginable blessings He has prepared. Tears become joy as God molds us into instruments pure and holy, worthy of a Master's hand.

Marshall—SOUTH AMERICA

> Prayer is repeating the victor's name into the
> ears of Satan and insisting on his retreat.
> *S. D. Gordon*

PRAISE & THANKSGIVING

Worship by using the name of God mentioned in
this Scripture—"maker of all things."

> *I, the LORD, am the maker of all things, stretching out the heavens*
> *by Myself and spreading out the earth all alone.*
>
> Isaiah 44:24 (NASB)

REPENTANCE

Search your heart as you meditate on this Scripture.
What is the Holy Spirit revealing to you?

> *We know that when he appears, we shall be like him, for we shall see him as he is.*
> *Everyone who has this hope in him purifies himself, just as he is pure.*
>
> 1 John 3:2–3

ASKING

Read the following Scripture. Rewrite it, personalizing it
for missionary children, seeking the Lord for their purity.

> *This is my prayer: that your love may abound more and more in knowledge and*
> *depth of insight, so that you may be able to discern what is best and may be pure*
> *and blameless until the day of Christ.*
>
> Philippians 1:9–10

_____

_____

YIELDING

Now meditate on the Scripture again. Rewrite it below,
personalizing and praying it for yourself. How can you
respond to what God is saying to you in this Scripture?

_____

_____

_____

_____

Pray for missionary work on
THE SOLOMON ISLANDS
(South Pacific islands, east of Papua New Guinea)

All the mighty interceding of the ages that has ever shaken the
kingdom of darkness has been based upon the promises of God.
Arthur Wallis

PRAISE & THANKSGIVING

Worship Him today—the "maker of all things."

*I, the LORD, am the maker of all things, stretching out the heavens
by Myself and spreading out the earth all alone.*

Isaiah 44:24 (NASB)

REPENTANCE

Search your heart as you meditate on this Scripture.

*We know that when he appears, we shall be like him, for we shall see him as he is.
Everyone who has this hope in him purifies himself, just as he is pure.*

1 John 3:2–3

ASKING

Rewrite this Scripture, personalizing it for missionary
children, seeking the Lord for their purity.

*Rather, clothe yourselves with the Lord Jesus Christ, and do not think about
how to gratify the desires of the sinful nature.*

Romans 13:14

_____

_____

_____

_____

YIELDING

Rewrite it again, personalizing and praying it for yourself.
Respond to what God is saying to you in this Scripture.

_____

_____

_____

_____

Pray for missionary work in SOMALIA
(Eastern Africa, on the Indian Ocean, east of Ethiopia)

> Inarticulate prayer, the impulsive prayer that looks so futile,
> is the thing God always heeds. The habit of ejaculatory
> prayer ought to be the persistent habit of each one of us.
> *Oswald Chambers*

PRAISE & THANKSGIVING

> *I, the LORD, am the maker of all things, stretching out the heavens*
> *by Myself and spreading out the earth all alone.*
>
> Isaiah 44:24 (NASB)

REPENTANCE

> *We know that when he appears, we shall be like him, for we shall see him as he is.*
> *Everyone who has this hope in him purifies himself, just as he is pure.*
>
> 1 John 3:2–3

ASKING

Personalize this Scripture for missionary children,
rewriting it, seeking the Lord regarding their purity.

> *Flee from sexual immorality. All other sins a man commits are outside*
> *his body, but he who sins sexually sins against his own body. Do you not*
> *know that your body is a temple of the Holy Spirit, who is in you, whom*
> *you have received from God? You are not your own; you were bought*
> *at a price. Therefore honor God with your body.*
>
> 1 Corinthians 6:18–20

_____

_____

_____

YIELDING

Now personalize and pray it for yourself. How can you
respond to what God is saying to you?

_____

_____

_____

_____

Pray for missionary work in SOUTH AFRICA
(Southern Africa, at the southern tip of the continent)

The place of real prayer is the Christian's treasure chamber.
He is there in the midst of the treasures of grace which God has
given him, and it is there that God enriches him more and more.
Amzi Clarence Dixon

PRAISE & THANKSGIVING

I, the LORD, am the maker of all things, stretching out the heavens
by Myself and spreading out the earth all alone.

Isaiah 44:24 (NASB)

REPENTANCE

We know that when he appears, we shall be like him, for we shall see him as he is.
Everyone who has this hope in him purifies himself, just as he is pure.

1 John 3:2–3

ASKING

Rewrite this Scripture, personalizing it for missionaries.

It gave me great joy to have some brothers come and tell about your faithfulness
to the truth and how you continue to walk in the truth. I have no greater joy
than to hear that my children are walking in the truth.

3 John 3–4

_____

_____

_____

_____

YIELDING

What is God saying to you in this Scripture?

_____

_____

_____

_____

_____

_____

Pray for missionary work in SOUTH KOREA
(Eastern Asia, bordering the Sea of Japan and the Yellow Sea)

> Our prayers are heard, not because we are in earnest,
> not because we suffer, but because Jesus suffered.
>
> *Oswald Chambers*

PRAISE & THANKSGIVING

> *I, the LORD, am the maker of all things, stretching out the heavens*
> *by Myself and spreading out the earth all alone.*
>
> Isaiah 44:24 (NASB)

REPENTANCE

> *We know that when he appears, we shall be like him, for we shall see him as he is.*
> *Everyone who has this hope in him purifies himself, just as he is pure.*
>
> 1 John 3:2–3

ASKING

Personalize this Scripture today for missionaries.

> *Since we have these promises, dear friends, let us purify ourselves from everything*
> *that contaminates body and spirit, perfecting holiness out of reverence for God.*
>
> 2 Corinthians 7:1

_____

_____

_____

_____

_____

YIELDING

Personalize and pray this same Scripture for yourself.

_____

_____

_____

_____

_____

_____

_____

Pray for missionary work in SOUTHERN SUDAN
(Northern Africa, a region of Sudan comprising
ten of its provinces)

Week 40
Thoughts and Prayers

Week 41

RELATIONSHIPS

God has an amazing way of working through circumstances only He can divinely ordain.

On December 29, 2002, my family was driving to Virginia after spending Christmas in Texas. Car trouble delayed our return, and we were sitting in an auto repair shop on December 30 when we heard the tragic news of three missionaries killed in Yemen. Early reports confirmed our fears that our dear friend Kathy Gariety was among the dead.

We arrived home later that night and listened to updates from Yemen as we unloaded our car. We returned home with boxes that had been stored in the attic of family members while we lived overseas. The forgotten memories were of special interest to my daughters. I watched the news as they sorted through boxes.

Lesley, my youngest daughter, found a small, yellow piece of paper in her memory box. "Happy Gram" was written at the top, then a scripture from Isaiah 40:29 (KJV): "He giveth power to the faint, and to them that have no might He increaseth strength." A short prayer ended the note: "Dear Jesus, help me walk in the courage of my faith."

As I glanced at the note, Lesley said, "Mom, turn the paper over and read the other side." These words were written on the back: From Kathy Gariety, May 1992.

In 1992, my family went through missionary appointment and orientation with Kathy. Now, ten years later, God allowed us to find this small note on the day of her death. It was God's perfect timing that orchestrated the events that led my daughter to go through an old box of memories on that particular day. A note written to encourage a missionary kid (MK) at age nine was now a testimony to a young adult MK and her family of God's power for the faint and His strength for those who have no might.

That same evening, Kathy's brother was interviewed on national news. He said that Kathy's love for the children kept her in Yemen. I believe her love for children and for God was far greater than any fear. Kathy Gariety, Martha Myers, and Bill Koehn all died that day in Yemen. They each walked in the courage of their faith.

"Though the mountains be shaken and the hills be removed, yet my unfailing love for you will not be shaken nor my covenant of peace be removed," says the LORD, who has compassion on you. (Isa. 54:10)

Debbie—SOUTH AMERICA

> We like the company of men more than the
> company of God. . . . We love to play more than pray.
> *Leonard Ravenhill*

PRAISE & THANKSGIVING

Worship by using the name of God mentioned in
this Scripture—"my fortress."

> *I will say of the LORD, "He is my refuge
> and my fortress, my God, in whom I trust."*
>
> Psalm 91:2

REPENTANCE

Search your heart as you meditate on this Scripture.
What is the Holy Spirit revealing to you?

> *He who walks with the wise grows wise, but a companion of fools suffers harm.*
>
> Proverbs 13:20

ASKING

Read the following Scripture. Rewrite it, personalizing it
for missionary children, seeking the Lord for their various
relationships.

> *Do not be yoked together with unbelievers. For what do righteousness and
> wickedness have in common? Or what fellowship can light have with darkness?
> What harmony is there between Christ and Belial? What does a believer
> have in common with an unbeliever?*
>
> 2 Corinthians 6:14–15

_____

_____

YIELDING

Now meditate on the Scripture again. Rewrite it below,
personalizing and praying it for yourself. How can you
respond to what God is saying to you in this Scripture?

_____

_____

_____

Pray for missionary work in SPAIN
(Southwestern Europe, southwest of France)

Prayer is the key to success. Not to pray is to fail.
To pray aright is never to fail.

Amzi Clarence Dixon

PRAISE & THANKSGIVING

Worship Him today, for He is your "fortress."

I will say of the LORD, "He is my refuge
and my fortress, my God, in whom I trust."

Psalm 91:2

REPENTANCE

Search your heart as you meditate on this Scripture.

He who walks with the wise grows wise, but a companion of fools suffers harm.

Proverbs 13:20

ASKING

Rewrite this Scripture, personalizing it for missionary
children, seeking the Lord for their relationships.

Don't fool yourselves. Bad friends will destroy you.

1 Corinthians 15:33 (CEV)

_____

_____

_____

_____

YIELDING

Rewrite it again, personalizing and praying it for yourself.
Respond to what God is saying to you in this Scripture.

_____

_____

_____

_____

_____

_____

Pray for missionary work in SRI LANKA
(Southern Asia, island in the Indian Ocean, south of India)

God answers prayer on the ground of redemption and on no other ground.
Oswald Chambers

PRAISE & THANKSGIVING

I will say of the LORD, "He is my refuge
and my fortress, my God, in whom I trust."
Psalm 91:2

REPENTANCE

He who walks with the wise grows wise, but a companion of fools suffers harm.
Proverbs 13:20

ASKING

Personalize this Scripture for missionary children,
rewriting it, seeking the Lord for their relationships.

Don't be tempted by sinners or listen [to them].
Proverbs 1:10 (CEV)

_____

_____

_____

_____

YIELDING

Now personalize and pray it for yourself. How can you
respond to what God is saying to you?

_____

_____

_____

_____

_____

_____

_____

_____

Pray for missionary work in SUDAN
(Northern Africa, between Egypt and Eritrea)

> God does nothing but by prayer, and everything with it.
> *John Wesley*

PRAISE & THANKSGIVING

I will say of the LORD, "He is my refuge
and my fortress, my God, in whom I trust."
    Psalm 91:2

REPENTANCE

He who walks with the wise grows wise, but a companion of fools suffers harm.
    Proverbs 13:20

ASKING

Rewrite this Scripture, personalizing it for missionaries.

Be completely humble and gentle; be patient, bearing with one another in love.
    Ephesians 4:2

_____

_____

_____

_____

YIELDING

What is God saying to you in this Scripture?

_____

_____

_____

_____

_____

_____

_____

_____

Pray for missionary work in SURINAME
(Northern South America, between French Guiana and Guyana)

> Next to the wonder of seeing my Savior will be, I think,
> the wonder that I made so little use of the power of prayer.
> *Dwight L. Moody*

PRAISE & THANKSGIVING

> *I will say of the LORD, "He is my refuge*
> *and my fortress, my God, in whom I trust."*
> Psalm 91:2

REPENTANCE

> *He who walks with the wise grows wise, but a companion of fools suffers harm.*
> Proverbs 13:20

ASKING

Personalize this Scripture today for missionaries.

> *I pray that you may be active in sharing your faith, so that you will have*
> *a full understanding of every good thing we have in Christ.*
> Philemon 6

_____

_____

_____

_____

YIELDING

Personalize and pray this same Scripture for yourself.

_____

_____

_____

_____

_____

_____

_____

_____

Pray for missionary work in SVALBARD
(Northern Europe, islands north of Norway)

Thoughts and Prayers

_____

_____

_____

_____

_____

_____

_____

_____

_____

_____

_____

_____

_____

_____

_____

_____

_____

_____

_____

_____

_____

_____

_____

_____

_____

_____

_____

_____

Week 42

SPIRITUAL GROWTH

When we moved to South Asia, we went as a family of seven: my husband, five children ages five to ten, and myself. Being a homeschooling, lover-of-learning Mom, I thought, what a great field trip! The Taj Mahal, Gandhi, Mother Teresa! Our children would experience the culture as they studied it. I could hardly wait to see their eyes shine with the delight of learning.

After a year and a half in South Asia, some of my highest hopes and educational goals were realized. Simultaneously, some of my ideas laid trampled under the stress and adjustment of living in a new culture. The issues we faced include ways you can pray for missionary kids and families.

· *Breaks will be needed for illness.* As our bodies adjusted to the new environment, there was an increase in illnesses. We were encountering a new set of germs, diseases, and often less than standard drinking water. We had to learn to be flexible with our yearly schedule when we encountered frequent physical delays. How did God answer prayer? Just before we moved here, a new clinic opened that provided quality medical care.

· *Temperature changes put a real drain on energy levels.* We moved here from a climate with four distinct seasons to a year-round tropical climate. Heat and humidity, combined with newly developed allergies, often made us feel like we were moving in slow motion. Our children needed an extra dose of grace for days when they did not feel like doing anything. How did God answer prayer? The Lord provided an inverter that allows our fans to run even when the electricity is out. The movement of air is a huge help!

· *Our family needed to be prepared to deal with the ugly things that are part of every culture.* Along with the beautiful tourist sites, there was the daily challenge of addressing issues of poverty. We asked our prayer network to pray for a way to address those who approached us at stoplights. We needed a system that would help meet the need but not contribute to the problem. We decided to put small snack bags in our glove compartment. When we were approached at stoplights by needy children or a handicapped adult, we gave them food. How did God answer prayer? We have learned to speak in their heart language. We can tell them we are giving in the name of Jesus.

· *No matter how enthusiastic I was about our new culture, I had to realize there were times when our children needed a break from their adopted culture.* The issues of discomfort are different in each culture. For our children, it was the staring, pinches to the cheek, and being picked up by strangers. These experiences were outside my children's comfort level. There is not much enthusiasm for a field trip to a museum or the oldest market area in the city when they anticipate such discomfort. How did God answer prayer? We asked for much prayer regarding our children. Now we love to watch them run and play in the parks interacting with everyone.

It may not seem like it would ever be a good idea to live in an international setting. But the fact is that sometimes, as adults, we feel God directing us to make such a move. The right response is always obedience. Thankfully, God's Word encourages us in our daily walk.

Sherra—South Asia

> Quit playing, start praying. Quit feasting, start fasting.
> Talk less with men, talk more with God.
> *Leonard Ravenhill*

PRAISE & THANKSGIVING

Worship by using the aspect of God mentioned in this Scripture—"stronghold."

> *The LORD is good, a stronghold in the day of trouble, and He knows those who take refuge in Him.*
>
> Nahum 1:7 (NASB)

REPENTANCE

Search your heart as you meditate on this Scripture. What is the Holy Spirit revealing to you?

> *But the seed on good soil stands for those with a noble and good heart, who hear the word, retain it, and by persevering produce a crop.*
>
> Luke 8:15

ASKING

Read the following Scripture. Rewrite it, personalizing it for missionary children, seeking the Lord for their spiritual growth.

> *Speaking the truth in love, we will in all things grow up into him who is the Head, that is, Christ. From him the whole body, joined and held together by every supporting ligament, grows and builds itself up in love, as each part does its work.*
>
> Ephesians 4:15–16

_____

_____

YIELDING

Now meditate on the Scripture again. Rewrite it below, personalizing and praying it for yourself. How can you respond to what God is saying to you in this Scripture?

_____

_____

_____

Pray for missionary work in SWAZILAND
(Southern Africa, between Mozambique and South Africa)

> It is a tremendously hard thing to pray aright,
> yea, it is verily the science of all sciences.
>
> *Martin Luther*

PRAISE & THANKSGIVING

Worship Him today, for He is your "stronghold."

The LORD is good, a stronghold in the day of trouble, and He knows those
who take refuge in Him.

Nahum 1:7 (NASB)

REPENTANCE

Search your heart as you meditate on this Scripture.

But the seed on good soil stands for those with a noble and good heart,
who hear the word, retain it, and by persevering produce a crop.

Luke 8:15

ASKING

Rewrite this Scripture, personalizing it for missionary
children, seeking the Lord for their spiritual growth.

Teach me your ways, O LORD, that I may live according to your truth!
Grant me purity of heart, that I may honor you. With all my heart I will
praise you, O Lord my God. I will give glory to your name forever.

Psalm 86:11–12 (NLT)

_____

_____

_____

YIELDING

Rewrite it again, personalizing and praying it for yourself.
Respond to what God is saying to you in this Scripture.

_____

_____

_____

_____

Pray for missionary work in SWEDEN
(Northern Europe, between Finland and Norway)

Before you intercede, be quiet first, and worship God in His glory. Think of what He can do, and how He delights to hear the prayers of His redeemed people. Think of your place and privilege in Christ, and expect great things!
Andrew Murray

PRAISE & THANKSGIVING

> *The LORD is good, a stronghold in the day of trouble, and He knows those who take refuge in Him.*
>
> Nahum 1:7 (NASB)

REPENTANCE

> *The name of the LORD is a strong tower; the righteous run to it and are safe.*
>
> Proverbs 18:10

ASKING

Personalize this Scripture for missionary children, rewriting it, seeking the Lord for their strength.

> *Even youths grow tired and weary, and young men stumble and fall; but those who hope in the LORD will renew their strength. They will soar on wings like eagles; they will run and not grow weary, they will walk and not be faint.*
>
> Isaiah 40:30–31

_____

_____

_____

_____

YIELDING

Now personalize and pray it for yourself. How can you respond to what God is saying to you?

_____

_____

_____

_____

Pray for missionary work in SWITZERLAND
(Central Europe, east of France, north of Italy)

> The devil is not put to flight by a courteous request.
> He meets us at every turn, contends for every inch, and
> our progress has to be registered in heart's blood and tears.
> *Mrs. Charles E. Cowman*

PRAISE & THANKSGIVING

*The LORD is good, a stronghold in the day of trouble, and He knows those
who take refuge in Him.*

 Nahum 1:7 (NASB)

REPENTANCE

The name of the LORD is a strong tower; the righteous run to it and are safe.

 Proverbs 18:10

ASKING

Rewrite this Scripture, personalizing it for missionaries.

*I love you, O LORD, my strength. The LORD is my rock, my fortress and
my deliverer; my God is my rock, in whom I take refuge. He is my shield
and the horn of my salvation, my stronghold. I call to the LORD, who is
worthy of praise, and I am saved from my enemies.*

 Psalm 18:1–3

_____

_____

_____

_____

_____

YIELDING

What is God saying to you in this Scripture?

_____

_____

_____

_____

_____

Pray for missionary work in SYRIA
(Middle East, between Lebanon and Turkey)

We usually pray more for things than we do for men.
Our prayers should be thrown across their pathway
as they rush in their downward course to a lost eternity.
E. M. Bounds

PRAISE & THANKSGIVING

The LORD is good, a stronghold in the day of trouble, and He knows those
who take refuge in Him.

Nahum 1:7 (NASB)

REPENTANCE

Be sure to fear the LORD and serve him faithfully with all your heart;
consider what great things he has done for you.

1 Samuel 12:24

ASKING

Personalize this Scripture today for missionaries.

When I am afraid, I will trust in you. In God, whose word I praise,
in God I trust; I will not be afraid. What can mortal man do to me?

Psalm 56:3–4

_____

_____

_____

_____

YIELDING

Personalize and pray this same Scripture for yourself.

_____

_____

_____

_____

_____

_____

Pray for missionary work in TAIWAN
(Eastern Asia, islands off the southeastern coast of China)

Week 42
Thoughts and Prayers

Week 43

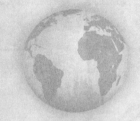

WHEN THEY'RE AWAY

My heart was heavy about our son leaving for college in the United States, 12,000 miles away. I asked friends in the States to pray with me that God would work a peace in my heart concerning this. I knew my son would go when someone said, "Let's go!"

I had already spent time teaching him to separate colors from whites for laundry and how to sew on a button. But what about all the rest, Lord?

In my morning quiet time I was reading through the book of Jeremiah. God gave me a verse that comforted and strengthened me. He gave me the peace I had asked others to pray for. The verse was Jeremiah 23:23: "Am I only a God nearby, declares the Lord, and not a God far away?"

God did prove Himself faithful, and I praise Him.

Prayer made a difference.

Glenn—Pacific Rim

This was not the missionary life I imagined. I was in an unfamiliar land struggling to learn language amid the heat, bugs and sickness. I was just beginning a two-year assignment overseas. I did enjoy traveling overseas and at that time had been to 19 countries; but the thrill and excitement of living in a remote location waned as I struggled with the new surroundings and loneliness. Long days brought me to a point of brokenness. Going home was not an option. This was not a decision I had considered lightly; this was God's call.

One afternoon, needing time alone, I took a small boat out on the lake located near the village where I was working. Making friends had always been easy, but friendships came slowly in this culture, especially with limited knowledge of the language. I sat in the boat, watching dolphins swim around me until it began to rain. I prayed and called out to the Lord. An hour passed and the blue skies grew dark as a storm blew in and strong winds began to rock the boat. Suddenly I realized I should get back to the shore, but the engine wouldn't start. After repeated tries, the engine started and I headed for the shore. Arriving home I reached for my Bible and turned to Psalm 18:6–15. I couldn't believe my eyes!

The words described exactly what I had just experienced—rain clouds, thunder, bolts of lightning. Yet the words were filled with love, and God's message was clear, "I know you are here, and I am here with you." From that day forward, I looked at life differently. I could see the fingerprint of God even in the small things of life—the brilliant color of a flower, the majesty of creation or the intricate colors of a rainbow. God allowed me to celebrate in His creation around me. Each new discovery was a reminder of God's presence. Little things like the sight of a rare flower or a smile on a child's face were reminders of God's hand reaching out to me. It was God's fingerprint upon my life.

Marshall—South America

> Prayer lays hold of God's plan and becomes the link
> between His will and its accomplishment on earth.
> *Elisabeth Elliot*

PRAISE & THANKSGIVING

Worship by using the name of God mentioned in this Scripture—"my witness."

Even now, behold, my witness is in heaven, and my advocate is on high.

Job 16:19 (NASB)

REPENTANCE

Search your heart as you meditate on this Scripture. What is the Holy Spirit revealing to you?

Do not be angry beyond measure, O Lord; do not remember our sins forever. Oh, look upon us, we pray, for we are all your people.

Isaiah 64:9

ASKING

Read the following Scripture. Rewrite it, personalizing it for missionary children, seeking the Lord for them when they're away from home.

Do not offer the parts of your body to sin, as instruments of wickedness, but rather offer yourselves to God, as those who have been brought from death to life; and offer the parts of your body to him as instruments of righteousness.

Romans 6:13

_____

_____

_____

YIELDING

Now meditate on the Scripture again. Rewrite it below, personalizing and praying it for yourself. How can you respond to what God is saying to you in this Scripture?

_____

_____

_____

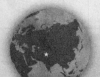

Pray for missionary work in TAJIKISTAN
(Central Asia, west of China)

There is no way that Christians, in a private capacity, can do so much to
promote the work of God and advance the kingdom of Christ as by prayer.
Jonathan Edwards

PRAISE & THANKSGIVING

Worship Him today, for He is your "witness."

Even now, behold, my witness is in heaven, and my advocate is on high.

Job 16:19 (NASB)

REPENTANCE

Search your heart as you meditate on this Scripture.

Do not be angry beyond measure, O LORD; do not remember our sins forever.
Oh, look upon us, we pray, for we are all your people.

Isaiah 64:9

ASKING

Rewrite this Scripture, personalizing it for missionary
children, seeking the Lord for them when they're away
from home.

Then I acknowledged my sin to you and did not cover up my iniquity. I said, "I
will confess my transgressions to the LORD"—and you forgave the guilt of my sin.

Psalm 32:5

_____

_____

_____

_____

YIELDING

Rewrite it again, personalizing and praying it for yourself.
Respond to what God is saying to you in this Scripture.

_____

_____

_____

_____

Pray for missionary work in TANZANIA
(Eastern Africa, between Kenya and Mozambique)

> When a Christian shuns fellowship with other Christians,
> the devil smiles. When he stops studying the Bible, the devil laughs.
> When he stops praying, the devil shouts for joy.
> *Corrie ten Boom*

PRAISE & THANKSGIVING

Even now, behold, my witness is in heaven, and my advocate is on high.

Job 16:19 (NASB)

REPENTANCE

Do not be angry beyond measure, O LORD; do not remember our sins forever.
Oh, look upon us, we pray, for we are all your people.

Isaiah 64:9

ASKING

Personalize this Scripture for missionary children,
rewriting it, seeking the Lord for their well-being.

Keep me from deliberate wrongs; help me to stop doing them.
Only then can I be free of guilt and innocent of some great crime.

Psalm 19:13 (TLB)

_____

_____

_____

_____

YIELDING

Now personalize and pray it for yourself. How can you
respond to what God is saying to you?

_____

_____

_____

_____

_____

_____

Pray for missionary work in THAILAND
(Southeastern Asia, southeast of Burma)

Oh, for closest communion with God, till soul and body,
head, face, and heart shine with divine brilliancy!
But oh! for a holy ignorance of our shining!
Robert Murray McCheyne

PRAISE & THANKSGIVING

Even now, behold, my witness is in heaven, and my advocate is on high.

Job 16:19 (NASB)

REPENTANCE

Do not be angry beyond measure, O LORD; do not remember our sins forever.
Oh, look upon us, we pray, for we are all your people.

Isaiah 64:9

ASKING

Rewrite this Scripture, personalizing it for missionaries.

The one thing I want from God, the thing I seek most of all, is the privilege of
meditating in his Temple, living in his presence every day of my life, delighting
in his incomparable perfections and glory. There I'll be when troubles come.
He will hide me. He will set me on a high rock out of reach of all my enemies.
Then I will bring him sacrifices and sing his praises with much joy.

Psalm 27:4–6 (TLB)

_____

_____

_____

YIELDING

What is God saying to you in this Scripture?

_____

_____

_____

_____

_____

Pray for missionary work in TIMOR-LESTE
(Southeastern Asia, at the eastern end of Indonesia)

How we have prayed for a revival—we did not care whether it was
old-fashioned or not—what we asked for was that it should be such that
would cleanse and revive His children and set them on fire to win others.
Mary Warburton Booth

PRAISE & THANKSGIVING

Even now, behold, my witness is in heaven, and my advocate is on high.
Job 16:19 (NASB)

REPENTANCE

Do not be angry beyond measure, O LORD; do not remember our sins forever.
Oh, look upon us, we pray, for we are all your people.
Isaiah 64:9

ASKING

Personalize this Scripture today for missionaries.
Tell me where you want me to go and I will go there. May every fiber of my
being unite in reverence to Your name. With all my heart I will praise you.
I will give glory to your name forever, for you love me so much! You are
constantly so kind! You have rescued me from deepest hell.
Psalm 86:11–13 (TLB)

_____

_____

_____

_____

YIELDING

Personalize and pray this same Scripture for yourself.

_____

_____

_____

_____

_____

_____

Pray for missionary work in TOGO
(Western Africa, between Benin and Ghana)

Week 43
Thoughts and Prayers

I thank my God every time I remember you.

In all my prayers for all of you, I always pray with joy

because of your partnership in the gospel from the first day until now,

being confident of this, that he who began a good work in you

will carry it on to completion until the day of Christ Jesus.

It is right for me to feel this way about all of you,

since I have you in my heart; for whether I am in chains

or defending and confirming the gospel, all of you share

in God's grace with me. God can testify how I long

for all of you with the affection of Christ Jesus.

And this is my prayer: that your love may abound

more and more in knowledge and depth of insight,

so that you may be able to discern what is best

and may be pure and blameless until the day of Christ,

filled with the fruit of righteousness that comes

through Jesus Christ—to the glory and praise of God.

PHILIPPIANS 1:3–11

THE
MISSIONARY'S
PARENTS

Week 44

HEALTH & PROTECTION

As I hung up the phone, the realization of what I had just heard began to sink in. My sister called to tell me our mother had just gone through a series of exams, and there was a high probability that she had Alzheimer's.

Our mother was the love of our life, our hero of the faith, and our dearest friend. As I sat thousands of miles away in our South American mission apartment, I began to cry out to God. I was not so much asking why my mother had contracted this dreaded disease, but why I was so far away when she and my dad needed me the most.

At this very critical time in my life, God's mercy and love were showered down on me. People all around the world began to pray. Churches in the United States where my husband and I served prior to becoming missionaries were praying for God's wisdom in our lives. People we did not know, with similar family situations, began to pray. Our mission family was praying, calling, and sharing words of comfort and love with us. Through prayer, God provided all we needed.

I was blessed to have a sister who, along with my father, cared for my mom in the initial stages of the disease. My two brothers were very attentive to my mother's needs, and other relatives and church members helped my family. God was so gracious to allow me to travel back to the United States several times to relieve other family members for a little while. Because of my mother's illness, doors were opened for me to minister and witness to people who were going through the same situation.

As I look back at this experience, I know God brought me through it because of the prayers of churches, my missionary colleagues, and the national believers. He sustained me through the prayers of others. Through answered prayer, I realized once again that "his compassions never fail. They are new every morning; great is your faithfulness" (Lam. 3:22–23).

Evelyn—SOUTH AMERICA

> No blessing of the Christian life becomes continually possessed unless we
> are men and women of regular, daily, unhurried secret lingerings in prayer.
> *J. Sidlow Baxter*

PRAISE & THANKSGIVING

Worship by using the name of God mentioned in
this Scripture—"my help."

> *I am poor and needy; come quickly to me, O God.*
> *You are my help and my deliverer; O LORD, do not delay.*
> Psalm 70:5

REPENTANCE

Search your heart as you meditate on this Scripture.
What is the Holy Spirit revealing to you?

> *Do not be wise in your own eyes; fear the LORD and shun evil.*
> *This will bring health to your body and nourishment to your bones.*
> Proverbs 3:7–8

ASKING

Read the following Scripture. Rewrite it, personalizing it
for the missionary's parents, seeking the Lord for their
health.

> *My son, pay attention to what I say; listen closely to my words.*
> *Do not let them out of your sight, keep them within your heart;*
> *for they are life to those who find them and health to a man's whole body.*
> Proverbs 4:20–22

_____

_____

YIELDING

Now meditate on the Scripture again. Rewrite it below,
personalizing and praying it for yourself. How can you
respond to what God is saying to you in this Scripture?

_____

_____

_____

Pray for missionary work in TOKELAU
(South Pacific islands, halfway between Hawaii
and New Zealand)

> Prayer is not conquering God's reluctance,
> but taking hold of God's willingness.
> *Phillips Brooks*

PRAISE & THANKSGIVING

Worship Him today, for He is your "help."

> *I am poor and needy; come quickly to me, O God.*
> *You are my help and my deliverer; O LORD, do not delay.*
>
> Psalm 70:5

REPENTANCE

Search your heart as you meditate on this Scripture.

> *Do not be wise in your own eyes; fear the LORD and shun evil.*
> *This will bring health to your body and nourishment to your bones.*
>
> Proverbs 3:7–8

ASKING

Rewrite this Scripture, personalizing it for the missionary's parents, seeking the Lord for their health.

> *Dear friend, I pray that you may enjoy good health and that all may go well*
> *with you, even as your soul is getting along well.*
>
> 3 John 2

_____

_____

_____

_____

YIELDING

Rewrite it again, personalizing and praying it for yourself. Respond to what God is saying to you in this Scripture.

_____

_____

_____

_____

Pray for missionary work in TONGA
(South Pacific island, halfway between Hawaii
and New Zealand)

> The best prayers often have more groans than words.
> *John Bunyan*

PRAISE & THANKSGIVING

> *I am poor and needy; come quickly to me, O God.*
> *You are my help and my deliverer; O LORD, do not delay.*
>> Psalm 70:5

REPENTANCE

> *"For I know the plans I have for you," declares the LORD, "plans to prosper*
> *you and not to harm you, plans to give you hope and a future."*
>> Jeremiah 29:11

ASKING

Personalize this Scripture for the missionary's parents,
rewriting it, seeking the Lord for their protection.

> *If you make the Most High your dwelling— even the LORD, who is my refuge—*
> *then no harm will befall you, no disaster will come near your tent.*
>> Psalm 91:9–10

_____

_____

_____

_____

YIELDING

Now personalize and pray it for yourself. How can you
respond to what God is saying to you?

_____

_____

_____

_____

_____

_____

_____

Pray for missionary work in
TRINIDAD and **TOBAGO**
(Caribbean islands, northeast of Venezuela)

Throughout our history, Americans of faith have always turned to prayer
for wisdom, prayer for resolve, prayers for compassion and strength,
prayers for commitment to justice and for a spirit of forgiveness.
George W. Bush

PRAISE & THANKSGIVING

I am poor and needy; come quickly to me, O God.
You are my help and my deliverer; O LORD, do not delay.
Psalm 70:5

REPENTANCE

"For I know the plans I have for you," declares the LORD, "plans to prosper
you and not to harm you, plans to give you hope and a future."
Jeremiah 29:11

ASKING

Rewrite this Scripture, personalizing it for missionaries.

Let all who take refuge in you be glad; let them ever sing for joy. Spread your
protection over them, that those who love your name may rejoice in you.
For surely, O LORD, you bless the righteous; you surround them with
your favor as with a shield.
Psalm 5:11–12

_____

_____

_____

_____

YIELDING

What is God saying to you in this Scripture?

_____

_____

_____

_____

_____

Pray for missionary work in TUNISIA
(Northern Africa, between Algeria and Libya)

> Prayer is not an exercise. It is the life of the saint.
> *Oswald Chambers*

PRAISE & THANKSGIVING

I am poor and needy; come quickly to me, O God.
You are my help and my deliverer; O LORD, do not delay.
Psalm 70:5

REPENTANCE

"For I know the plans I have for you," declares the LORD, "plans to prosper
you and not to harm you, plans to give you hope and a future."
Jeremiah 29:11

ASKING

Personalize this Scripture today for missionaries.

Keep me as the apple of your eye; hide me in the shadow of your wings.
Psalm 17:8

_____

_____

_____

_____

YIELDING

Personalize and pray this same Scripture for yourself.

_____

_____

_____

_____

_____

_____

_____

_____

Pray for missionary work in TURKEY
(Southwestern Asia, between Greece and Syria)

Week 44
Thoughts and Prayers

_____
_____
_____
_____
_____
_____
_____
_____
_____
_____
_____
_____
_____
_____
_____
_____
_____
_____
_____
_____
_____
_____
_____
_____

Week 45

OVERCOMING LONELINESS

Every day was filled with packing, selling belongings, and saying good-byes to a loving church family. Our family was moving overseas, and it was an exciting and often stressful time.

Just six years earlier, God blessed us with an opportunity to start a new church. The small church was like family. In the midst of transition, we failed to recognize the feelings our parents were experiencing. My husband's parents lived across the street from us. When we began the work of starting a new church, my in-laws stepped up to help.

Our daughters were blessed by the godly influence of their grandparents as we worked together in the new church. So it was especially difficult when our parents learned that God was calling us to be missionaries. Of course, they were happy God had answered their prayers for us, but the thought of the grandchildren living an ocean away seemed unbearable.

Before we left the United States, my mother-in-law took my youngest daughter on a shopping trip, just the two of them. It was not an easy transition for our children either, so "Granny" wanted to buy something special for the plane trip. The two of them returned home with a small stuffed animal that would just fit in my daughter's carry-on bag. It wasn't until the first flight out of the country that my daughter told me the name of her new treasure. She chose the name "Granny." From that day on, any time she missed her grandmother, she would give "Granny" a hug. The special gift was a constant reminder of her grandmother's love and influence, and "Granny" followed her all the way to college.

It wasn't until our first trip back to the United States that we realized how difficult our move had been for the grandparents. They were such a big part of our children's lives, so a vacuum was left when we moved away. But we were overjoyed to learn that God had not wasted all the love they had to give away. A young family in their neighborhood had a new baby boy. His only living grandmother lived in Asia, so Granny and Papa became "adopted" grandparents to Charlie. This worked well for our children, because after all, this was their "Granny and Papa," but they were willing to share their love.

My daughters are now grown and married. We have not had the blessing of living near grandparents since that initial move, but God graciously continues to bring "adopted" grandchildren into Granny and Papa's lives. Every one of them lives a long distance from his or her grandparents. Right now, the family across the street has two children and their grandmother lives in Mexico. And yes, they love our "Granny and Papa."

God is a personal God who meets our needs in very personal and unique ways. My dear in-laws still have a lot of love to give, and I am overjoyed to know that God has a plan for them as well. God provided for grandchildren who needed the love of very special grandparents.

There may be parents of missionaries in your church or neighborhood. They have a lot of love to give, and they really miss their children and grandchildren. Pray for them by name and find ways to reach out and minister to them.

Debbie—SOUTH AMERICA

> Prayer power has never been tried to its full capacity. Let us answer
> God's standing challenge, "Call unto me, and I will answer thee,
> and show thee great and mighty things which thou knowest not."
> *Hudson Taylor*

PRAISE & THANKSGIVING

Worship by using the characteristic of God mentioned
in this Scripture—"near."

> *The LORD is near to all who call upon Him, to all who call upon Him in truth.*
>
> Psalm 145:18 (NASB)

REPENTANCE

Search your heart as you meditate on this Scripture.
What is the Holy Spirit revealing to you?

> *The LORD is my strength and my shield; my heart trusts in him, and I am helped.*
> *My heart leaps for joy and I will give thanks to him in song.*
>
> Psalm 28:7

ASKING

Read the following Scripture. Rewrite it, personalizing it
for the missionary's parents, seeking the Lord regarding
their loneliness.

> *God has said, "Never will I leave you; never will I forsake you."*
>
> Hebrews 13:5

_____

_____

_____

YIELDING

Now meditate on the Scripture again. Rewrite it below,
personalizing and praying it for yourself. How can you
respond to what God is saying to you in this Scripture?

_____

_____

_____

Pray for missionary work in TURKMENISTAN
(Central Asia, on the Caspian Sea,
between Iran and Kazakhstan)

I have often said it would be a thing very desirable . . . that there should be an agreement of all God's people in America to keep a day of fasting and prayer to God; wherein, we should all unite on the same day.
Jonathan Edwards

PRAISE & THANKSGIVING

Worship Him today, for He is "near."

The LORD is near to all who call upon Him, to all who call upon Him in truth.
Psalm 145:18 (NASB)

REPENTANCE

Search your heart as you meditate on this Scripture.

The LORD is my strength and my shield; my heart trusts in him, and I am helped.
My heart leaps for joy and I will give thanks to him in song.
Psalm 28:7

ASKING

Rewrite this Scripture, personalizing it for the missionary's parents, seeking the Lord regarding their loneliness.

The Lord is good, a refuge in times of trouble. He cares for those who trust in him.
Nahum 1:7

_____

_____

_____

YIELDING

Rewrite it again, personalizing and praying it for yourself. Respond to what God is saying to you in this Scripture.

_____

_____

_____

_____

_____

_____

Pray for missionary work on
THE TURKS and CAICOS ISLANDS
(Caribbean islands, southeast of the Bahamas, north of Haiti)

Persons never need hesitate, because of their past sins, to approach
God with the fullest confidence. If they now repent . . . they have
no reason to fear being repulsed from the footstool of mercy.
Charles G. Finney

PRAISE & THANKSGIVING

The LORD is near to all who call upon Him, to all who call upon Him in truth.
Psalm 145:18 (NASB)

REPENTANCE

The LORD is my strength and my shield; my heart trusts in him, and I am helped.
My heart leaps for joy and I will give thanks to him in song.
Psalm 28:7

ASKING

Personalize this Scripture for the missionary's parents,
rewriting it, seeking the Lord regarding their loneliness.
I will praise the LORD, who counsels me; even at night my heart instructs me.
I have set the LORD always before me. Because he is at my right hand, I will
not be shaken.
Psalm 16:7–8

_____

_____

_____

YIELDING

Now personalize and pray it for yourself. How can you
respond to what God is saying to you?

_____

_____

_____

_____

_____

Pray for missionary work in TUVALU
(South Pacific islands, halfway between Hawaii and Australia)

Prayer is . . . a two-way relationship in which man should not only talk to God but also listen to Him. Prayer to God is like a child's conversation with his father. It is natural for a child to ask his father for the things he needs.
Billy Graham

PRAISE & THANKSGIVING

The LORD is near to all who call upon Him, to all who call upon Him in truth.
Psalm 145:18 (NASB)

REPENTANCE

The LORD is my strength and my shield; my heart trusts in him, and I am helped. My heart leaps for joy and I will give thanks to him in song.
Psalm 28:7

ASKING

Rewrite this Scripture, personalizing it for missionaries.

On my bed I remember you; I think of you through the watches of the night. Because you are my help, I sing in the shadow of your wings. My soul clings to you; your right hand upholds me.
Psalm 63:6–8

_____

_____

_____

_____

YIELDING

What is God saying to you in this Scripture?

_____

_____

_____

_____

_____

_____

Pray for missionary work in UGANDA
(Eastern Africa, west of Kenya)

> In every storm there is a "Peace! Be still" that Christ
> will speak where prayer's call invites Him.
> *Jack Hayford*

PRAISE & THANKSGIVING

> *The LORD is near to all who call upon Him, to all who call upon Him in truth.*
>
> Psalm 145:18 (NASB)

REPENTANCE

> *The LORD is my strength and my shield; my heart trusts in him, and I am helped.*
> *My heart leaps for joy and I will give thanks to him in song.*
>
> Psalm 28:7

ASKING

Personalize this Scripture today for missionaries.

> *Hear my cry, O God; listen to my prayer. From the ends of the earth I call to you,*
> *I call as my heart grows faint; lead me to the rock that is higher than I.*
>
> Psalm 61:1–2

_____

_____

_____

YIELDING

Personalize and pray this same Scripture for yourself.

_____

_____

_____

_____

_____

_____

_____

Pray for missionary work in UKRAINE
(Eastern Europe, between Poland, Romania,
Moldova, and Russia)

Week 45
Thoughts and Prayers

Week 46

SPIRITUAL NEEDS

Encouraging the parents of missionaries has been a passion of mine since I returned to the United States after twenty-three years of service in Asia. When I have the opportunity to speak to parents whose children are answering God's call to go to the ends of the earth, I invariably tell them that God indeed has a special grace for missionary parents.

The Lord has been faithful to allow me the challenge and joy of "walking in that of which I talk." Both of my children, along their spouses, surrendered their lives to serve overseas as missionaries, taking my two grandsons to the other side of the world. When my husband and I were appointed as missionaries and were preparing to move to Indonesia with our two small children, I was perplexed by the question asked repeatedly by well-meaning supporters: "Are you going to take the children with you?" However, when I put my own two children and their families on an airplane to Asia, the question did not seem inappropriate at all. I also wanted to say, "You aren't taking the young 'uns with you, are you?"

After what seemed like an eternity of separation, the time came for my son's family to have a brief visit to the United States. As I flew to Dallas to meet them, I began to experience an inexplicable anxiety and sense of uneasiness. Getting in touch with my gnawing fears, I realized that my sense of unsettledness was triggered by doubts that my grandchildren would really know who I was. They knew what to call me, of course, but did they really know my relationship to them? Did they realize how important they were to me and how closely I was connected to them? Was that familial bond firmly established in their little hearts?

As I walked from the ramp, those two precious children, ages five and almost two, were waiting for me. Zachary is one of those effervescent, spontaneous children who often does not know what he's going to say until he hears himself say it. He looked as if he were laboring under an undelivered message! As we ran toward each other, he loudly exclaimed, "You are BuBob! We'll never forget that you are our grandmother!"

Oh, Lord, the two things my heart desired and needed on that special day, You so profoundly gave. Zachary affirmed first my name, "BuBob," the name uniquely coined for him and other grandchildren who would follow. Secondly, he defined our "till-death-do-us-part" relationship. By calling me "Grandmother," he automatically identified himself as my grandson!

In reflecting on that encounter, indelibly etched on my mind, I was reminded of the powerful names of God that are revealed to us, His children, in Scripture.

Oh, Father, thank You for Your covenantal names which help us to know You in a more intimate, personal relationship. I praise You, Lord, that your name is that "strong tower" into which we can run for refuge and find eternal safety. Giver of wonderful gifts, thank You that You do indeed grant a special grace to parents. For answered prayers and for fulfilling even the desires of our hearts, I praise and gratefully worship You.

Bobbye—Pacific Rim

> May all fear as to our being able to fulfill our vocation vanish
> as we see Jesus, living ever to pray, living in us to pray.
> *Andrew Murray*

PRAISE & THANKSGIVING

Worship by using the name of God mentioned in this
Scripture—"tower of deliverance."

> *He is a tower of deliverance to His king, and shows lovingkindness*
> *to His anointed, to David and his descendants forever.*
>
> 2 Samuel 22:51 (NASB)

REPENTANCE

Search your heart as you meditate on this Scripture.
What is the Holy Spirit revealing to you?

> *Jesus answered, "It is written: 'Man does not live on bread alone,*
> *but on every word that comes from the mouth of God.'"*
>
> Matthew 4:4

ASKING

Read the following Scripture. Rewrite it, personalizing
it for the missionary's parents, seeking the Lord regarding
their spiritual needs.

> *Love the LORD your God with all your heart and with all your soul and*
> *with all your strength.*
>
> Deuteronomy 6:5

_____

_____

_____

YIELDING

Now meditate on the Scripture again. Rewrite it below,
personalizing and praying it for yourself. How can you
respond to what God is saying to you in this Scripture?

_____

_____

_____

Pray for missionary work in
THE UNITED ARAB EMIRATES
(Middle East, between Oman and Saudi Arabia)

Prayer is not intended to change God's purpose, nor is it to move Him to form fresh purposes. God has decreed that certain events shall come to pass through the means He has appointed for their accomplishment.
Arthur W. Pink

PRAISE & THANKSGIVING
Worship Him as your "tower of deliverance."
> *He is a tower of deliverance to His king, and shows lovingkindness*
> *to His anointed, to David and his descendants forever.*
>
> 2 Samuel 22:51 (NASB)

REPENTANCE
Search your heart as you meditate on this Scripture.
> *Jesus answered, "It is written: 'Man does not live on bread alone,*
> *but on every word that comes from the mouth of God.'"*
>
> Matthew 4:4

ASKING
Rewrite this Scripture, personalizing it for the missionary's parents, seeking the Lord regarding their spiritual needs.
> *Trust in the LORD with all your heart and lean not on your own understanding;*
> *in all your ways acknowledge him, and he will make your paths straight.*
>
> Proverbs 3:5–6

_____

_____

_____

_____

YIELDING
Rewrite it again, personalizing and praying it for yourself. Respond to what God is saying to you in this Scripture.

_____

_____

_____

_____

Pray for missionary work in
THE UNITED KINGDOM
(Western Europe, northwest of France)

> I have benefited by my praying for others; for by making an errand
> to God for them, I have gotten something for myself.
> *Samuel Rutherford*

PRAISE & THANKSGIVING

> *He is a tower of deliverance to His king, and shows lovingkindness*
> *to His anointed, to David and his descendants forever.*
>
> 2 Samuel 22:51 (NASB)

REPENTANCE

> *Jesus answered, "It is written: 'Man does not live on bread alone,*
> *but on every word that comes from the mouth of God.'"*
>
> Matthew 4:4

ASKING

Personalize this Scripture for the missionary's parents,
rewriting it, seeking the Lord regarding their spiritual
needs.

> *I love you, O LORD, my strength. The LORD is my rock, my fortress and my*
> *deliverer; my God is my rock, in whom I take refuge. He is my shield and the*
> *horn of my salvation, my stronghold. I call to the LORD, who is worthy of praise,*
> *and I am saved from my enemies.*
>
> Psalm 18:1–3

_____

_____

_____

_____

YIELDING

Now personalize and pray it for yourself. How can you
respond to what God is saying to you?

_____

_____

_____

_____

Pray for missionary work in URUGUAY
(Southern South America, between Argentina and Brazil)

> The preacher of the gospel asks your prayers, and it is a part of
> the duties arising out of the relationship between Christian men that
> those who are taught should pray for those who teach God's Word.
> *Charles Spurgeon*

PRAISE & THANKSGIVING

> *He is a tower of deliverance to His king, and shows lovingkindness*
> *to His anointed, to David and his descendants forever.*
>
> 2 Samuel 22:51 (NASB)

REPENTANCE

> *There is a time for everything, and a season for every activity under heaven . . .*
> *a time for war and a time for peace.*
>
> Ecclesiastes 3:1, 8

ASKING

Rewrite this Scripture, personalizing it for missionaries.

> *You will keep him in perfect peace, whose mind is stayed on You,*
> *because he trusts in You.*
>
> Isaiah 26:3 (NKJV)

_____

_____

_____

YIELDING

What is God saying to you in this Scripture?

_____

_____

_____

_____

_____

_____

_____

Pray for missionary work in UZBEKISTAN
(Central Asia, north of Afghanistan)

More tears are shed over answered prayers than unanswered ones.
Mother Teresa

PRAISE & THANKSGIVING

He is a tower of deliverance to His king, and shows lovingkindness
to His anointed, to David and his descendants forever.

2 Samuel 22:51 (NASB)

REPENTANCE

There is a time for everything, and a season for every activity under heaven . . .
a time for war and a time for peace.

Ecclesiastes 3:1, 8

ASKING

Personalize this Scripture today for missionaries.

Do not be anxious about anything, but in everything, by prayer and petition,
with thanksgiving, present your requests to God. And the peace of God,
which transcends all understanding, will guard your hearts and your minds
in Christ Jesus.

Philippians 4:6–7

_____

_____

_____

_____

YIELDING

Personalize and pray this same Scripture for yourself.

_____

_____

_____

_____

_____

_____

Pray for missionary work in VANUATU
(South Pacific islands, between Hawaii and Australia)

Week 46
Thoughts and Prayers

Week 47

UNITED TO THE CALL

I don't exactly know when my grandmothers started praying for me. My maternal grandmother probably started while I was still in my mother's womb. My paternal grandmother likely began praying for me by name from the first day she met her son's five-year-old prospective stepson. This I do know: my grandmothers prayed for me every day. When my wife, Susan, and I went to the mission field, we knew Grandmother Cox and Grandmother Coffey were tops on our list of faithful prayer warriors.

The last time I saw Grandmother Coffey, my dad's mother, was in 1989, just a few months before she died. As we left, she said the same thing she had said every time we said good-bye since Susan and I first left as young missionaries to Venezuela in 1977: "I don't write much, but I pray for you every day. If I don't see you here again, I'll see you in heaven."

When she died a few months later, I shared with our church family in Mexico City that I had lost one of my most faithful prayer warriors. After the service, two ladies came up to say they would take my grandmother's place to pray for me every day. Between the two of them, they might make up for her.

Grandmother Cox suffered her first crippling stroke in 1980 when she lost the use of her right hand. Over the next twenty-three years, her speech slurred, she lost the use of her legs, and she could no longer read. In her last years, she was confined to bed and could only say, "Yeah" or shake her head for "No" whenever we asked her a question. But she still lit up with a big smile whenever I visited her.

On one visit, she grabbed my hand and held it tightly the whole time we talked. (Actually, Susan and I talked, I read from Grandmother Cox's old Pilgrim Bible, and she occasionally said, "Yeah.") Before we prayed for her at the end of our visit, she was trying so hard to speak, but the words just wouldn't come out. I leaned over and said in her ear, "I know. You still pray for me every day."

"Yeah!" she said with a tear in her eye, "Yeah." She went home to the Lord just a few months later at age ninety-three.

If the Spirit intercedes for us with groans that words cannot express (Rom. 8:26-27), then I am confident that my grandmother's prayers were heard, understood, and are effective still. I know she prayed for me faithfully—and God says, "Yeah."

Larry—Pacific Rim

The story is told of a little guy valiantly but futilely trying to move a heavy log to clear a pathway to his favorite hideout. . . . His dad told him he was not using all his strength, because he hadn't asked [his dad] to help.

Zig Ziglar

PRAISE & THANKSGIVING

Worship by using the characteristic of God mentioned in this Scripture—"zealous."

Thus says the LORD of hosts: "I am zealous for Zion with great zeal; with great fervor I am zealous for her."

Zechariah 8:2 (NKJV)

REPENTANCE

Search your heart as you meditate on this Scripture. What is the Holy Spirit revealing to you?

By this all men will know that you are my disciples, if you love one another.

John 13:35

ASKING

Read the following Scripture. Rewrite it, personalizing it for the missionary's parents, seeking the Lord regarding encouraging relationships.

As for me, far be it from me that I should sin against the LORD by failing to pray for you. And I will teach you the way that is good and right.

1 Samuel 12:23

_____

_____

_____

YIELDING

Now meditate on the Scripture again. Rewrite it below, personalizing and praying it for yourself. How can you respond to what God is saying to you in this Scripture?

_____

_____

_____

Pray for missionary work in VATICAN CITY
(a sovereign city-state within the city of Rome)

Only those who see the invisible can attempt the impossible.
Dick Eastman

PRAISE & THANKSGIVING

Worship Him today—the One who is "zealous" for all His people.

> *Thus says the LORD of hosts: "I am zealous for Zion with great zeal; with great fervor I am zealous for her."*
>
> Zechariah 8:2 (NKJV)

REPENTANCE

Search your heart as you meditate on this Scripture.

> *By this all men will know that you are my disciples, if you love one another.*
>
> John 13:35

ASKING

Rewrite this Scripture, personalizing it for the missionary's parents, seeking the Lord regarding encouraging relationships.

> *I am convinced that neither death nor life, neither angels nor demons, neither the present nor the future, nor any powers, neither height nor depth, nor anything else in all creation, will be able to separate us from the love of God that is in Christ Jesus our Lord.*
>
> Romans 8:38–39

_____

_____

_____

YIELDING

Rewrite it again, personalizing and praying it for yourself. Respond to what God is saying to you in this Scripture.

_____

_____

_____

_____

Pray for missionary work in VENEZUELA
(Northern South American, between Colombia and Guyana)

It is the habit of faith, when she is praying, to use pleas. Mere prayer sayers,
who do not pray at all, forget to argue with God; but those who prevail
bring forth their reasons and their strong arguments.
Charles Spurgeon

PRAISE & THANKSGIVING

Thus says the LORD of hosts: "I am zealous for Zion with great zeal;
with great fervor I am zealous for her."
Zechariah 8:2 (NKJV)

REPENTANCE

By this all men will know that you are my disciples, if you love one another.
John 13:35

ASKING

Personalize this Scripture for the missionary's parents,
rewriting it, seeking the Lord regarding encouraging
relationships.

We know that in all things God works for the good of those who love him,
who have been called according to his purpose.

Romans 8:28

_____

_____

_____

YIELDING

Now personalize and pray it for yourself. How can you
respond to what God is saying to you?

_____

_____

_____

_____

_____

_____

Pray for missionary work in VIETNAM
(Southeastern Asia, alongside China, Laos, and Cambodia)

Work as if you were to live a hundred years.
Pray as if you were to die tomorrow.
Benjamin Franklin

PRAISE & THANKSGIVING

Thus says the LORD of hosts: "I am zealous for Zion with great zeal;
with great fervor I am zealous for her."
Zechariah 8:2 (NKJV)

REPENTANCE

By this all men will know that you are my disciples, if you love one another.
John 13:35

ASKING

Rewrite this Scripture, personalizing it for missionaries.
I prayed for this child, and the LORD has granted me what I asked of him. So
now I give him to the LORD. For his whole life he will be given over to the LORD.
1 Samuel 1:27–28

_____

_____

_____

YIELDING

What is God saying to you in this Scripture?

_____

_____

_____

_____

_____

_____

_____

_____

Pray for missionary work in THE VIRGIN ISLANDS
(Caribbean islands, east of Puerto Rico)

Learn to worship God as the God who does wonders, who wishes
to prove in you that He can do something supernatural and divine.
Andrew Murray

PRAISE & THANKSGIVING

Thus says the LORD of hosts: "I am zealous for Zion with great zeal;
with great fervor I am zealous for her."
Zechariah 8:2 (NKJV)

REPENTANCE

By this all men will know that you are my disciples, if you love one another.
John 13:35

ASKING

Personalize this Scripture today for missionaries.

I have no greater joy than to hear that my children are walking in the truth.
3 John 4

_____

_____

_____

_____

YIELDING

Personalize and pray this same Scripture for yourself.

_____

_____

_____

_____

_____

_____

_____

_____

Pray for missionary work in
WALLIS and FUTUNA
(South Pacific islands, between Hawaii and New Zealand)

Week 47
Thoughts and Prayers

May God be gracious to us and bless us

and make his face shine upon us,

that your ways may be known on earth,

your salvation among all nations.

May the peoples praise you, O God;

may all the peoples praise you.

May the nations be glad and sing for joy,

for you rule the peoples justly and guide

the nations of the earth.

May the peoples praise you, O God;

may all the peoples praise you.

Then the land will yield its harvest, and God,

our God, will bless us. God will bless us,

and all the ends of the earth will fear him.

PSALM 67:1–7

Part Two

THE HARVEST
THE NATIONS

Week 48

GOVERNMENTAL LEADERS

[The following experience was written by a worker visiting
Yemen shortly after three missionaries were killed
at Jibla Baptist Hospital on December 30, 2002.]

I've had many Yemenis tell me how sorry they were for what
happened at Jibla Baptist Hospital. The immigration man at the
airport when I first entered Yemen, the police at the road block, the
grocery man in Jibla town, the cleaner at the hospital—all of these
expressed deep sympathy over what happened.

The people of Jibla town where the hospital is located seem to
be kinder than ever! I think what amazed them most is the fact that
we were still kind to them and showed the same manner of love as
before. But even more amazing to them, I think, was the fact that
we had not lost our joy despite this tragic event. It's true that everyone at the hospital was shocked and saddened, but they did not lose
their joy. The people in the town noticed this, and they were asking
questions.

The apostles went through difficult times at the beginning of
their ministry. Peter was persecuted, Stephen was martyred, and
Paul was shipwrecked and imprisoned, but they carried on with the

task. In Acts 5:41–42 we can read their story: "The apostles left the Sanhedrin, rejoicing because they had been counted worthy of suffering disgrace for the Name. Day after day, in the temple courts and from house to house, they never stopped teaching and proclaiming the good news that Jesus is the Christ."

Look at their attitude after being whipped, after being told not to continue preaching. They left the Sanhedrin rejoicing! Why? Because they had been "counted worthy of suffering disgrace." They weren't rejoicing because they were released. They weren't rejoicing because they were not hurting. They rejoiced because they considered it an honor to suffer disgrace. The Lord Jesus had only recently modeled suffering to them. They had shared just a little of what Jesus shared, so they counted it an honor and they rejoiced.

The people of Jibla noticed something different with our missionaries at the hospital. When the townspeople expressed anger towards the killer, the missionaries expressed love. When the townspeople said the killer must be executed, the missionaries told them that God loves him, cares for him, and forgives him. This is a strange concept to a Muslim. How can God love and forgive such a person?

Taking the gospel to Jerusalem and beyond does not stop or diminish as a result of persecution or setbacks. The Scripture says, "Day after day, in the temple courts and from house to house, they never stopped teaching and proclaiming the good news that Jesus is the Christ." The apostle's commitment to take the gospel to Jerusalem after the "flogging" recorded in verse 40 of the same chapter did not diminish. They went to the temple court and from house to house, teaching and proclaiming Christ.

We live in a spoiled society. We want things to go just right—no persecution. We expect things to go right all the time, every time, and in the way we expect them to go. When things do not go well, we complain and often lose our focus. My prayer is that in the midst of trials and persecution, we will remain focused on taking the gospel to the whole world.

—A *Christian worker in the Middle East*

The evangelization of the world depends first of all upon a revival of prayer.
Andrew Murray

PRAISE & THANKSGIVING

Worship by using the name of Christ mentioned in this
Scripture—"chosen one."

> *Behold, My Servant, whom I uphold; My chosen one in whom My soul delights.*
> *I have put My Spirit upon Him; He will bring forth justice to the nations.*
>> Isaiah 42:1 (NASB)

REPENTANCE

Search your heart as you meditate on this Scripture.
What is the Holy Spirit revealing to you?

> *May the words of my mouth and the meditation of my heart be pleasing*
> *in your sight, O LORD, my Rock and my Redeemer.*
>> Psalm 19:14

ASKING

Read the following Scripture. Rewrite it, personalizing it
for believing governmental leaders, seeking the Lord in
prayer on their behalf.

> *The God of Israel spoke, the Rock of Israel said to me: "When one rules over*
> *men in righteousness, when he rules in the fear of God, he is like the light of*
> *morning at sunrise on a cloudless morning, like the brightness after rain that*
> *brings the grass from the earth."*
>> 2 Samuel 23:3–4

_____

_____

YIELDING

Now meditate on the Scripture again. Rewrite it below,
personalizing and praying it for yourself. How can you
respond to what God is saying to you in this Scripture?

_____

_____

_____

Pray for missionary in the WEST BANK
(Middle East, west of Jordan)

I have so much to do that I shall spend the first three hours in prayer.
Martin Luther

PRAISE & THANKSGIVING
Worship Jesus today—the "chosen one"

Behold, My Servant, whom I uphold; My chosen one in whom My soul delights.
I have put My Spirit upon Him; He will bring forth justice to the nations.
Isaiah 42:1 (NASB)

REPENTANCE
Search your heart as you meditate on this Scripture.

May the words of my mouth and the meditation of my heart be pleasing
in your sight, O LORD, my Rock and my Redeemer.
Psalm 19:14

ASKING
Rewrite this Scripture, personalizing it for believing
governmental leaders, seeking the Lord in prayer on
their behalf.

He has showed you, O man, what is good. And what does the LORD require
of you? To act justly and to love mercy and to walk humbly with your God.
Micah 6:8

_____

_____

_____

_____

YIELDING
Rewrite it again, personalizing and praying it for yourself.
Respond to what God is saying to you in this Scripture.

_____

_____

_____

_____

Pray for missionary work in WESTERN SAHARA
(Northern Africa, between Mauritania and Morocco)

It matters little what form of prayer we adopt or how many words we use.
What matters is the faith which lays hold on God, knowing that
He knows our needs before we even ask Him.
Dietrich Bonhoeffer

PRAISE & THANKSGIVING

*Behold, My Servant, whom I uphold; My chosen one in whom My soul delights.
I have put My Spirit upon Him; He will bring forth justice to the nations.*
Isaiah 42:1 (NASB)

REPENTANCE

*May the words of my mouth and the meditation of my heart be pleasing
in your sight, O LORD, my Rock and my Redeemer.*
Psalm 19:14

ASKING

Personalize this Scripture for believing governmental
leaders, rewriting it, seeking the Lord in prayer on
their behalf.

*Give me wisdom and knowledge, that I may lead this people, for who
is able to govern this great people of yours?*
2 Chronicles 1:10

_____

_____

_____

_____

YIELDING

Now personalize and pray it for yourself. How can you
respond to what God is saying to you?

_____

_____

_____

_____

_____

Pray for missionary work in YEMEN
(Middle East, on the Gulf of Aden, between Oman
and Saudi Arabia)

The greatest blow sent Satan-ward is made by weeping warriors of prayer.
Dick Eastman

PRAISE & THANKSGIVING
> *Behold, My Servant, whom I uphold; My chosen one in whom My soul delights.*
> *I have put My Spirit upon Him; He will bring forth justice to the nations.*
> Isaiah 42:1 (NASB)

REPENTANCE
> *The fruit of the righteous is a tree of life, and he who wins souls is wise.*
> Proverbs 11:30

ASKING
Rewrite this Scripture, personalizing it for unbelieving governmental leaders.
> *All the ends of the earth will remember and turn to the LORD, and*
> *all the families of the nations will bow down before him, for dominion*
> *belongs to the LORD and he rules over the nations.*
> Psalm 22:27–28

_____

_____

_____

_____

_____

YIELDING
What is God saying to you in this Scripture?

_____

_____

_____

_____

_____

_____

_____

_____

Pray for missionary work in ZAMBIA
(Southern Africa, east of Angola)

It is possible to move men, through God, by prayer alone.
Hudson Taylor

PRAISE & THANKSGIVING

Behold, My Servant, whom I uphold; My chosen one in whom My soul delights.
I have put My Spirit upon Him; He will bring forth justice to the nations.
Isaiah 42:1 (NASB)

REPENTANCE

The fruit of the righteous is a tree of life, and he who wins souls is wise.
Proverbs 11:30

ASKING

Personalize this Scripture today for unbelieving governmental leaders.

The LORD foils the plans of the nations; he thwarts the purposes
of the peoples. But the plans of the LORD stand firm forever,
the purposes of his heart through all generations.
Psalm 33:10—11

_____

_____

_____

_____

_____

YIELDING

Personalize and pray this same Scripture for yourself.

_____

_____

_____

_____

_____

_____

_____

Pray for missionary work in ZIMBABWE
(Southern Africa, between South Africa and Zambia)

Week 48
Thoughts and Prayers

Week 49

CHURCH PLANTING

The owner of the boat refused to take us unless we narrowed our group to only four people. This was all that would fit in his small boat. Our team consisted of eight, plus 5,000 copies of the Gospel of Luke and 120 Bibles. He finally agreed to provide a bigger boat, but he would not go with us. He thought we were fools to even attempt the trip.

We waited until the boat crew transferred the engine from the small boat onto the bigger one. The owner kept insisting we would not be able to go one mile due to low water levels in the river.

Sure enough, about a mile down the river we ran into very shallow water. Everyone got out and pushed the huge rowboat-shaped vessel until the water level increased. We jumped back in, and away we went for about another half a mile. Again and again we had to get out and push. We covered less than five miles the first day.

As we traveled, we stopped at villages along the way. Many of these villages are totally isolated. The river is their only means of communication with the outside world. Many villagers had never seen a white man before, let alone a boatful of them! They welcomed us into their homes and were exceptional hosts to the strange-looking men from afar.

As we arrived at each village, we split in teams of two and went in different directions. Each team carried 200 copies of Luke to distribute. One team looked for the local village leader and presented him with a copy of the entire Bible. We wrote down his name and village contact information. Our objective was to gain an invitation for a national evangelist to return to the village. In eight days we collected more than fifty names, and the evangelist was invited back into every village.

The boat trip resulted in the forming of eight churches because we knew where to send the evangelists. There have been more than 280,000 decisions for Christ since 1998.

—*A Christian worker in South Asia*

> Our prayers may be very beautiful in appearance and
> might appear to be the very paragon of devotion, but unless
> there is a secret spiritual force in them, they are vain things.
> *Charles Spurgeon*

Praise & Thanksgiving

Worship by using the name of God mentioned in this
Scripture—"victorious warrior."

> *The Lord your God is in your midst, a victorious warrior. He will exult over you
> with joy, He will be quiet in His love, He will rejoice over you with shouts of joy.*
> Zephaniah 3:17 (NASB)

Repentance

Search your heart as you meditate on this Scripture.
What is the Holy Spirit revealing to you?

> *You are the salt of the earth. But if the salt loses its saltiness,
> how can it be made salty again? It is no longer good for anything,
> except to be thrown out and trampled by men.*
> Matthew 5:13

Asking

Read the following Scripture. Rewrite it, personalizing
it for church planting movements, seeking the Lord in
prayer on their behalf.

> *Declare his glory among the nations, his marvelous deeds among all peoples.*
> Psalm 96:3

_____

_____

_____

Yielding

Now meditate on the Scripture again. Rewrite it below,
personalizing and praying it for yourself. How can you
respond to what God is saying to you in this Scripture?

_____

_____

Pray for missionary work in
THE EASTERN and NORTHEASTERN
UNITED STATES

Importunate praying is the earnest inward
movement of the heart toward God.
E. M. Bounds

PRAISE & THANKSGIVING

Worship Him today as the "victorious warrior."

*The LORD your God is in your midst, a victorious warrior. He will exult over you
with joy, He will be quiet in His love, He will rejoice over you with shouts of joy.*
Zephaniah 3:17 (NASB)

REPENTANCE

Search your heart as you meditate on this Scripture.

*You are the salt of the earth. But if the salt loses its saltiness,
how can it be made salty again? It is no longer good for anything,
except to be thrown out and trampled by men.*
Matthew 5:13

ASKING

Rewrite this Scripture, personalizing it for church planting
movements, seeking the Lord in prayer on their behalf.

*The LORD will be awesome to them when he destroys all the gods of the land.
The nations on every shore will worship him, every one in its own land.*
Zephaniah 2:11

_____

_____

_____

_____

YIELDING

Rewrite it again, personalizing and praying it for yourself.
Respond to what God is saying to you in this Scripture.

_____

_____

_____

_____

Pray for missionary work in
THE MIDWESTERN UNITED STATES

> If your faith does not make you pray, have nothing to do with it:
> get rid of it, and God help thee to begin again.
> *Charles Spurgeon*

PRAISE & THANKSGIVING

*The LORD your God is in your midst, a victorious warrior. He will exult over you
with joy, He will be quiet in His love, He will rejoice over you with shouts of joy.*
Zephaniah 3:17 (NASB)

REPENTANCE

*You are the salt of the earth. But if the salt loses its saltiness,
how can it be made salty again? It is no longer good for anything,
except to be thrown out and trampled by men.*
Matthew 5:13

ASKING

Personalize this Scripture for church planting movements,
rewriting it, seeking the Lord in prayer on their behalf.

*The God of our fathers has chosen you to know his will and to see
the Righteous One and to hear words from his mouth. You will be
his witness to all men of what you have seen and heard.*
Acts 22:14–15

_____
_____
_____
_____

YIELDING

Now personalize and pray it for yourself. How can you
respond to what God is saying to you?

_____
_____
_____
_____
_____

Pray for missionary work in
THE SOUTHEASTERN UNITED STATES

Men may spurn our appeals, reject our message, oppose our arguments, and despise our person, but they are helpless against our prayer. Christians who love the cause of Christ—to prayer! The times are calling us to it.
J. Sidlow Baxter

PRAISE & THANKSGIVING

The LORD your God is in your midst, a victorious warrior. He will exult over you with joy, He will be quiet in His love, He will rejoice over you with shouts of joy.
Zephaniah 3:17 (NASB)

REPENTANCE

You are the salt of the earth. But if the salt loses its saltiness, how can it be made salty again? It is no longer good for anything, except to be thrown out and trampled by men.
Matthew 5:13

ASKING

Rewrite this Scripture, personalizing it for church planters.

Pray for us, too, that God may open a door for our message, so that we may proclaim the mystery of Christ, for which I am in chains. Pray that I may proclaim it clearly, as I should.
Colossians 4:3–4

_____

_____

_____

_____

YIELDING

What is God saying to you in this Scripture?

_____

_____

_____

_____

_____

Pray for missionary work in
THE SOUTHWESTERN UNITED STATES,
including HAWAII

> We think of prayer as a preparation for work, or a calm after
> having done work, whereas prayer is the essential work. It is the
> supreme activity of everything that is noblest in our personality.
> *Oswald Chambers*

PRAISE & THANKSGIVING

*The LORD your God is in your midst, a victorious warrior. He will exult over you
with joy, He will be quiet in His love, He will rejoice over you with shouts of joy.*
Zephaniah 3:17 (NASB)

REPENTANCE

*You are the salt of the earth. But if the salt loses its saltiness,
how can it be made salty again? It is no longer good for anything,
except to be thrown out and trampled by men.*
Matthew 5:13

ASKING

Personalize this Scripture today for church planters.

*I will raise up for them a prophet like you from among their brothers; I will
put my words in his mouth, and he will tell them everything I command him.*
Deuteronomy 18:18

_____

_____

_____

_____

YIELDING

Personalize and pray this same Scripture for yourself.

_____

_____

_____

_____

_____

_____

Pray for missionary work in
THE WESTERN and NORTHWESTERN
UNITED STATES, including ALASKA

Week 49
Thoughts and Prayers

_____

_____

_____

_____

_____

_____

_____

_____

_____

_____

_____

_____

_____

_____

_____

_____

_____

_____

_____

_____

_____

_____

_____

_____

_____

_____

_____

Week 50

LABORERS

A young co-worker from the Philippines spent several years abroad in a Southeast Asian country. The first year went pretty well as a missionary. She taught and loved her college-age students. However, when her first Christmas season arrived, she became very lonely for the Philippines. She missed being in a country that celebrated the season with so much fun and festivity, gift-giving, religious services and Christmas carols. And, of course, she missed her friends and family. To make things worse, her birthday was at the end of November and she had celebrated it alone.

One morning before Christmas, the starkness and loneliness of Christmas in a Buddhist country so far away from home overwhelmed her. She found herself walking down an empty street at 7 a.m. Tears welled up in her eyes and then there was no stopping them. She started weeping.

All of a sudden she heard a voice say, "I am Christmas" in the Filipino language, Tagalog. She immediately thought, "There is another Filipino around!" so she turned to see who had said it. There was no one on the street. Immediately her tears stopped. She knew God had spoken to her. She was able to really experience "Christmas" that year, even through she was far from home.

Diana—Pacific Rim

Our church was located in a large city in Southeast Asia. We had never conducted a discipleship program among the women, so I asked for prayer that I might choose the right women to build a foundation that would be ongoing. After much prayer, I determined the six women to choose. I asked for continued prayer from partners at home that if there were anyone else, the Lord would show me. We were to start on Monday.

On Sunday after church, Mettie approached me with a shy smile. "I hear you are going to work with a group of women. Could I be one of them?"

"Yes!" I replied.

"But," she said, "it will be hard for me because I was only able to go through second grade."

"That's all right," I told her. "I'll help you and God will help us." So we began. Who do you think knew every single memory passage given—and word perfect at that?

When training was over, the women were asked to consider leading others in discipleship while continuing training. Mettie was one of the few who was willing to do so. I asked that the group write out a prayer to ask God whom they should train. Many were specifically in prayer for this small group of women. This was Mettie's prayer: "God, I ask you to give me some women that are much smarter than I am so they can help many others." What a prayer from a society that never wants to admit a weakness.

God answered that prayer. In Mettie's group was our leading deacon's wife, two young women who were leaders in our church— a teacher, and the superintendent of our Sunday school! What a joy to know that she continues to disciple. When we had to leave our city because of visa denial, I confidently left my group in Mettie's capable hands. Only God could do this!

Glenn—Southeast Asia

> The story of every great Christian achievement
> is the history of answered prayer.
> *E. M. Bounds*

PRAISE & THANKSGIVING

Worship by using the characteristic of God mentioned
in this Scripture—"power."

God is my strength and power, and He makes my way perfect.

2 Samuel 22:33 (NKJV)

REPENTANCE

Search your heart as you meditate on this Scripture.
What is the Holy Spirit revealing to you?

Therefore, since we are surrounded by such a great cloud of witnesses,
let us throw off everything that hinders and the sin that so easily entangles,
and let us run with perseverance the race marked out for us.

Hebrews 12:1

ASKING

Read the following Scripture. Rewrite it, personalizing it
for laborers, seeking the Lord in prayer on their behalf.

You will receive power when the Holy Spirit comes on you; and you will be my
witnesses in Jerusalem, and in all Judea and Samaria, and to the ends of the earth.

Acts 1:8

_____

_____

_____

_____

YIELDING

Now meditate on the Scripture again. Rewrite it below,
personalizing and praying it for yourself. How can you
respond to what God is saying to you in this Scripture?

_____

_____

_____

Pray for missionary work throughout
THE CARIBBEAN

> The greatest gift we can give to others is our prayers.
> *Anonymous*

PRAISE & THANKSGIVING

Worship Him today as your all-sufficient source of "power."

> *God is my strength and power, and He makes my way perfect.*
>
> 2 Samuel 22:33 (NKJV)

REPENTANCE

Search your heart as you meditate on this Scripture.

> *Therefore, since we are surrounded by such a great cloud of witnesses,
> let us throw off everything that hinders and the sin that so easily entangles,
> and let us run with perseverance the race marked out for us.*
>
> Hebrews 12:1

ASKING

Rewrite this Scripture, personalizing it for laborers, seeking the Lord in prayer on their behalf.

> *They will rebuild the ancient ruins and restore the places long devastated;
> they will renew the ruined cities that have been devastated for generations.*
>
> Isaiah 61:4

_____

_____

_____

YIELDING

Rewrite it again, personalizing and praying it for yourself. Respond to what God is saying to you in this Scripture.

_____

_____

_____

_____

_____

If I should neglect prayer but a single day,
I should lose a great deal of the fire of faith.
Martin Luther

PRAISE & THANKSGIVING

God is my strength and power, and He makes my way perfect.
2 Samuel 22:33 (NKJV)

REPENTANCE

Therefore, since we are surrounded by such a great cloud of witnesses,
let us throw off everything that hinders and the sin that so easily entangles,
and let us run with perseverance the race marked out for us.
Hebrews 12:1

ASKING

Personalize this Scripture for laborers, rewriting it,
seeking the Lord in prayer on their behalf.

Jesus came to them and said, "All authority in heaven and on earth
has been given to me. Therefore go and make disciples of all nations,
baptizing them in the name of the Father and of the Son and of the
Holy Spirit, and teaching them to obey everything I have commanded
you. And surely I am with you always, to the very end of the age."
Matthew 28:18–20

_____

_____

_____

YIELDING

Now personalize and pray it for yourself. How can you
respond to what God is saying to you?

_____

_____

_____

_____

_____

Pray for missionary work throughout
CENTRAL AMERICA

> Prayer continues in the desire of the heart, though
> the understanding be employed on outward things.
> *John Wesley*

PRAISE & THANKSGIVING

> *God is my strength and power, and He makes my way perfect.*
> 2 Samuel 22:33 (NKJV)

REPENTANCE

> *Therefore, since we are surrounded by such a great cloud of witnesses,*
> *let us throw off everything that hinders and the sin that so easily entangles,*
> *and let us run with perseverance the race marked out for us.*
> Hebrews 12:1

ASKING

Rewrite this Scripture, personalizing it for laborers.

> *Therefore, my dear brothers, stand firm. Let nothing move you.*
> *Always give yourselves fully to the work of the Lord, because you*
> *know that your labor in the Lord is not in vain.*
> 1 Corinthians 15:58

_____

_____

_____

_____

_____

YIELDING

What is God saying to you in this Scripture?

_____

_____

_____

_____

_____

_____

Pray for missionary work throughout
CENTRAL ASIA

Whether we think of or speak to God, whether we act
or suffer for Him, all is prayer, when we have no other
object than His love, and the desire of pleasing Him.
John Wesley

PRAISE & THANKSGIVING

God is my strength and power, and He makes my way perfect.
2 Samuel 22:33 (NKJV)

REPENTANCE

Therefore, since we are surrounded by such a great cloud of witnesses,
let us throw off everything that hinders and the sin that so easily entangles,
and let us run with perseverance the race marked out for us.
Hebrews 12:1

ASKING

Personalize this Scripture today for laborers.

But thanks be to God, who always leads us in triumphal procession in Christ
and through us spreads everywhere the fragrance of the knowledge of him.
2 Corinthians 2:14

_____

_____

_____

_____

YIELDING

Personalize and pray this same Scripture for yourself.

_____

_____

_____

_____

_____

_____

Pray for missionary work throughout
CENTRAL EUROPE

Week 50
Thoughts and Prayers

Week 51

PEOPLE GROUPS

At the invitation of Asian friends, my husband and I traveled to a country closed to the gospel where few people are followers of Christ. One night while worshiping in a church there with our friends living abroad, a young man gave this testimony:

The previous day, this young man and another Asian believer were working on an oil rig. Exhausted after a long shift, they climbed down into the sleeping quarters of a ship for a seven-hour trip back to land. Almost immediately, a rough sea developed and the ship began to toss. The young man said he was so tired he just prayed and went to sleep. When he woke up the vessel was rocking violently. He heard his Christian coworker praying out loud, "In Jesus' name, in Jesus' name, in JESUS' NAME!" The young man felt assured the Lord would take care of them and he trusted the prayers of his friend, so he put on his headphones and went back to sleep.

The next time he awakened he knew something was quite wrong. He pulled himself up to the deck. When he saw the fear on the faces of the crew, he realized the danger they were in. The boat was listing at a sharp angle. The cargo had shifted. Several ships had pulled up nearby to watch what seemed like an inevitable catastrophe. At that point, the sea calmed and the ship moved slowly back to land.

The exhausted crew came down into the quarters below. A Tanzanian man started a DVD in his language. The young Asian noticed a church and people praying in the movie. He asked the man in English, "Are you a Christian?" The man said, "No." He was from another world religion and had been given the video while in port. At the same time, a group of Indonesian crew members were watching a video in their language. Our friend noticed this video was also a Christian movie. When he asked about their beliefs, they told him they were from the same world religion as the first man. Someone had given them the DVD.

The crew asked if the young Asian was a Christian. For the next few hours, the African man and the Indonesians questioned the two Asian believers about Christ and discussed what it means to follow Him. With the power of the storm and the testimony of two believers, all the crew walked away that day seriously considering the claims of Christ to be their Savior.

Think of how many people, most unknown to each other, worked together to make that powerful witness a possibility. The two Asians were willing to do more than merely seek a job abroad. They responded to the challenge to be prepared to give an account in the workplace for the hope that is in them. There was a church that provided training for their members. There were others who gave financially and prayed faithfully so my husband and I could live abroad to mobilize and train others. God was at work, perhaps even stirring up a rolling sea, for no other purpose than to bring seamen to the end of themselves. There was probably a believing friend, relative, or stranger who prayed for these men. And it moves me to think of the various individuals, even farther removed, who had the vision and faith to make Christian movies, translate them into many languages, or personally hand them to a sailor. And, of course, there is Jesus Christ who made salvation possible.

May God multiply your influence as you give, pray, witness and live in such a way that reaches people.

Diana—PACIFIC RIM

> Prevailing, or effectual prayer, is that prayer
> which attains the blessing that it seeks.
> *Charles G. Finney*

Praise & Thanksgiving

Worship by using the name of God mentioned in this Scripture—"I AM."

> *God said to Moses, "I AM WHO I AM"; and He said, "Thus you shall say
> to the sons of Israel, 'I AM has sent me to you.'"*
>
> Exodus 3:14 (NASB)

Repentance

Search your heart as you meditate on this Scripture. What is the Holy Spirit revealing to you?

> *Do nothing out of selfish ambition or vain conceit, but in humility consider
> others better than yourselves.*
>
> Philippians 2:3

Asking

Read the following Scripture. Rewrite it, personalizing it for the people groups of the world, seeking the Lord in prayer on their behalf.

> *See, I have given you this land. Go in and take possession of the land that the LORD
> swore he would give to your fathers—to Abraham, Isaac and Jacob—and to their
> descendants after them.*
>
> Deuteronomy 1:8

_____

_____

Yielding

Now meditate on the Scripture again. Rewrite it below, personalizing and praying it for yourself. How can you respond to what God is saying to you in this Scripture?

_____

_____

_____

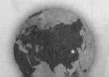

Pray for missionary work throughout
EAST ASIA

> Prayer is not a device for imposing our will upon God, or bending
> his will to ours, but the prescribed way of subordinating our will to his.
> *John R. W. Stott*

PRAISE & THANKSGIVING

Worship Him today—the "I AM."

> *God said to Moses, "I AM WHO I AM"; and He said, "Thus you shall say*
> *to the sons of Israel, 'I AM has sent me to you.'"*
>
> Exodus 3:14 (NASB)

REPENTANCE

Search your heart as you meditate on this Scripture.

> *Do nothing out of selfish ambition or vain conceit, but in humility consider*
> *others better than yourselves.*
>
> Philippians 2:3

ASKING

Rewrite this Scripture, personalizing it for the people
groups of the world, seeking the Lord in prayer on
their behalf.

> *I am sending you to them to open their eyes and turn them from darkness to light,*
> *and from the power of Satan to God, so that they may receive forgiveness of sins*
> *and a place among those who are sanctified by faith in me.*
>
> Acts 26:17–18

_____

_____

_____

_____

YIELDING

Rewrite it again, personalizing and praying it for yourself.
Respond to what God is saying to you in this Scripture.

_____

_____

_____

_____

Pray for missionary work throughout
EASTERN EUROPE

> The secret of all failure is our failure in secret prayer.
> *The Kneeling Christian*

PRAISE & THANKSGIVING

God said to Moses, "I AM WHO I AM"; and He said, "Thus you shall say to the sons of Israel, 'I AM has sent me to you.'"

Exodus 3:14 (NASB)

REPENTANCE

Do nothing out of selfish ambition or vain conceit, but in humility consider others better than yourselves.

Philippians 2:3

ASKING

Personalize this Scripture for the people groups of the world, rewriting it, seeking the Lord in prayer on their behalf.

For God so loved the world that he gave his one and only Son, that whoever believes in him shall not perish but have eternal life.

John 3:16

_____

_____

_____

_____

YIELDING

Now personalize and pray it for yourself. How can you respond to what God is saying to you?

_____

_____

_____

_____

_____

_____

Pray for missionary work throughout
THE MIDDLE EAST

If you want that splendid power in prayer, you must remain in loving, living,
lasting, conscious, practical, abiding union with the Lord Jesus Christ.
Charles Spurgeon

PRAISE & THANKSGIVING

*God said to Moses, "I AM WHO I AM"; and He said, "Thus you shall say
to the sons of Israel, 'I AM has sent me to you.'"*

Exodus 3:14 (NASB)

REPENTANCE

*Do nothing out of selfish ambition or vain conceit, but in humility consider
others better than yourselves.*

Philippians 2:3

ASKING

Rewrite this Scripture, personalizing it for unreached
people groups.

*Salvation is found in no one else, for there is no other name under heaven given
to men by which we must be saved.*

Acts 4:12

_____

_____

_____

_____

YIELDING

What is God saying to you in this Scripture?

_____

_____

_____

_____

_____

_____

Pray for missionary work throughout
NORTH AMERICA

> If the spiritual life be healthy, under the full power of the
> Holy Spirit, praying without ceasing will be natural.
> *Andrew Murray*

PRAISE & THANKSGIVING

*God said to Moses, "I AM WHO I AM"; and He said, "Thus you shall say
to the sons of Israel, 'I AM has sent me to you.'"*
    Exodus 3:14 (NASB)

REPENTANCE

*Do nothing out of selfish ambition or vain conceit, but in humility consider
others better than yourselves.*
    Philippians 2:3

ASKING

Personalize this Scripture today for unreached people
groups.

*Seek the LORD while he may be found; call on him while he is near. Let the
wicked forsake his way and the evil man his thoughts. Let him turn to the LORD,
and he will have mercy on him, and to our God, for he will freely pardon.*
    Isaiah 55:6–7

_____

_____

_____

_____

YIELDING

Personalize and pray this same Scripture for yourself.

_____

_____

_____

_____

_____

_____

Pray for missionary work throughout
NORTHERN AFRICA

Week 51
Thoughts and Prayers

Week 52

PERSECUTED CHURCH

During our visit to the United States one year, we shared the story of R.M.* who had been translating the Bible into simple Urdu. He would speak the translation onto computer wave files, and a scribe would write out the Urdu script. R.M. was raised a Muslim but became a believer while living in the United States. He had recently returned to his home country and won several family members to the Lord. He wanted to give them a version of the Bible they could understand.

When we returned from our visit, we learned that R.M. and his younger brother A.M.* were being persecuted by their other brothers. They were threatened and beaten. The youngest brother had organized an armed gang to come and threaten them at gunpoint. Their lives were probably saved when the youngest brother's wife stood in front of them to protect them.

The translation came to a standstill because of the danger for the scribe. We sent out an emergency request, asking people to pray for their safety and protection, praying that the Lord would give them wisdom to know what to do in this volatile situation.

Soon after we sent out that request, we had to evacuate to another country due to unrelated circumstances. Upon our return several months later, we learned of the wonderful answer to our prayers. The youngest brother and his wife, their sister and her husband, and their mother had all come into the kingdom. R.M. had started a local fellowship, and eight Muslims were attending, drawn to the teaching there.

—*A missionary serving among Last Frontier peoples*
*Names changed

I live in the spirit of prayer; I pray as I walk, when I lie down
and when I rise, and the answers are always coming.
George Mueller

PRAISE & THANKSGIVING

Worship by using the aspect of God mentioned in this
Scripture—"refuge."

The LORD has been my stronghold, and my God the rock of my refuge.

Psalm 94:22 (NASB)

REPENTANCE

Search your heart as you meditate on this Scripture.
What is the Holy Spirit revealing to you?

*Love your enemies and pray for those who persecute you, that you may
be sons of your Father in heaven. He causes his sun to rise on the evil
and the good, and sends rain on the righteous and the unrighteous.*

Matthew 5:44–45

ASKING

Read the following Scripture. Rewrite it, personalizing it
for the persecuted church, seeking the Lord in prayer on
their behalf.

*On account of me you will stand before governors and kings as witnesses to them.
And the gospel must first be preached to all nations.*

Mark 13:9–10

_____

_____

_____

YIELDING

Now meditate on the Scripture again. Rewrite it below,
personalizing and praying it for yourself. How can you
respond to what God is saying to you in this Scripture?

_____

_____

_____

Pray for missionary work throughout
THE PACIFIC RIM

> Prayer breaks all bars, dissolves all chains, opens all prisons,
> and widens all straits by which God's saints have been held.
>
> *E. M. Bounds*

PRAISE & THANKSGIVING

Worship Him today—your "refuge."

> *The LORD has been my stronghold, and my God the rock of my refuge.*
>
> Psalm 94:22 (NASB)

REPENTANCE

Search your heart as you meditate on this Scripture.

> *Love your enemies and pray for those who persecute you, so that you may
> be sons of your Father who is in heaven; for He causes His sun to rise on
> the evil and the good, and sends rain on the righteous and the unrighteous.*
>
> Matthew 5:44–45

ASKING

Rewrite this Scripture, personalizing it for the persecuted
church, seeking the Lord in prayer on their behalf.

> *I am not ashamed of the gospel, because it is the power of God for the salvation
> of everyone who believes: first for the Jew, then for the Gentile.*
>
> Romans 1:16

_____

_____

_____

YIELDING

Rewrite it again, personalizing and praying it for yourself.
Respond to what God is saying to you in this Scripture.

_____

_____

_____

_____

_____

Pray for missionary work throughout
SOUTH AMERICA

> All things else being equal, our prayers are only as powerful as our lives.
> In the long pull we only pray as well as we live.
>
> *A. W. Tozer*

PRAISE & THANKSGIVING

> *The LORD has been my stronghold, and my God the rock of my refuge.*
>
> Psalm 94:22 (NASB)

REPENTANCE

> *Love your enemies and pray for those who persecute you, so that you may
> be sons of your Father who is in heaven; for He causes His sun to rise on
> the evil and the good, and sends rain on the righteous and the unrighteous.*
>
> Matthew 5:44–45

ASKING

Personalize this Scripture for the persecuted church,
rewriting it, seeking the Lord in prayer on their behalf.

> *Pray also for me, that whenever I open my mouth, words may be given me so
> that I will fearlessly make known the mystery of the gospel, for which I am
> an ambassador in chains. Pray that I may declare it fearlessly, as I should.*
>
> Ephesians 6:19–20

_____

_____

_____

_____

YIELDING

Now personalize and pray it for yourself. How can you
respond to what God is saying to you?

_____

_____

_____

_____

_____

Pray for missionary work throughout
SOUTH ASIA

As is the business of tailors to make clothes and cobblers
to make shoes, so it is the business of Christians to pray.
Martin Luther

PRAISE & THANKSGIVING

The LORD has been my stronghold, and my God the rock of my refuge.
Psalm 94:22 (NASB)

REPENTANCE

*Love your enemies and pray for those who persecute you, so that you may
be sons of your Father who is in heaven; for He causes His sun to rise on
the evil and the good, and sends rain on the righteous and the unrighteous.*
Matthew 5:44–45

ASKING

Rewrite this Scripture, personalizing it for the persecuted
church.

*I consider my life worth nothing to me, if only I may finish the race and
complete the task the Lord Jesus has given me—the task of testifying to
the gospel of God's grace.*
Acts 20:24

_____

_____

_____

YIELDING

What is God saying to you in this Scripture?

_____

_____

_____

_____

_____

_____

_____

Pray for missionary work throughout
WEST AFRICA

> God's mercy visits every house where night and morning prayers
> are made, but where these are neglected, sin is incurred.
> *Charles Spurgeon*

PRAISE & THANKSGIVING

The LORD has been my stronghold, and my God the rock of my refuge.
Psalm 94:22 (NASB)

REPENTANCE

Love your enemies and pray for those who persecute you, so that you may
be sons of your Father who is in heaven; for He causes His sun to rise on
the evil and the good, and sends rain on the righteous and the unrighteous.
Matthew 5:44–45

ASKING

Personalize this Scripture today for the persecuted church.

Remember those in prison as if you were their fellow prisoners,
and those who are mistreated as if you yourselves were suffering.
Hebrews 13:3

_____

_____

_____

_____

YIELDING

Personalize and pray this same Scripture for yourself.

_____

_____

_____

_____

_____

_____

_____

_____

Pray for missionary work throughout
WESTERN EUROPE

Week 52
Thoughts and Prayers

_____

_____

_____

_____

_____

_____

_____

_____

_____

_____

_____

_____

_____

_____

_____

_____

_____

_____

_____

_____

_____

_____

_____

In Appreciation

I am so humbled to have had this opportunity to serve alongside some of the most faithful, dedicated and God-fearing saints that I will ever know on this earth. I am reminded how God told Moses to "make this tabernacle and all its furnishings exactly like the pattern" he was shown (Exod. 25:9). In order for this book to be like the "pattern" God intended, it took many saints whose hearts were prompted to give (Exod. 25:2).

I am convinced by the Holy Spirit that there were many who cried up to the Lord before I was even born for the church to engage in God's Word to pray and make intercession from the Word of God in behalf of the kingdom work God intended to be done on this earth as it is in heaven. I am grateful for their prayers.

I am greatly appreciative for the prayer team who labored endless hours with me on their knees. Thank you Charlene, Debbie, Sandi, JoBeth, Linda, Deloris, Illy, Becky, and CJ. I love you so much! Debbie Floyd, "for such a time as this" God placed you strategically, having served as a State-side Prayer Advocate for Western South America for the International Mission Board. Bless you, my dear sister in Christ, for all the hours of communication and work you initiated in gaining testimonies from IMB missionaries. I am ever so grateful for the willingness of these missionaries to share from their hearts about the work they are accomplishing through the power of the Holy Spirit to fulfill the Great Commission!

Sandi Moncure, I have been blessed by endless hours of your pressing in with me, bringing forth the formatting and reformatting of this book. I am thankful to the many missionaries I had the opportunity to meet with, who willfully spent time with me sharing their heartfelt needs for prayer.

My heart has continued to be bowed before the throne of grace for the men and women at B&H Publishing Group. The confirmation of how God was placing this resource on your hearts before I ever met with you is amazing! Ken, David, Tom, Lawrence, Jeff Cooley, Jeff Godby, Craig, Phill, Jim, George, John, Paul—your earnest and fervent prayers have made an impact on my life forever and, I believe, will impact the world as well.

Finally, I am humbled and greatly encouraged for the partnerships God has allowed me to have with the International Mission Board and Living Proof Ministries. The heart of these two ministries beat fervently for the kingdom of God to come on this earth as it is in heaven!

To Help You Keep Praying

You can continue your prayer impact on the peoples of the world by accessing resources such as those provided by the International Mission Board, an entity of the Southern Baptist Convention. To find out more about these hotlines, e-mail updates, and many other helpful prayer tools on a wide range of interest areas—perfect for keeping yourself and your church informed about the current needs of today's missionaries and their various ministries—visit imb.org/compassionnet.

For more information on Mary Ann Bridgwater and Pray the Word Ministries, visit praytheword.org. You can also get immediate, ongoing access to other materials and services by going to PrayersForTheFaithful.com.